Praise for *The Unlikely*

"*The Unlikely Village of Eden* is a wonderful read: lyrical, funny, heartbreaking, heart-healing, and deeply inspiring. With her writing and her life, Emma Nadler has created a testament to the resiliency of parents, children, friendships, marriage, and every other manifestation of human love."
  —Martha Beck, *New York Times* bestselling author of *Expecting Adam* and *Leaving the Saints: How I Lost the Mormons and Found my Faith*

"Such a gorgeous book. An honest, difficult, and hopeful look at what it means to create a family."
  —Jenny Lawson, #1 *New York Times* bestselling author of *Furiously Happy* and *Broken (in the Best Possible Way)*

"A stunning debut memoir by a gifted writer and psychotherapist. Emma Nadler has written a truly poignant read that shines a light on the humanity in neurodivergence, the heart of parenting, and the soul of psychotherapy."
  —Adam Grant, #1 *New York Times* bestselling author of *Think Again* and host of the TED podcast Re:Thinking

"This is a heartbreaking but evermore heartwarming book. Parents everywhere will see themselves in Emma, and her story is inspiring, yes, but it is also instructional for navigating the pandemic of loneliness all around us. A triumphant story of the sacred spirit in our human connections, parenting, and profoundly loving community."
  —Dr. Lisa Miller, *New York Times* bestselling author of *The Spiritual Child*

"Emma Nadler is a natural storyteller, and her memoir, *The Unlikely Village of Eden*, reads like a nail-biting tale that your best friend tells you over a cup of tea. With wit, wisdom, humility, and heart, Nadler chronicles her family's experience of raising a neurodivergent child with multiple disabilities. The real gift of this engaging memoir is that Nadler's lessons belong to all of us: letting go of perfection, building community, celebrating our children exactly as they are, and surviving the inevitable trials and disappointments of life. Not only did I fall in love with the author, but also her whole family and the village that rallied around them all."

—Christie Tate, bestselling author of *Group*

"*The Unlikely Village of Eden* is the undeniable proof that community empathy is how we thrive—and Emma and Eden are guiding lights, showing us how we can create a world that is more compassionate. I wept, I laughed, I felt the strength in her vulnerability as she told this story—I cannot recommend it enough."

—Rosanna Arquette, award-winning actress

"As a writer, Emma Nadler expertly masters the ability to convey the full range of her experiences as a mother, wife, friend, therapist, advocate, human. *The Unlikely Village of Eden* leaves the reader with a greater sense of understanding of families with special needs children and, just as importantly, reminds us that humans, especially parents, are more than the sum of their parts."

—Justin Vernon, founder and lead singer of
Grammy-winning folk band Bon Iver

"Emma Nadler is the perfect voice—unique, funny, fiercely intelligent—to show that when life doesn't go to plan, community and connection is the answer. Her memoir should be required reading not just for parents, but for people everywhere."

—Mark Daley, foster child advocate and founder of One Iowa

"As parents we often feel that we are the sole source of our children's wellbeing, and when things don't go to 'plan,' we inevitably have to contend with the weight of that responsibility. Emma's immensely authentic memoir shows that the strive for perfectionism is never the answer, and the gifts of community and connection are what matter most. Her story will touch anyone with the privilege to read it."

—Tina Payne Bryson, PhD, *New York Times* bestselling author of *The Whole-Brain Child* and *Bottom Line for Baby*

THE UNLIKELY VILLAGE OF EDEN

THE

UNLIKELY

VILLAGE

OF

EDEN

A Memoir

EMMA NADLER

CENTRAL RECOVERY PRESS

Las Vegas, Nevada

Central Recovery Press (CRP) is committed to publishing exceptional materials addressing addiction treatment, recovery, and behavioral healthcare topics.

For more information, visit www.centralrecoverypress.com.

27 26 25 24 23   1 2 3 4 5

Library of Congress Cataloging-in-Publication Data

Names: Nadler, Emma, author.
Title: The unlikely village of Eden : a memoir / Emma Nadler.
 Identifiers: LCCN 2022055028 (print) | LCCN 2022055029 (ebook) | ISBN
  9781949481815 (hardcover) | ISBN 9781949481822 (ebook)
Subjects: LCSH: Nadler, Emma. | Parents of developmentally disabled
  children--United States--Biography. | Parents of chronically ill
  children--United States--Biography. | Women psychotherapists--United
  States--Biography. | Caregivers--United States--Biography. | Mother and
  child--United States.
Classification: LCC HQ759.913 .N324 2023 (print) | LCC HQ759.913 (ebook)
  | DDC 649/.15 [B]--dc23/eng/20230130
LC record available at https://lccn.loc.gov/2022055028
LC ebook record available at https://lccn.loc.gov/2022055029

Photo of Emma Nadler by Meghan Doll.

Publisher's Note:
This book contains general information about relationships, parenting, and psychotherapy. The information contained herein is not medical advice. This book is not an alternative to medical advice from your doctor or other professional healthcare provider.

Our books represent the experiences and opinions of their authors only. Every effort has been made to ensure that events, institutions, and statistics presented in our books as facts are accurate and up to date. To protect their privacy, the names of some of the people, places, and institutions in this book have been changed.

Cover design by The Book Designers and interior by Deb Tremper, Six Penny Graphics.

For anyone who thought it would be one way, and then it wasn't
and for Cedar

TABLE OF CONTENTS

PREFACE

I am endlessly amazed by how one unexpected moment can lead to another and how each moment can shape a day or a week or even a whole life. I sometimes soak in Eden's gleaming almond-shaped eyes or behold her funky swagger and think, *Wow, who knew*?

Who knew I was going to be here, in a life that didn't seem like it was going to be mine? I certainly didn't. But that's both the adventure and calamity of life. You just never know how it's going to turn out. Sometimes not knowing feels like an incredible mystery. Emphasis on *sometimes*.

I grappled with the language to use around the concept of disability, which reflects, in part, how flawed this language is. I use the terms *disabled and disability*, using person-first language (i.e., person with disabilities vs. disabled person) to put emphasis on the individual as a whole person. *Special needs* is commonly used in some circles, but I don't believe it fully encapsulates the challenges that Eden and so many others face. The term has been critiqued as a euphemism—unintentionally adding stigma. I like the idea of reclaiming disability as something that is not derogatory or less than. I suspect, like most of the words that came before, these terms will also drift in and out of fashion and become obsolete. This is what time does, it reinvents us. And sometimes it just makes us embarrassed about the past.

Putting our story into words has been an imperfect process. People are complex and dynamic, and labels cannot ever fully capture the human experience. There's no one else like Eden, at least no one I've ever met. She's part magic.

The other parts are harder to explain.

CHAPTER ONE

This Feels Like a Lot

When the neurologist called, I was standing in the bedroom of a one-story adobe vacation rental in Palm Springs, California. The photos online had done an incredible job of making the place look vintage glam; it supposedly once belonged to an elegant Old Hollywood star.

In person, it was just plain dirty.

Thick, musty curtains blocked out most of the sunlight in our bedroom, adding an overcast feel to what was actually a bright morning. It was one of the last, lingering days of the year. Eden, my blonde, big-headed angel, was seven months old. And I do mean big-headed—her head was notably large—so large that she was often the target of unhelpful comments from strangers.

"Wow, now there's a noggin!"

Yep. Thank you for your (highly unsolicited) feedback. For going out of your way to inform me, her actual mother, of my daughter's obvious physical state.

Eden, who was in the living room with my parents, couldn't yet roll over from her back to her front or sit up on her own. She wore a thick cotton-candy pink helmet most of her waking hours to correct the flattening of her head (technically known as positional plagiocephaly), which was a result of her limited mobility and subsequent difficulty changing positions.

Our girl may not have been meeting milestones, but with her cool blue-gray eyes and wide, toothless grin, she really rocked that helmet.

I called it her roller girl look.

I recognized the number on the phone and picked up with a chirpy hello. I had liked this warm and cheerful neurologist when we'd first met a few weeks earlier.

But the voice on the phone spoke in a soft, delicate tone very different from the one in our last conversation.

"I have your daughter's test results," he said. I looked at Cedar. My tenderhearted husband was rummaging for something in his suitcase with a focused look on his face, skin glowing from a full week of vacation. I put the call on speaker and sat down on the twisted sheets of the unmade bed.

At Eden's pediatrician's recommendation, we had—just in case—sought out genetic testing. Something had been off since Eden was just a few weeks old, when she would choke and sputter and pull off my breast in the middle of nursing. Then she would jolt awake repeatedly, sometimes every fifteen minutes, all through the night. She was only able to consume small amounts of milk.

Still, nobody expected anything big. For months, the pediatrician, a well-versed, no-nonsense practitioner with a tight ponytail, seemed to imply that the root cause of the feeding issues was me.

"Keep on trying, Mom," she said, then made a referral to a lactation consultant, and eventually, occupational therapy.

The occupational therapist, too, placed her focus on me. "Your anxiety about her not eating might be causing some of these feeding issues."

But I had breastfed our first child Avi for almost a year, and by the age of three, he was a roaring combination of curls and sheer will. He would gobble up whatever snappy foods were set in front of him—even things like asparagus or bright chunks of green avocado. Eventually, we had to cut him off lox because a preschooler should probably not finish off an entire package of smoked salmon in one sitting. Even for a Jew, it seemed overboard.

I swore off dairy, hoping Eden's feeding difficulties had something to do with my commitment to cheese. I tried various breast pumps to slow the flow of milk, along with more than a handful of hypoallergenic formulas, bottles, levels, shapes of nipples, burping techniques, and time intervals between feeds. None of these changes made a difference, at least for Eden's well-being. She was bony, born under six pounds, and still in the first percentile for weight.

All of this meant she was earning the most ominous of labels: *failure to thrive.*

"Failure" probably should not be used to describe anybody under the age of one.

Or anyone over the age of one, for that matter.

And so, I wondered if the real failure was me at thirty-six years old. After all, I was the mother. Wasn't I responsible for keeping her safe and well?

On the phone, the neurologist's voice was stiff and minimal. "Your daughter has a substantial genetic deletion. It's very rare."

"What does that mean?" I asked. I stood up and started to pace, the tiles cold beneath my bare feet.

I stared at the thick burgundy brocade bedspread.

"I'm sorry. I don't know enough to tell you very much about it. You can schedule an appointment with a geneticist to learn more."

"We're gone, out of town right now, visiting family. We aren't even in Minnesota. I can't imagine waiting weeks, wondering what this means. Do you know how much it will affect Eden? Will she be . . . like, compromised?" My voice started to crack and then came a rush of tears. I didn't try to push them away. Cedar had stopped rummaging through his bag, and I felt his hand on my back, steadying me. There was a pause on the phone and a breath.

The doctor responded softly, "I can't tell you exactly what it means, but she's missing DNA. A sizable amount. I wasn't expecting this. It's likely going to have a strong impact on her development."

His speech was thick with caution, as if he was greeting us at a shiva. As if he didn't want to overstep. As if he was acutely aware that this phone call would be something I would remember for the rest of my life.

I understood what he was saying, in his not saying it.

"What do you mean?" I asked. "Will she be developmentally delayed?" I knew enough to understand that DNA is the essential foundation for functioning.

"That appears to be the most likely outcome. I'm sorry, I really am. I wish I could give you more information."

I winced. I could tell that he was sincerely sorry.

I didn't want anyone to be sorry about my one luminous daughter.

"But I can't tell you how it will play out. As I shared, it's a large deletion. But I have no way to predict the future, and I'm not an expert in this type of deletion. It's extremely rare."

I looked at Cedar, who was staring at the phone, cupping his forehead. His face, usually warm and open, was tight, his jaw clenched. I raked my long hair back behind my ears, ordering it, and went through the motions of politely ending the call.

Cedar opened his arms. I leaned against his warm body, sobbing into his chest. I could feel his stubble against my cheek. I pushed my fingers into his choppy hair, which I had cut in our bathroom the morning before our trip. He smelled as always, like wood spice, and as if he had recently brushed his teeth. He set his black thick-rimmed glasses on the nightstand beside us.

We sat for a few minutes together like that until Cedar said, "This feels like a lot." I looked into his wide, steel blue eyes. Yes, it did.

We had done the routine genetic screenings and appointments, the bloodwork, the prenatal vitamins. Every test had come back just fine. I had done all the right things to grow a hearty, thriving child. I exercised, ate well, and avoided alcohol. I hadn't had so much as a turkey sandwich during Eden's pregnancy to avoid foodborne illness.

The second child was supposed to be less intense—nearly every parent I knew said so—because we were seasoned now, more experienced.

And yet, at this moment, none of the planning, none of the "supposed to," none of what we hoped for, counted on, or prepared for meant a thing.

Until that moment, I hadn't been aware of my own expectations for parenthood. I had assumed that my children would be rosy-cheeked and strong, friendly and curious, and maybe—in a best-case scenario—they would also find the cure to Alzheimer's or spearhead a social justice movement.

Only then did I realize my vision of success was based on achievement, the kind of achievement I thought was most valuable—an active contribution to the greater good. It became apparent to me, most clearly only now that it seemed so precarious, that I saw good health as a form of wholeness.

Even our baby's name, Eden, was airy and utopian: the first garden, paradise. My vision of who my daughter would be had been informed in part by my family, my stalwart Jewish Midwestern upbringing, and my grandmother, Edith, Eden's namesake. As Edith used to often declare, "If you don't have your health, you don't have anything."

In the wake of the neurologist's call, I couldn't help but think that we didn't know what we had.

Cedar and I sat for a while on that lumpy, itchy bed together, not knowing what to do or say, and then we walked down the hall toward the kitchen. My mother was coming out of the bathroom, petite and sporty as ever in all-black Spandex and a ponytail. As we locked eyes, I looked away. I felt my mother stiffen. Of course, she would sense something was wrong from the look on my face. She followed us down the hall into the next room.

Cedar and I walked into the family room together holding hands and sat down on a floral loveseat. My parents stood next to our son, bright-eyed Avi. My dad's hand rested on his shoulder, just below Avi's white-blond curlicues as he perched on the large stuffed rocking horse that came with the place.

"Hi Mama," he said and smiled his big full-face grin. His eyes squinted just like mine, crinkling downward a bit at the far edges.

"Hi baby," I said quietly, rubbing my cheeks. He rocked back and forth with gusto, his usual frequency.

I looked at my parents, took a big breath, and let it all out. "Eden has a genetic deletion," I said. "It sounds intense. The neurologist said it was too rare to know much more. But he said that it would affect her development. Probably a lot."

My mother sighed. Jet-black streaks appeared on her face, this moment beyond the power of waterproof mascara. "Oh, Emma." She breathed out slowly, and I could hear everything she felt for us inside of that sigh.

I was already halfway gone in my grief, but Cedar was more present. "Well, I mean, who knows how it will be? It seems unclear at this point. It could be intense. But look at her . . . she's the sweetest." Eden lay on a gauzy blanket with her feet in the air. Her gray hand-me-down onesie, emblazoned with the words "I heart art," fit loose on her delicate frame. I lifted her up; she smelled faintly of French toast. I kissed the top of her warm forehead.

My mom jumped in. "Maybe it's not so bad? I mean, there's so much we don't know yet about DNA. And there may be new developments soon. There is unbelievable scientific research happening right now."

My father looked at us pensively. With his perennially tan skin, he appeared much younger than his sixty-nine years. When he shook his head, his dark curls stayed in place, "I feel for you guys. But I know you will figure it out. You know, it's never the things we worry about." This was one of his classic sayings. Right now, it resonated.

I put Eden back on the floor on her stomach and propped *The Very Hungry Caterpillar* open underneath her. I looked over at Avi, who was rolling one of his favorite trucks around by the sliding glass door, and felt a sharp sting settle into my stomach. "Two healthy children, that's what we were going to have," I said. "That's what we were supposed to have."

I already knew my life had been cleaved in two—the one before the phone call from the neurologist and then the one afterward. This new life existed in various shades of unknown.

Cedar stayed with the kids while I walked outside alone for a long time, trailing my fingers along fences dotted with blooming bougainvillea. Sobbing, I called my friend Sara, whom I'd known since our days of not paying attention together in Hebrew school. I tried to speak between heaving breaths. "The neurologist was like, 'I don't know what to tell you, basically.' I mean, just living with this uncertainty? For days, weeks, who knows how long? I don't want it. I really don't."

Sara listened, asked questions—most of which I could not answer— and added some empathetic swearing for good measure. (She was the kind of person who tossed f-bombs around freely, like glitter.) While we talked, I could picture her strolling around her uptown Minneapolis neighborhood after work. Since she was her own boss, and had been for years, she generally did what she wanted when she wanted, and even though she had two children, she still somehow pulled it off. This was one of the many reasons I loved her.

After we ended the call, I lay down on a dusty hill outside of the house we had rented, looking up at a cluster of palm trees. My whole body ached as if I had the flu. As if those postcard-worthy date palms would never again be as beautiful as they used to be.

Later, while my parents took Avi and Eden to a nearby park, Cedar and I walked for miles, all over Palm Springs. We passed gates and fences, residential streets and stretches of stores, cacti, and palm trees. All I wanted to do was keep moving. We eventually came to an ultra-modern cafe with white walls and too much sunshine. I didn't want to eat, but Cedar got us a table for two anyway. I ordered a cheeseburger because I didn't know what else to do. I wasn't about to order a salad at a time like this.

It tasted empty, far away, a memory of a lighter time.

—⁓—

We returned to cold, reliable Minnesota and our creaky house in Minneapolis. We loved the city—it brimmed with parks and natural areas and was hip but still affordable. It had a vibrant art scene and pioneering restaurants, yet it was too far north to be pretentious. People wore winter hats and snow boots indoors; anyone who chose this place as home had to be hearty enough to deal with blizzards.

We lived in a creaky Arts and Crafts style home with beautiful beadboard and miserable insulation. Cedar and I thought it was our forever house. We liked to walk everywhere, even in the winter, especially to get a dipped cone at Sebastian Joe's even though it took at least twenty minutes one way.

Against this backdrop, we carried on with the tasks of living. I went back to my job as a staff psychotherapist at a Jewish nonprofit, and Cedar returned to his work as a music teacher at an arts high school.

One snow-encrusted January morning, we both took a sick-day, armed ourselves with parkas and a notebook full of questions we'd written ahead of time. We nervously piloted our trusty Prius across the icy city

streets to an appointment with a well-regarded geneticist and her team
at a nearby hospital.

"It's a very large deletion," a physician's assistant explained, gripping
her clipboard tightly. "It's on the 12th Q arm from the 21.2 all the way to
22. You can see it here." She flipped the clipboard toward us, pointing to
a black-and-white printout picture of the strands of DNA.

Deletions happen around conception as a random force of nature.
It wasn't anything we did or did not do. It was pure chance. During cell
division, a portion of Eden's DNA simply didn't copy. The larger the
deletion, the more genes are likely to be involved, which generally creates
a more acute impact.

"You need to be prepared. With this size of deletion, your daughter
will be cognitively impaired. It could be moderate, but it will likely be
severe. She may not walk; she may not talk. We don't exactly know how it
will affect her, but we do know she will be seriously affected."

She then listed all our daughter's possible problems, enunciating each
syllable in a stony monotone: heart conditions, skin conditions, muscle
weakness, brain abnormalities, kidney issues, degenerative hearing loss
that could result in deafness, substantial behavioral concerns, significant
developmental delays.

Each word was a hammer to my gut. Heart conditions, smash.
Degenerative hearing loss, smash smash. Substantial behavioral concerns,
smash smash SMASH.

The emotional intensity buzzed with a deep physical ache.

The clinical geneticist entered the room and, after she introduced
herself, began a physical exam on Eden. As she listened to her lungs,
I tried to breathe.

"She does appear to have the almond shaped eyes and hooded eyelids
that characterize a deletion like this. Her feet, are they webbed?"

Webbed? I shook my head slowly. The room smelled sharply of
rubbing alcohol.

I sat there, trying to listen, yet wondering all the while, *Is this really
happening? Is this really happening to us? This must be someone else's life,
and we were just dropping in. This couldn't be ours. Mine. Eden's.*

We were given a red folder containing a few poorly photocopied research articles that chronicled the handful of children with a similar atypical DNA deletion. There were so few others with this specific deletion that it did not even have a name.

Only now it did.

Eden.

I flipped through the articles, hooked into one paragraph that detailed a girl who was learning to tie her shoes at age fourteen. I quickly tucked the papers back into the folder. I could not look at them.

"How do you know she'll be so impaired?" I asked. "Maybe it won't affect her very much."

"I don't think so. It's a lot of missing DNA," she replied quickly, as if she was predicting the weather. There was no "Your daughter is still a worthy, beautiful, human." No reassurances that she was so much more than a deletion, more than whatever her disabilities would or would not be. No "There is still a path to joy or purpose or a good life."

There was no we; there was only us.

A family that would have to weather this on our own.

Sitting across from her on that hard, plastic chair, even with Cedar right beside me, I felt alone. Solitary in my grief. Crushed. Hollow.

I was the mother. I was supposed to make everything okay.

When she left the room, she sent in a genetic counselor with long smooth hair. "I can't imagine," she said from the rolling stool, her body perched toward us. "If I were you, if I was dealing with this with my daughter, who is twelve, I would be devastated."

She meant to be compassionate, but it felt like pity. I hated her I-feel-bad-for-you attitude. I envisioned her golden, healthy daughter with some nice, regular life somewhere. Did she know how precious it all was? Did she fully appreciate it? At that moment, I would have given anything for Eden to have been born with a complete set of DNA. Anything. Take a kidney (do I really need two?), my eyes, even my heart—though what good was it now anyway?

I wanted her, the girl I had longed for, dreamed about, prepared for—a daughter who would someday argue with me about politics, who could have babies of her own (if she wanted to), who might eventually take care of me when I was too old to care for myself. The daughter who could, eventually, do anything she wished to do with her own existence.

I wanted the future I had imagined, one of infinite possibilities.

I took a deep breath and tried to focus. Cedar asked a few tentative questions about the hearing loss, as this played on some of his biggest fears; his younger brother became deaf suddenly when he was two and a half as a result of childhood meningitis. Cedar, a musician and composer, was understandably alarmed.

He was no stranger to the ways this type of change could isolate a person.

"We don't know, exactly. We will have to continue to monitor it. Because her condition is so rare, there is no known trajectory for her," she said. I searched her face for some clue, something she maybe wasn't saying, but there was nothing. "The hearing loss is just something we are learning about now, with new research continuing to emerge. Like most everything in your daughter's case, we really aren't sure about how she will be affected. There is no crystal ball." She looked over at me, my face a ruddy, splotchy mess.

"Of course, it is normal to experience grief."

I already didn't like this labeling of things as "normal," since it suggested there was another side, its less desirable opposite. I bawled through the rest of the appointment. Short, gasping, successive breaths, and full-on heaving into the thin, scratchy tissues from the box on the table. It was a very un-Minnesotan display of emotion, unleashing that intensity into a bright, cold room full of strangers.

Eden, content in her bucket car seat, was as calm as a lullaby.

After the appointment, I walked with Cedar through the antiseptic hallways of the hospital and rode the elevator down toward the parking lot. I felt a tightening all over my body—heaviness in my stomach, my chest, my neck, slithering around my shoulders.

It was grief, of course, and I could feel it burrowing inside me.

―――∞――――

Another month. Another windowless basement hospital room. This time, a neurosurgery appointment to explore possible brain abnormalities. Eden balanced contentedly on my lap, observing, her face open and her mouth closed. The gray-haired surgeon, in blue scrubs, had a bit of a gut—but I still declared later, on the car ride home, that I thought he was a silver fox. Cedar chuckled and I smiled; for a second our banter felt good again, like before.

The surgeon looked at us tenderly, asking us the details of Eden's developmental and medical history. It was all the usual inquiries: "When did she first hold a toy?" But still, he seemed to be giving us his condolences, tilting his head ever so slightly.

Flanked by a diligent scribe who stood by the door silently, feverishly typing, the surgeon pointed to the MRI pictures of Eden's brain. I nodded along, as if I could fully comprehend it, like I saw snapshots of my child's brain all the time. "These are two arachnoid cysts," he said, gesturing to two masses in the globe of her brain. The one in her cerebellum hovered like Greenland on a world map.

"A lot of people have them and don't even know it. They often get discovered accidentally. Most don't need intervention. There's a 15 percent chance that she will need surgery on these at some point in her lifetime. We'll have to watch them to see if they grow in size."

"They look pretty large. I mean, that seems like a lot of brain real estate," I said.

"Well, maybe it appears that way in that particular image," he said, snapping along to show various viewpoints. "The brain has a way of working around them."

"There's also a 75 to 80 percent chance your daughter will need a spinal surgery within two years. Eden may have a tethered cord, which could require surgical intervention. We will have to continue to monitor it. And there's the matter of her cerebrospinal fluid, which is higher than normal. It could become hydrocephalus."

"Hydrocephalus?" Cedar asked.

"It's a condition that occurs when higher than normal levels of cerebrospinal fluid accumulate, which puts pressure on the brain," he said. "You'll have to watch for certain symptoms. It can be an emergency situation that would need immediate intervention." He listed the various symptoms that would help us discern whether our daughter's brain was malfunctioning.

All of this was such a contrast to Eden's mellow nature. A sweet-tempered, cuddly little baby, Eden was so agreeable and portable; you could tuck her in your arms and go anywhere. Even throughout these long appointments, she was steadfast in her giggles and gentle gazes.

"But this is relatively good news. Compared to all the bigger problems she will face in her life; this isn't so bad." And then he looked at us with kindness in his eyes, eyes that had seen thousands of children and families during their most harrowing moments. He had spent over an hour with us, and I understood it was just one of many hours he would spend at the hospital that day—and probably that night.

But . . . bigger problems? The comment darted around in my mind long after he had said it. The stinging in my stomach intensified. The only thing that seemed clear was that much of Eden's future was unknown, and likely, would be arduous. Painful. Possibly excruciating.

Questions ricocheted off one another in a cacophony of uncertainty inside me. Would Eden ever be able to carry on a conversation, eat a meal, go for a hike? How long would her life even last? And how would Cedar and I manage, now that our life was straying so far from plan? How the hell could we endure it? We were both sensitive, emotional. You could call it—generously—artsy, or—to use a term from my work as a psychotherapist—highly attuned. Perhaps overly so. Cedar even hated stepping on ants, and I was not much better, especially when humans were involved. I could interpret the emotions of anyone within a one-hundred-foot radius, regardless of whether I wanted to or not.

How would we weather this unknown road?

How *could* we?

How could *anyone*?

Whatever this road even was or would turn out to be.

CHAPTER TWO

Cheeseburger in a Coma

Mothering a child with exceptional medical challenges is a little like being on a low dose of a hallucinogenic drug. I went to college at University of California-Santa Cruz, so I should know.

On college move-in day, I heaved my two duffel bags onto the unoccupied bed and said a shy "Hi," to my new roommate. She took one look at me and asked breathlessly, "Is *that* all you have?" as she plunked another crate down next to her standard-issue dorm desk. Her face glistened with sweat from hauling in crate after crate of books, which, as I soon learned, contained the best of the Beat generation. Once she arranged her library around her side of our small white room, it was like the iconic indie bookstore City Lights had set up shop across from my sparse single bed.

I prided myself on having just a few material goods, which seemed like it would suit our dynamic just fine. We made small talk; I took a long time making the bed with my brother's hand-me-down blue comforter because I didn't know what else to do with myself. It was a good thing Kerouac and Ginsberg took up so much space—I hadn't brought anything to put up on the walls.

That first year I studied like I was getting paid by the hour, but my roommate did not have the same (obsessive) approach. When her parents visited mid-year, she had to ask me for directions to the library. I saw her do a lot of serious bong rips, and I heard her blast the song "Under Pressure" on repeat whenever one of her term papers was due. One afternoon we ended up belting out "Why can't we give love that one more chance" in unison, holding a water bottle as a microphone, closing our eyes for dramatic effect. We sang together in our dorm room that day as if we were drunk on stage at a dimly lit karaoke bar. I wasn't 100 percent sure about my roommate's level of intoxication—it was sometimes hard to discern—but I was stone cold sober and very into it.

Despite the Bowie moments, eventually I was ready to get out of the dorms. I found a housing co-op with twenty-eight other people and three cats, and I thought, *Home, sweet home.* And I was at home, in a suddenly very scrappy village, with a family of rats and a boyfriend who introduced me to Marxism, *Kind of Blue*, and sex (in that order).

The co-op was called Chavez House, named after local labor hero Cesar Chavez. It was a sprawling yellow Victorian with green and purple trim plus the back house, which appeared to be crumbling before our eyes. In what might have been an attempt at radical hospitality or pure laziness or both, there were no locks on the main doors. An extensive hand-painted mural of a naked goddess covered the walls of the common space. The house also included a large infestation of rats that dashed around the kitchen freely like it was the *Ratatouille* movie set.

We each had chores that we did—or were supposed to do—weekly, for the betterment of the co-op. Each Thursday night, I cooked dinner for everyone with my housemate, who had bright reddish curls. She was the type of person who always looked flushed and joyful; it was the highlight of the week. We would blast hip hop from the dented black CD player and dance like no one was watching (and really, they weren't). We also were on garden duty together and planted veggies that never seemed to grow.

During our weekly Sunday night meetings, which were mandatory, the house would erupt with tense exchanges regarding what to do about the rats. Decision-making was based on consensus—everyone had to agree to every single house decision. One meeting became a battle between those who wanted to use poison and those who believed the only humane way to deal with the vermin was by catch and release.

"I am going to move out if we don't finally deal with these rats," angled my boyfriend.

One of the other guys, a surfer, declared, "Well, I'm going to move out if we do."

You haven't really lived until you've argued for extermination to a roomful of vegans. When a rat scurried over my upstairs neighbor's face when he was trying to sleep, it got real. I knew it was only a matter of time until it would be my face underneath a long scaly tail. I ended up being the one who called the pest control service.

This was during an era where I got most of my clothes from what we called "The Free Bin," an old clawfoot tub in a filthy bathroom of the co-op. You could drop something off that you were sick of wearing, and you could pick something up to take with you. My uniform then was generally a mini skirt over stretchy pants, so that I could still bike everywhere and not flash the town of Santa Cruz. I found one of my favorite tight shimmery shirts in that bin, which I wore as much as possible, both at night and in the day. Glitter could be daywear, with the right attitude.

I was happy at the co-op and thought I might always live communally. There was always someone to talk to, someone who would consider the topic of fate or Burning Man or self-actualization on the front porch. I thrived in community. I even majored in Community Studies. A lot of my classes were independent study, which meant I was able to get credit for doing things that I probably would have been doing anyway, like volunteering at the Homeless Garden Project, and mentoring while working at a garden. I probably should have minored in gardening (or horticulture, which is basically the same thing but sounds fancier). In many ways, I was the same back then as I am today, only I showered a lot less.

I also spent too much time reading and more than that, belaboring over upcoming tests and papers. Just like high school, I would hit the books for hours at a time, hunkered down at an underground study center. My friends were out smoking weed and staying up most of the night at drum circles, and I was working on turning in those term papers early—weeks early, just to be sure I would get them in on time. It wasn't even for the grades; I had opted for narrative evaluations.

It was just the way I did things, by overdoing them, even in a place where a Banana Slug was the school mascot. If you would have asked me, I would have said that I wanted to get the most out of my education, that I loved ideas. That was part of it. My diligence was also motivated by fear, the fear of not being good enough. Or maybe it was more that I needed to *stay* good, by any means necessary.

I had a motor hum in my heart that was too revved up. At least, that's what it felt like, as if I was driven by an unstoppable and frenetic force. I had an itch to be productive, to do more and be more—and to do it faster, better, more perfectly.

Perfectionism was my native language.

This relentless drive to be perfect was something I inherited, something that was never mine in the first place. But I brought it with me nearly everywhere I went. I could have passed it down to the next generation, without trying.

I think I would have, if not for Eden.

—⟋⟍—

During the spring of my first year, after I had chosen a major but before I had a solid friend group, I completed a nearly three-month long wilderness adventure. Well, I didn't *fully* complete it.

In what initially struck me as miraculous luck, my university offered a program that was focused on studying the ecosystems of California; it seemed like a way to go camping and get academic credit for it. I filled out the registration forms quickly. I was in, without a doubt.

Back then, I loved everything about camping: the deliberate, unmarked hours and the tribal feeling of a small pack. I also liked the routines of life on the trail, i.e., waking up early, spending the whole day outside, eating dinner in front of a campfire, and then watching the sunset explode into the sky every single evening. The occasional, no-shame nudity that came with a trek like this was also a plus. I didn't even mind going without a shower for an indefinite amount of time. Soap was overrated.

Throughout high school, I attended a wilderness summer camp in Northern Minnesota. This is where I met my friends Quinn and Solvay, at a trip-planning meeting when I was fourteen.

"I heard you're a rebel," Quinn said to me immediately, her hair cropped short, her smile gigantic. Her head tilted just so, as if it was a question or an actual challenge. Quinn's friend had spotted me smoking cloves on a bench outside of a McDonald's in Uptown, and word got around fast.

Quinn and Solvay were city kids, and I was a suburban Jew who went to private school, so it was surprising they found me exciting in that way. Of course, I liked their attention. I had a short blond pixie cut, recently dyed platinum, and freckles. I was almost always barefaced and didn't wear a bra or shave, just for the principle of it. My style icons were Janis Joplin meets Ann Bancroft, a polar explorer from nearby St. Paul—polyester-leaning thrift store finds with a dash of high-tech fleece. Standing in the school lounge one day, I overheard a senior, a starter on the football team, motion to me from his chair, "You could be really pretty, if you tried." I looked at him, rolled my eyes, and walked away.

I didn't want to be that kind of pretty.

My mother was also not impressed with the way I dressed, and I don't blame her. "Are you trying to make yourself look unattractive?" she asked one day as I sauntered around in a worn-out pair of men's Levi's three sizes too big. Maybe I was. She had a point, as usual.

She nurtured me so affectionately early on—carried extra granola bars in her bag and initiated midweek treasure hunts just because. She even did things like design her own storyboards and puppet shows for me, my brother, and any of our friends who happened to be over for a playdate, of which there were many. When I was younger, she rubbed my back every night before I fell asleep while she read *Vogue* magazine. And here I was separating myself from her through, basically, an impersonation of the original cast of *Hair: The American Tribal Love-Rock Musical*. Back in her high school days, she was closer to a cheerleader, but not quite. She was too busy earning money for college. I was everything but one.

The camping trips were hardcore backcountry treks. When I was sixteen, Solvay, Quinn, and I canoed thirty-seven-days through Northern Ontario with a kind-hearted, confident guide in her early twenties.

Because these trips were so adventurous—and so polar bear adjacent—it was surprising my parents allowed me to participate. All this was before we carried cell phones or had access to online maps. There was, except for the few fishermen we encountered every week or so, no one else for miles around. We probably brought along bear spray. We did not bring a gun or anything else to protect ourselves beyond our Leatherman pocketknives. We used paper maps and an analog compass, which now seems reminiscent of a Wes Anderson film.

We canoed all day, nearly every day. I liked the rhythm of the strokes and the smell of the clear pine air, but mostly, I liked the conversations. Six weeks of uninterrupted paddling meant that we got to know each other in the least filtered way possible.

Late one night, as the sun was setting, we finally found a place to set up camp. We had already pitched the tent, gathered firewood, and started a fire when we realized we weren't alone. A giant, lumbering black bear was lurking curiously a few feet away. Immediately, we circled up to brainstorm in hushed voices about what to do. As the bear continued to approach us, we didn't have time to overthink it. This bear had no fear.

Quinn started singing a steady, subdued version of *Amazing Grace*. We stayed close in that circle formation and went with it. All five of us harmonized desperately, as if our lives depended on it. I do not know if we actually sounded great, or if with all of the adrenaline it just appeared that way to me, but we were, no question, giving this bear the best acapella concert she had ever seen. The bear listened, watching us intently, but did not come any closer. We got through several verses as we swiftly gathered up our stuff, threw it in the canoes, and set off down the river.

As we paddled in sync under the stars that night, we were aware of how powerful we were, so much so that we didn't even need to talk about it. We kept on singing for many miles. Finally, we found a semi-suitable place to camp near the shore of the river, and we pitched our tent once more for the night. We woke up to wolf tracks circling our makeshift campsite.

I found all this exhilarating. When we thought we might be lost during the last few days of the trip and started to run out of food, it still seemed like things would likely work out just fine. I don't remember worrying about the future or grappling with doubt. We rationed out the food we had left—a sweaty old block of cheese and some chunks of waxy chocolate, nibbling on each as we plugged on down the river. I slept well every night, despite the snores of the other girls, the intermittent buzz of the mosquitos, and our mummy-style sleeping bags scrunched up together. I felt safe out there. I was at home among these gutsy girls. And even more than that, I felt safe within myself.

During the college wilderness-for-credit program, we went into the field for a few weeks, slept in tents or right under the stars, and then drove our van to a dusty small town to reload our food and gear, and a day or so later headed into the backcountry again. I remember finding it a little soft because of the breaks between trail time, but I wouldn't have said that out loud. We hiked through stunning remote landscapes—Death Valley, the backwoods of Southern Oregon, then the Yolla Bolly Mountains.

Everybody picked trail names, which were basically nicknames with an earthy flair. There was Luna, Meadow, and Fawn, among others. One by one, over a series of days, everyone in the group had selected their nature-related throwback monikers. I was the last to decide. I didn't want to pick something predictable. Finally, I made my announcement to the group over our dinner of curried lentils and rice. "I'm going with Cheeseburger," I said with a grin. It got a good laugh, which was my main goal, and it stuck.

We spent our days belting out Paul Simon and Fleetwood Mac songs together as we hiked. In the afternoons, we read about forest and desert ecosystems. The women of the group argued about the divine feminine with the guys during our daily circle, and we all hoped to avoid any encounters with mountain lions.

We didn't get pounced on like prey, as I'd feared. On the last day of our group trip, the plan was this: first, we would do a sweat lodge together and then each of us would head out with our backpacks for several nights solo.

I knew the sweat lodge was a spiritual practice appropriated from Native people and that didn't seem right. As a Jew, I was raised with culturally informed rituals; I didn't need or want to adopt anyone else's. But because I didn't want to ruin the group tradition, I went along with it.

It was a sweltering hot day in mid-May, and we were hunkered down in a dusty, hilly valley. We were already sweating when we started building the structure out of a few tarps early in the morning.

Everyone else was fasting that day, as our instructors recommended, but, for me, eating felt vital. I got faint after skipping breakfast when I was in the comfort of air conditioning. I ate my normal breakfast, a cup of granola. Later, before the sweat, I devoured a few handfuls of trail mix.

Once the fire was fully stoked, we crawled in together in the steamy, small dimly lit space. The air was hot and smoky. I sat, uncomfortable, and tried to focus on my breathing. I would come out for breaks, chug water from my Nalgene water bottle, jump in the river, and then head back in. I don't know how long this went on for. My fellow group members were around me, all doing the same thing, except they were calm and pink-cheeked. I started to feel something like vertigo, the world spinning as if I was drunk, and then I became extraordinarily giddy. Suddenly, as I leaned forward in the sand of the riverbank, I could not stop throwing up.

My legs went completely numb; I couldn't shake them back to feeling again. I could hardly move. The lower half of my body was rubbery, seemingly detached. "I can't feel my legs," I moaned as everyone stood around me staring. The puke just kept coming, watery and pale. Someone helped me find my way inside of my sleeping bag.

One of the instructors asked me if I knew my name and what day it was. It was May 19. Eden would be born, many years later, on almost the same day—May 18.

Someone else asked me what my trail name was, and my voice sounded low and far away, in slow motion. *Cheeeseburrrger.* Somehow, I still knew this. And I knew enough at that moment to know these questions were a very, very bad sign. People don't ask you if you know your own name unless things are really going south.

I'm going to die here, I thought. *So, this is how it happens.*

I still knew my name, until I didn't anymore.

Two fellow group members hiked miles in the dark to the van and then drove to a phone to call for help. Before all of this happened, I didn't think they liked me much.

A helicopter was able to land on a patch of flat ground near our campsite. The only reason it was able to see clearly enough to safely land was because of the full moon. The light of the moon saved me—along with the guys who I used to bicker with about politics and feminist theory.

In the helicopter, I suffered a grand mal seizure because my brain was rapidly swelling. I had a collapsed lung, so I was intubated and put on a respirator. My kidneys stopped working. I was first airlifted to a smaller hospital in Ukiah but turned away because I needed a higher level of trauma care. I was then given another helicopter ride to Santa Rosa Memorial Hospital and finally admitted to the ICU.

My parents flew out to Santa Rosa first thing the next morning. They didn't know if they would be bringing me home alive or if I would be sent back via domestic funeral shipping.

My parents came to the hospital every day after their workout at the hotel gym and waited. My mother used the hairbrush from her overflowing purse to slowly work the chunks of dirt and sandy debris out of my hair. She waited and brushed, hopeful as ever.

I got a spinal tap because of concern about meningitis, which I did not have. What I had was acute hyponatremia, which is an electrolyte imbalance. In short, I drank too much water. I thought by chugging all those water bottles I was preventing something bad from happening, but instead my body started to shut down.

The doctors could not predict if I would ever wake up, and if I did, how much damage there would be. They would not speculate on my ability to recover, partially or fully.

I laid there, unresponsive, dreaming of mountain lions.

One early morning, a nurse called my mother, "I told her to squeeze my hand if she could hear me. Your daughter squeezed," she gushed. "You should come now." My parents rushed over, breathless.

When I finally opened my eyes, I was startled by the fluorescent lights and medical equipment. I heard beeping next to me and noticed the slick gray linoleum floor. The room was so bright, polished, and sterile. There were so many tubes attached to me, seemingly everywhere. A catheter snaked down the bed. Where were the campfires and towering redwoods?

My mother sat beside me in a shiny nylon FILA tracksuit. She saw my eyes dart around and spoke quickly. Her voice was loud, strained. "It's okay. You're in the hospital. There was an accident, Emma."

My whole body throbbed. It was hard to move anything—an arm, a leg, even my fingers. My head was a sandbag, dead weight. I closed my eyes. An hour passed, and then another. She waited by my bedside. I was in a coma for four or five days, although even my mother cannot recall the exact timeline. I certainly wasn't tracking.

An intensivist who had recently graduated from Stanford, originally from India, took a special interest in me. He checked in frequently with my parents, assuring them, "I want to bring her out of this slowly. You can't rush it; that causes lasting trauma to the brain." His meticulous care helped me resurface in a steady way.

The next day, around midmorning, I opened my eyes again. Then I finally spoke, "What? You're here?" I lifted my head abruptly, and then laid back on the pillows, hit with a swell of nausea. My voice was hoarse from being intubated, and it shocked me. It sounded like I was someone else entirely—as if I had aged decades.

"Try to eat a few ice chips," my mother encouraged, as she held up a plastic spoon and a Styrofoam cup. "Just a few. That's it, good," she motioned to me to open my mouth.

I took the cold chunks into my mouth, and they melted on my tongue. It hurt just to move toward the spoon. I thought, *Enough with the ice chips, already.* "I'm done," I replied. I closed my eyes. I drifted in and out of consciousness.

My older brother, Geoff, drove up from Los Angeles. He looked fresh, like he'd just had a haircut, smelling of his familiar aftershave. "Check out my new tattoo, Sis. What do you think?" He grinned, flexing for me. It was the letter G, nearly as big as a playing card. "Wow," I muttered. He raised his eyebrows and winked.

"It's good to be bold. Confidence, like it's all good." He shrugged, and then looked at me with crinkled, worried eyes. "I hope you feel better soon. We need to get you up and running again. Maybe you can get a matching tattoo. An E." I think I was able to laugh a little.

Friends drove up from Santa Cruz to visit me. One, with shaggy blond hair and a laid-back strut, who would later become my housemate, made the trip in his white VW bug. He stayed for several hours and read to me from Dr. Seuss's book *Oh, the Places You'll Go*. I really wasn't sure where I was going from there.

I stayed in the hospital for two weeks, weeks in which I remember very little.

With different luck or moon cycles or medical care I could have been disabled for life, cared for by my doting parents, my canoe paddle hanging dryly on the wall. Or maybe I wouldn't have made it that far.

We are all closer than we think to becoming disabled. As others have said before me: if we live long enough, ultimately, we will be. We aren't so far away from anything, really, especially each other.

———✎———

The night before we returned to Minnesota, I shared a hotel room near the airport with my mother. My dad had flown home to get back to work once I had made it out of the ICU. We were watching the movie *Shakespeare in Love* while laying on our respective beds. I couldn't understand the plot but didn't want to let on that this movie seemed so complicated. It was like watching something while stoned. I just couldn't follow it.

Toward the end of the movie, I turned to my mother. There was something I had always wanted to talk with her about, but it was never the right time. I'd heard her throwing up after meals sometimes during my early years. I was terrified, yet never could think of the right thing to say. "I just, I wanted to ask you. Are you okay? I mean, about the throwing up." I sighed. I kept going, even though I could feel a hard tightening in my chest.

What did I have to lose at this point?

"I thought it was cancer. I really . . . I thought you were going to die. Until I was older, and then I understood it was just . . ." I stopped, and I looked at her in her nightgown, with her soft skin, smelling of soap. Seeing her in that long, thick white fabric reminded me of my entire childhood, all at once.

"I'm better now," she said, hardly looking at me. And I could tell, she was.

"I haven't been in that place for a long time. It was a lot of pressure back then, being a woman. Twiggy was the big thing, the model of the times, back when I started. And I felt so anxious, and well, that was the way I learned to deal with it."

I thought about how it was *still* a lot of pressure—being a woman and also just being alive, but it was hard to put all that into words.

"Oh," I said, the fatigue settling in again. "I never felt like it was your fault. You know, the standards are so high." I ached for her.

More than high, the standards are impossible. How many millions of women were just like her, so why did she have to feel so alone? Why did she have to feel for even one minute, that this was her fault, something she did wrong? Why did this have to be a source of shame and embarrassment when clearly these standards were put on her, without her consent? My beautiful mother, thinking that she wasn't beautiful enough? This woman now next to me, forever near if I needed her—but somehow never hovering—who gave me my life.

I had always wanted to make it easier for her, especially when I was younger. Throughout elementary school, I often filled pages of paper with elaborate love notes laden with hearts and stars and rainbows, all the cheery things. I would slip one under the crack in her bedroom door at night, leave one on the kitchen table in the morning. I didn't know about smashing the patriarchy back then or even that my dolls were comparatively the measurements of starving women, but I knew I wanted my mother to feel what she deserved to feel: absolutely worthy. And not the kind of worthiness that has to be constantly maintained.

The conversation only lasted a few minutes. My head was gauzy and didn't know what else to say. I sunk back on a thick pillow and gazed at her face. "Thank you, Mom."

What exactly was I thanking her for? At that moment, it felt like I was thanking her for everything or anything or both. For showing up when I needed her. For understanding that when I didn't call her from college each Sunday like I'd promised, it wasn't because I didn't love her. For feeding me ice chips in the hospital, one by one, even though I pressed my lips tight and turned my face away. For lying next to me in this airport hotel, even though I had sometimes been sullen, somewhere else, entirely unaware of her efforts. She'd stuck by me through my fickle teenage years, and here we were now, in beds with thin sheets in a town we'd never planned on visiting. Together. When I looked over at her and took it all in, something snapped into place.

—— w ——

Instead of arriving home with the typical dorm room junk, like a stained bean bag chair or a chipped lava lamp, I came back from that first year of college with a traumatic brain injury. Also, a never-washed gown I had worn in the ICU that smelled of sour sweat and puke and fear, which was placed on the highest shelf in my parents' closet.

I was supposed to spend the summer as a camp counselor alongside Solvay, back at my old summer camp in the Boundary Waters. Instead, I was struggling to walk, sleeping in my childhood bedroom with the gumball pink carpet. My parents drove me to my medical appointments— the neurologist, nephrologist, and the endocrinologist. They drove me everywhere because I couldn't drive myself.

My brain was swollen with trauma. Every part of me was heavy with fatigue and hard to lift. It got better each week, and I progressed quickly, in part because my mother made me stroll down the block with her daily. I resisted every step, which was like wading through clay. I complained almost the whole time, but there she was, steadfast, walking in her clean white sneakers right alongside me.

"Of course, you can do it," she said, urging me to venture out a little farther down their street each day. It was an unwritten rule of the household: keep going, no matter what.

After a few months, I took a job as a teacher's aide in the city and felt a strange survivor's guilt about my comfortable existence. I had always prided myself on my independence yet still wasn't cleared to drive. So, my mother drove me thirty-minutes there and back each day in her big gold Pontiac Bonneville with the A/C cranked up high. I was both grateful and embarrassed as I waited for my mom to roll up at the end of a shift to climb in the passenger seat again.

This was a hell of an introduction to humility.

It was also a specific developmental moment, the moment in which I saw my parents as people—flawed, trying, nowhere near invincible. I stopped criticizing my mother for the small things she did that used to bother me too much—the sound she made when she cleared her throat or the way she always wore a full face of makeup, even to her workout classes.

Now I could see her tenacity as a first-generation college student who left home at age sixteen. Her Norwegian family of pipefitters and farmers said, "If you go, you're on your own." She did it anyway and worked her way through a degree in Early Childhood Education. When she was my age, there was no one holding her hand all the way down the block, urging her for another step. Except for herself.

And simultaneously, the softer side of my father emerged when, sparked by my near-death experience, he sold his business so that he could be more available. In the evenings, and sometimes even in the afternoon, he would come sit next to me on the screen porch, in his favorite rocker. We were surrounded by soaring willow trees and a wide view of the bay. He would sit in his loose, stretched out comfy clothes, set aside his *Wall Street Journal*, and we'd talk. He listened and asked thoughtful follow-up questions. My father was so curious and carefully considered my perspective, even when it was way *way* out there. I'd never noticed that before.

It became obvious: this village was my foundation, the starting point for every other way that my village could grow.

While I was home that summer, my friends from California sent handwritten letters and art supplies like plaster of Paris. They were kind, but busy with various summer jobs and the typical college revelry. They didn't understand what it was like to be healing in my childhood home and grappling with what it all meant. How could they? We were only twenty years old, if that.

Miraculously, I was still alive and relatively unscathed. I had most of my life ahead of me; it seemed likely that I would heal completely over time. But what would I make of it? How would I justify these arbitrary breaks? It seemed only fair; I should pay it back somehow. I spent a lot of time in my parents' spacious house on the lake, considering my own mortality, hyperaware of my privilege. (In short, your usual freshman sorority party life.)

I also longed to sit in the driver's seat of my Volkswagen, to go where I wanted when I wanted, just like I'd been used to doing for years.

I wrote in journals and tried to read. I'd have to go back over a sentence several times to decode what it meant. Words with double meanings, even simple ones, such as *mean, leaves,* and *type* stopped me altogether.

My mother took me to a therapist downtown who had a large office filled with toys. This therapist had a big smile, flushed cheeks, and thick corduroy pants. I tried to pepper our conversation with some upbeat, light-hearted commentary. I also explained how I'd made meaning from the *accident*, as we called it, by reconnecting with my parents and that I was glad it had happened to me. This was a speech I had already shared with several people. It wasn't the full, unencumbered truth. I just didn't want to do therapy. After our hour was up, she looked at me and said, "Well, it seems like you are doing great!" I nodded vigorously and smiled. I really was not great; I didn't even know *how* I was doing, but I was a good salesperson for it.

I was a girl who took hardship and made it shine. That was our first and last session.

I waited until I was twenty-six, in graduate school to become a therapist myself, to talk in depth about the coma, the anxiety it sparked in me, and everything else. In the aftermath of the accident, I didn't want to seem overly dramatic, or worse, ungrateful, the biggest sin of all where I was from. I was alive, wasn't I? I had it easier than a lot of people.

I carried around a heavy gratitude, laced with worry. For the first time in my life, I no longer felt invincible. Things no longer felt as if they were going to work out. I was all too aware now: my safety was not guaranteed.

Once I left the familiar cushion of my parents' home, my anxiety spiked. It seemed fairly likely, once I went back to school in the fall, that I would be attacked by a mountain lion. Although the year before I used to walk alone for miles and rest comfortably underneath the redwoods, I began to peek around every corner. My heart leapt, even when I was still. I saw danger in every fallen log, every shadowy patch of land. Eventually, I went on more camping trips, up to Point Reyes and to Big Sur. But I never felt safe. When I went into town, I no longer sauntered down Pacific Avenue with my chest arched, all tanned muscles and a tank top, smelling like ylang ylang. I didn't want anyone to notice me, especially men. This feeling did not wear off, as I had expected. The world was now a dangerous place.

Because of my TBI (traumatic brain injury), I got accommodations from the campus Disability Resource Center for untimed testing and notetaking support. I decided to carry a full load and with those accommodations, I was able to swing it.

In December, while home for the holidays, I returned to the neurologist for some additional testing. After the assessment, the doctor looked squarely at my mother and I to share his findings. "There is good news and bad news," he began. "The good news is that you can drive again because it looks like your brain waves have resumed typical patterns of activity. The bad news is I'll likely never see you again." We wanted to hug him, and we probably did.

I was excited to have autonomy once more and about how far I'd come—my brain had, in most ways, recovered in a short amount of time. But I felt as if something awful, anything really, may happen again at any moment.

It loomed over me, like the sky.

CHAPTER THREE

As Shiny as Our Faces

When I was seventeen, I stood in the middle of my childhood bedroom in bell bottom jeans with my hands on my narrow hips and told my mother I would never, ever get married. "It's too conventional," I'd offered, along with a cavalier eye roll, as if that explained everything. I thought that conventionality was for people who had given up on being brave.

I used to date all kinds of people. Mostly guys, but some women, too. I crushed out on a few hotties who didn't define themselves in those binary terms at all. Marriage equality was still a long way off in those days.

I made other declarations of what I would and wouldn't do. I wouldn't go to graduate school. I *definitely* wouldn't move anywhere near where I grew up, which was at least ten miles from any skyscraper. And I *absolutely* would not marry. My mother always said, with her lipstick-coated smile, "We'll see." My mother was right, of course.

Regardless of whether I wanted a legally sanctioned marriage, I always wanted children. I wanted three, enough to fill the whole backseat. I don't remember ever discovering that I had a desire for mothering or ever reconsidering it. It was simply there, like the way I laughed.

One late summer evening, my friend Jeannie took me to Cafe Maude to see a band called Enormous. We were both approaching thirty and both single, wondering in that very specific torturous way if it would always be like this. Even though I wasn't sold on marriage, I wanted to find a partner, and I worried that I might not ever find anyone who really felt like home.

Jeannie had a thing for the saxophone player, so we needed to play it cool. We sat in a booth in the back, shared an order of fries, and drank the cheapest white wine on the menu. "He's just so *present*," she said, her eyes flicking on like a light. I looked him up and down (quite easy to do when a musician is performing). He seemed nice, but not too nice. At first, I didn't get it.

And then that saxophonist played up on that pocket stage like it was the best party he had ever experienced, like he existed for this very moment. Like he was a Prince song, and it was 1999 (it wasn't). Afterward, jolted and euphoric from playing, he approached our table. Jeannie introduced him: Chris, who I would eventually call Cedar. "It's really nice to meet you," he said heartily, as if I was someone notable to meet. The warmth radiated off him, like a city parking lot in July. It was clear: this was his way in the world. I started to get it.

Shortly after that gig, Jeannie brought me to a barbecue at Cedar's house, which was only five blocks from mine. It was a casual gathering with a handful of her yoga friends—they all knew each other from the regular Friday evening class. As the sun set, Cedar and I stood next to each other in the kitchen prepping the veggie kebabs. When the light got a little pinkish, everything changed. Cedar and I couldn't stop smiling while spearing those chunks of zucchini. I soaked up his earnestness; he treated everyone as if they were a cherished, lifelong friend, including me. I was wearing a clingy cardinal-red blouse. As Cedar slid a cherry tomato onto the skewer, he turned to me unexpectedly, and said, "That shirt looks really good on you." I beamed.

I was struck with a sudden longing that I felt in my knees, my forehead. He was an ocean riptide, and I was standing at the edge of the water, preparing to get carried away. The misty breeze was already on my tongue, in my eyes.

By the time dinner was ready, I wanted to know Cedar's favorite songs and stay up all night in his tiny attic bedroom listening to David Byrne records together. I wanted to hear all about his childhood, his favorite way to spend a Saturday, along with his plans for next year and the year after.

But I didn't do any of that, not then at least. I did keep that bright red top until it faded and started to fall apart.

After we finished the last of the charred dinner and had more than a few glasses of too-sweet cava, Jeannie and I sat next to each other on the brick stoop facing the street. It was nearly all the way dark, and we gazed out at the fading light as it hit King's Highway, a stretch of parkway in my favorite part of the city.

Her body was tense, a closed fist. I didn't get it, again, until she spelled it out, "You know I like him so much. And you're just going to go all out flirting like that?"

I felt her words right where I should have, in the gut. "I'm sorry. You're totally right." Jeannie and I had been roommates, twice. A few years before, she had invited me to share her apartment after I made the unfortunate choice to hook up with a housemate who I had recently met on Craigslist. Note: I couldn't recommend this less. And before that, I slept across the hall from her in an old four-square home so drafty that we covered the windows with plastic to avoid an indoor breeze. We spent a whole blustery evening trying to hold the material taut while we sealed it shut with a blow-dryer. Jeannie knew how to do things like that, like it was easy.

She was my *girl*, one of my dearest ones. On the day after her mother died in her arms, I made matzo ball soup for Jeannie and her siblings as they planned the funeral. I wasn't always pious—not even close (the truth is, before I had met Cedar, I hadn't *not* made out with Jeannie's charming older brother on the top floor of a parking garage), but here I knew what to do.

That night, I left with my dear friend, as I should have.

Cedar and I kept running into each other on the street in our neighborhood, Lake Harriet Farmstead. I biked by him twice on the corner near Gigi's coffee shop. Once I rode past him, waving. Once I stopped, but only briefly. I wanted to linger there with him on 36th Street so badly, but instead leaned my silver Bridgestone road bike for just a minute against his Honda. "See you around," I shouted over my shoulder.

Still, I thought of Cedar often, like when I was speeding down highway 35W and a raspy song full of brass instruments came on the radio. I didn't know him well, but I missed him.

All the while, Jeannie and Cedar stayed friends and went to yoga together. Before she met her Bay Area boyfriend, Jeannie hoped that Cedar would ask her out, but Cedar had a rule against making moves on any friends. He didn't want to come off as *that guy*; he didn't want to be disrespectful to women. It was considerate, but his approach really narrowed any dating prospects.

While putting herself through nursing school, Jeannie fell in love with a doting photographer who had a steady job in San Francisco. She decided to move there, as part of her unfolding adventure.

At Jeannie's going away party in September, there were a few effusive toasts to her new sunlit life, and, like most potlucks I've attended, too much hummus.

Before dinner, Cedar and I stood together alone in the den for almost half an hour, marveling, in part, over how close we lived to one another. He had moved since our first, fated barbecue the previous summer to a new apartment within the same neighborhood. We discovered, grinning, that his new place was even closer to my one-story bungalow on Harriet Avenue. He was in love with music, had been playing relentlessly since age seven, but never bragged about his talent. "It's just what I do," he offered, his eyes wide, bright and glacier blue.

"Tell me about your teaching schedule," I suggested. I mostly just wanted to keep talking. I knew he taught private saxophone and clarinet lessons and played gigs at least a few nights a week. He stood close enough for me to inhale his woodsy scent with every sentence. I tried not to stare at his sweet, open face.

He said, "Yeah, I'm working all over the place right now. I even teach one day a week at a military school. I like the kids. It's strict. But I like the variety, the different kinds of people."

Inside, I swooned. *He likes kids. He likes his work. And he likes all kinds of people.*

As Cedar leaned against the wall near a set of French doors, he offered, "I'd like to cook dinner for you sometime. You could walk over." He tossed this out casually, as if we had done it before. He didn't get my number right then, but I thought I would hear from him soon. Later, in bed, I replayed this in my mind. It made it hard to fall asleep, even hours later.

The morning after the going away party, I helped Jeannie pack up the last of her things in her second-floor apartment. I sat down on her bed as she folded up the thickest sweaters. I had worried all morning that she might feel angry with me, or possibly betrayed, so eventually I just blurted it. "Jeannie, is it okay if I go out with Cedar? He pretty much asked me out last night—said he wanted to *cook* for me." I waited for her response, sweating. She looked back at me with her always-surprising golden green eyes. They were so intense; it was like I could see everything she'd been through just by gazing over at her.

"I hoped that you would. You'd be good together."

I breathed out, finally. That was friendship, right there.

Cedar didn't call me, after all. After a week with no word from him, I reached out myself to arrange our first date. Unlike Cedar, I had absolutely no problem with making a move on a friend. None whatsoever.

———ᨠᨠ———

Eight months later, Cedar and I hightailed it to Madeline Island on Lake Superior during an unseasonably warm stretch of May. After loading up our backpacks, we were ready to hike into Big Bay State Park to stay for a few nights. There were lots of things we had remembered: my little gas stove, our sleeping bags, all the food we could possibly eat and then some. Once we made it all the way to our site to set up camp, we realized that someone hadn't packed the tent poles. And by we, I mean me.

We sat on a log and howled with laughter, and that's how I knew it was going to be a good life together. The mosquitos were out already, humming their high-pitched whirr. We decided: no poles, no camping. I wasn't *that* hardcore, not anymore. I was in some ways relieved.

So instead, as the sky grew dark, we found a tiny hotel on the beach with a king size bed and crisp white sheets. We cooked our meals in the sand outside on my portable propane stove and had a big bonfire, just the two of us, on the shore. One night we walked to the iconic island bar, Tom's Burned Down Cafe, and danced on the deck to dubstep. Every night we slept nine hours under a thick down comforter.

Our last morning of the trip, I was wearing sweats, or the equivalent. There certainly was no makeup involved, which was standard fare for me anyway. Cedar turned to me, handed me a paper to-go cup of coffee with 2 percent milk and said, "So, do you want to get married?"

It seemed a little casual. Maybe I had wanted a little more fanfare? Not like rose petals strewn over a diamond ring, nothing that could have ever appeared on *The Bachelor*, but maybe some preplanning on the experience?

Then I took a breath in and thought about how much I loved this person in front of me (who was definitely *not* on one knee). The dailiness of it made it feel real. At that moment, I was struck with affection and endless hope. I replied, "Of course." You could probably see my smile halfway across the lake.

I said I would never get married, especially to a man. But my mother was right. One blustery Friday in August, Cedar and I hightailed it to Decorah, just over the border into Iowa, for a civil ceremony at town hall. We were not eloping. We went to Iowa for solidarity because at the time, LGBTQ+ folks couldn't get legally married in Minnesota, but in nearby Iowa it was legal.

I wore a knee-length chiffon dress from H & M that draped surprisingly well. Cedar sported a collared shirt with a pink tie. We were sun-kissed from a long summer full of woodsy adventures, filled with joy, unselfconscious in nearly every way. During the drive, the rain pelted down on the car in sheets, and it did not matter.

As a person who had long identified as queer, the trip to Iowa felt like a way to acknowledge my sexuality and community, yet still marry the love of my life. It was, in a sense, a way to have my wedding cake, and eat it, too, even though we didn't actually have a wedding cake. Later, with our friends and family, we served luscious eclairs from our favorite bakery and not one person complained.

We should make the rules as we go, especially if the rules include pastries.

And also, we should make the rules as we go because creativity is a way to remember that we are alive.

Cedar happened to be a cisgender man. He didn't have to be. That's how it felt—all very love is love—although when I look back on it now, it seems more complicated than that. Though regardless, Cedar made me feel fully seen, alive to the point where it almost felt holy, the thing we had between us, a force pulling us toward each other, like I'd been waiting my whole life to meet him. At least my whole life before age twenty-eight. And somehow that led me to embrace the state-sanctioned institution of marriage, which I do not regret.

After the fifteen-minute event (including pictures), we caravanned with my parents over to Seed Savers, a nonprofit garden enterprise. When the rain let up, we strolled toward the orchard, flanked by giant sunflowers and sherbet-pink bursts of echinacea. It smelled of mud and tomato plants. Our friends Angela and Ben, yoga instructors who joined us for the trip, affably wound around the paths with us.

Near a patch of black-eyed Susans, Cedar and I stopped for a passionate kiss. We were elated, although we both had terrible colds and stopped to blow our noses roughly every five minutes. We tore through nearly a whole box of tissues during the trip. On the way home, it poured so hard that the roads flooded—some of them closed, even. We made it home just fine.

A few months later, we had a Jewish wedding near my childhood home, at Gale Woods Farm. While Cedar wasn't Jewish, we always said that he was "Jew-ish." There was no one I'd rather snuggle next to with my feet up, the heavy *New York Times* splayed out between us, and argue about who gets to read the "Sunday Review" first. He was also more willing than most to crack jokes about death, any kind of awkward experience, and himself, not necessarily in that order. I didn't care that he wasn't officially a Jew; he said he was happy to raise our children that way, and that was enough for me.

I was not overly concerned about the wedding details; I hadn't even seen the venue before we booked it. Cedar and my parents had all been there previously and said it was lovely. A wedding didn't strike me as stressful, probably because I didn't have any real expectations for it. I didn't find the planning to be difficult or the decisions to be onerous. Getting married was thrilling—we were planning a party, and Cedar and I loved a good party.

On a cold Saturday night on Thanksgiving weekend, we celebrated under a chuppah that my mother fashioned out of my late grandmother Edith's lace tablecloth and sticks she found in the woods near her house. It was officiated by our beloved Rabbi Zimmerman who also helped me become a Bat Mitzvah.

I wore broken-in cowboy boots with my off-white handmade dress; I wasn't about to enter this lifelong commitment while feeling uncomfortable. We took giddy pictures in the snow, despite the frigid late-November air. I hardly felt the cold at all against my bare shoulders. The bright red barn behind us was lit up like a beacon.

Cedar had composed a piece of music for the occasion—it was warm and breezy and free—and the whole barn was illuminated by candlelight. His musician friends played accordion, bass, and violin during the procession, and then later a band called Hookers and Blow (who went by Hava Nagila Monster for weddings, for obvious reasons) rocked us into dancing nearly the entire evening. For our first dance, Cedar stood on stage with the band to play Ray LaMontagne's "You Are the Best Thing" and then jumped down to join me on the floor.

My father made an exuberant toast. His olive skin looked polished, and his eyes were glossy when he spoke into the microphone, "Emma and I have a tradition of having lunch together almost every week or so. I always ask Emma, 'How are you?' Some days it's good, some days more of a *meh*. But since these two have been together, it's been, 'Dad, I'm *great*.' And that's what I want for her. To feel great and to be loved."

He was right. Cedar and I were deliriously, ridiculously happy when we found each other. I adored the way he could enter a room and have an engaged, wholehearted conversation with nearly anyone. He was so thoughtful about how he structured his time, how much he put our connection as a priority in his life. I was high on Cedar; I loved how he loved.

Did I also love that he was a man? Maybe there was a part of me that did. Since I could go any which way in my sexuality, I not-so-consciously thought, *I might as well please my parents.* Why *not* make it easy on everyone? This wasn't at the forefront of my mind. It was tucked away somewhere deep, and I would not find it until many years later.

Regardless, I had a blazing attraction to Cedar. And there was a part of me that didn't love that he was a man, a part that perhaps I tried to suppress. Conventionality has often rubbed me the wrong way. For starters, it's boring, and I knew that through this marriage—this monogamous relationship I chose—my queerness could become invisible. Like many, my queerness was not, *is* not, only a sexual identity. For some, it also encompasses gender identity and/or a defiance of the gender binary. It is an approach to life that embraces the questions, that challenges cultural scripts. It is a refusal to pretend I am some cookie-cutter person. It is a refusal to pretend any of us are.

When we married, Cedar and I had only been dating a year; I was hopped up on the dopamine that comes from that early, euphoric stage of love. I didn't feel like I was losing a part of myself by marrying a man. I wanted to become family with him, but after years of living communally and trekking around the wilderness in small groups, I never wanted just that nuclear family experience either. We would figure it out together.

At the peak of the night, Jay-Z's "Empire State of Mind" came on while we were dancing the hora. We started the raucous ritual while the band had gone on break. One of my father's dearest friends, a Holocaust survivor, said that he wasn't leaving until we did the hora because it wasn't a Jewish wedding without it, and that he was planning on leaving *soon*. When the dance mix—the one we had so carefully crafted ahead of time—turned from klezmer to hip hop royalty we kept on going, likely making this the first and last time Hava Nagila met Alicia Keys.

My mother was hoisted up on her chair, beaming in a bronze shimmery dress and knee-high boots, high above the crowd. Her dewy skin glowed with elation. As the night wore on, almost everyone was sweating together out on the dance floor for hours, gulping up all the kegs of Bell's Two Hearted until we ran out.

I never dreamed of a wedding. But being tossed around on a wooden folding chair, fully supported, knowing that Cedar and I chose each other? With the heat, bliss, and highly enthusiastic dance moves of our people right there with us? To do this whole life together, every single day? We were celebrating our connection to something bigger than our own individual selves.

As I looked out at the crowd, I saw my newer therapist friends dancing in a circle, laughing, and my old friends dapper in carefully curated outfits and/or artful tattoos, and Cedar's ever-loyal friends from childhood passing around a baby, and a whole lot of musicians.

From the view up there, anything felt possible.

It was Cedar and me, not against the world, but for it. We were going to have a blast. We had each other, and we had our plans—a creative, connected life together, and eventually, a few children. As we surfed sweatily above our friends and family, hoisted up in those rickety chairs, our future was limitless and thick with love, as shiny as our faces.

CHAPTER FOUR

A Very Natural Birth Story

When I was about twelve weeks pregnant with Avi, I went to one of Cedar's shows in Northern Minnesota at a resort in a little town called Lutsen. I pulled on a tight ballet neck t-shirt that revealed what I believed to be my baby bump and waited for the congratulations to roll in from Cedar's bandmates. *I'm really showing*, I thought. In reality, I think I just looked bloated. No one could decipher that I was pregnant.

I marched around there feeling proud *and* gorgeous.

There was also a part of me that was afraid; Cedar and I were waiting on important test results regarding my pregnancy.

On the night of the show, I waited alone with my fizzy water on the balcony for the concert to start. Seated next to me was an older man who had salt and pepper hair and a relaxed posture. This guy spent most of the show laughing and talking with his adolescent son, who appeared to have Down syndrome. I spent most of the show with a pit in my stomach, trying not to look at them.

I felt a tenderness toward the pair, a respect even, that made it hard to look away. But I remember also being struck by a strong and pressing feeling I could not shake. Pity. What I did not know then is that pity is the opposite of honoring a life.

I felt that pity, at least in part, because I didn't have much experience with people with disabilities. I did work as a personal care attendant one summer in Santa Cruz with a young woman my age who had cerebral palsy; we used to blast her favorite indie rock album on repeat in the kitchen of her cottage—we both knew all the words. We connected easily and spent a lot of time hanging around her beachside neighborhood. Yet that time I spent caring for her, while somewhat illuminating, was also short-lived.

I thought having a child with a significant disability was something like they tell you at the doctor: a terrible loss. Something you spend your whole life grieving over.

As it turns out, it's infinitely more complicated than that.

It depends on how you face it. It depends on how much you believe the dominant culture's messages about which lives are considered most valuable. And most of all, it depends on who is with you along the way.

—⁂—

The first bright June afternoon that I held Avi in my arms, I was still numb from the waist down from an unplanned C-section that came after over three days of labor. It wasn't exactly the magic moment of connection I'd been anticipating. I held him close, nuzzling his serious old man face. The scent of my baby, just as warm and earthy as I imagined. I already loved him in a primal way. But, also, it was hard for me to breathe after all that anesthesia. As I laid on the firm postoperative bed, there were several hours where I could not move my legs; I thought to myself, *I might die here.* My mind flashed to the last time my legs were numb like that: right before I went into that coma in college.

I had desperately wanted a natural birth. In preparation, Cedar and I had attended a six-session hypnosis class called Hypnobabies that met for three hours each Wednesday. In addition to the class, participants were expected to practice for thirty to forty minutes per day. Our facilitator Tara had four children and loved giving birth! For Tara, birth did not hurt at all! She was so excited to share this amazing pain-free experience with us!

I trained in hypnosis for countless hours so I could be prepared and comfortable throughout my drug-free water birth. I typed a double-sided document outlining my natural birth plan and presented it to the good-hearted nurses at St. Joseph's Hospital in Saint Paul, Minnesota.

There's an old Yiddish saying, "We plan, God laughs." Despite all that preparation for Avi's birth, I needed nearly every intervention known to humankind. Epidural? Yep. Morphine? Absolutely. I think I might have had nitrous. And no, it was not a water birth. Avi's head was cranked, chin fully extended up to what they called "military style," sending him ramming against me for roughly seventy-two hours.

Another word for it is back labor.

Another word for that is *ohmyfuckinggod*.

Down the cool gray hallways of the Maternity Care Center, we tried the rebozo, a large scarf made for jiggling the mama's belly, with the hope of repositioning the baby inside. I got on my hands and knees on the linoleum. I rocked. I hugged pillows. I took a shower. I even tried yoga, and I was not a yoga person.

I got in the hospital room's bleach-white bathtub naked. Not to be confused with the grand-finale birthing tub, it was just a regular hospital bathtub. A veteran nurse had at one point offered some hope when she announced, "Just one more centimeter and you'll be ready for the big tub." Earlier, a doctor broke the amniotic sack with what looked like a knitting needle. I got a shot of Pitocin, a medicine used to speed up labor.

I had been told by this nurse that I could wear a swimsuit for modesty. *Modesty*? The pain was so torrid and jolting that I didn't care if my teeming naked body was on display on Madison Avenue. I was far beyond caring about any such thing by that point, *days* into this birthing process.

Full bush on display, I got out of the bathtub. I got in it again next to Leah, the doula who had stuck it out with me nearly the whole time, only napping briefly in a room nearby at my mother's insistence, even though she had two young children at home.

The warm water was running, and it helped with the pain for a while, enough so that we could talk. She sighed from the edge of the tub and then said, "You are so beautiful pregnant." I felt anything but beautiful, and yet

I wanted to stay there with her for as long as possible. It was quiet, except for the water, and still. We had the light off, and there were no windows, so it looked like night was falling even though it was still daytime. As I leaned back on the cold porcelain, it was holy, just the two of us in that small bathroom, calm and defenseless. Such a needed break from the intensity.

Sometime later, I spiked a fever, huddled on the bed in my hospital gown, sweating and shivering, completely stalled out at seven centimeters. I had slept only a few hours since Sunday. It was now Wednesday.

The new nurse on-duty told us matter-of-factly, "Even if you could get to ten, you'd still have several hours of tough labor ahead of you. Do you have the energy to push a baby out? That can be the hardest part." My body was weak and shaky; I had already done twenty-six miles of a marathon, but the finish line was nowhere in sight.

Cedar, who had deferred to me for days, became resolute. He was still wearing a blue-green V-neck tee shirt and matching pants that looked like scrubs; he joked before getting to the hospital that he was posturing as a nurse, and maybe he would get asked to pick up a shift. "I hope not," he had cracked. "If there's blood, I'll be like *catch you later*."

His voice was serious now. He looked at me almost as if he was wincing. "I'm worried about you, Emma. I think we should go for the C-section." My mother looked at me with soft, pleading eyes, and agreed with Cedar. "You've been through enough. *Please*."

The whole thing ended with a four-hour wait for the surgeon. Once I finally got to the OR, the doctor cut a deep slice into my lower abdomen while I focused on breathing out of my mouth. It smelled like he was burning me alive. Afterward, I was given Oxycontin to manage the searing pain from the C-section. I was told to "Stay on top of the pain." I did not argue.

Obviously, this birth was totally, completely natural, just as I had planned!

I felt as if I'd failed. I had the belief that if I tried hard enough then I would absolutely get what I wanted. I was left wondering, *Did I not do enough*? This is how I was back then: determined, disciplined, unrealistic.

Thinking I had control of things that, of course, I didn't.

Later, on her postpartum visit to our house in Minneapolis, Leah sat with me on the couch as thick tears splashed down on my already stained nursing tank top. She looked in my eyes, which I knew were flanked by dark circles, and said, "I have never seen anyone work so hard for so long. I have never seen anyone fight so hard for what she wanted."

I appreciated her acknowledgment. I was touched by her generous, tireless care during the many hours I labored. And yet, there was something left unquestioned. What drove me to work that hard? To push myself that far, beyond my own sense of okay-ness, past the point of my own well-being? There are no awards for birth. Except, of course, the baby.

I was already thick with the longing of maternal perfection, weighed down by its all-encompassing promise of success. I wanted to feel good about myself, my choices. I wanted to feel like I'd done enough, the best that I could do, but that kind of enough was never done.

I didn't invent this mothering standard. It had been handed to me, just like it was handed to so many women who happened to be alive in this cultural climate.

For me, the type of parenting perfectionism that set in—even before Avi was in the world—wasn't easily discernible. It wasn't the traditional June Cleaver variety, full of hairspray and mild-mannered first impressions. It was a quirky offshoot, a type of mom-who-works-outside-the-home perfect—messy and inventive and full of my own dreams, but only to a point. What was required of me? Only that I give everything to my family, to my career, and ideally, to everyone else, as well.

I had these high expectations almost across the board. Going back to when I was in school, in my work, in nearly every area except for the way I kept my car—that was an unholy mess.

My therapist self knew I needed to let go more often; my mom self wasn't so sure.

After this arduous beginning, everything felt difficult. Moving my body, for one. I didn't fully know the extent of this beforehand, but a C-section is a major abdominal surgery. Everyday movements, like stepping into the shower, sent a shocking jolt of pain through me. Avi was not a strong sleeper, and since I was breastfeeding, I was up with him every two hours, shuffling over to his crib with stiff, forced movements. Then I spent forty-five minutes nursing him. The math on the time available to sleep was ridiculous.

For about a month, I sprawled on the couch whenever possible, relegated to my role as a human milk machine. My days (and the sustained, disrupted nights) began to revolve around breastfeeding. It wasn't as easy as I had originally anticipated. For the first few weeks, my nipples were like the skinned knees of an amateur skateboarder.

Cedar and I argued fiercely about whether he would go back to work right away; he was supposed to teach at a three-week jazz camp. "All I need to do is work this first camp, Emma," he told me. "Then I'll be around."

"That's when I need you most. Do you not even *care* about me? How am I supposed to tend to this baby, day, and night, like this?" I screamed.

I was clearly a blissed out, chill kind of mom. I could have been featured in *Tricycle: The Buddhist Review.* I was the goddamn mommy lama.

When he wasn't teaching at the summer music camp, Cedar whipped up turkey and pepper jack sandwiches for us, broiled in the toaster oven so that the cheese melted completely. It was the house specialty, the only specialty, during our early postpartum days. I would eat those sandwiches on the velvet sky-blue couch in the living room, sipping from a teal plastic oversized Big Gulp that came free with the purchase of a childbirth.

As the months rolled on, I became entrenched in an infant nap/nursing stronghold that I referred to as "baby jail." Avi wasn't the most flexible sleeper, and I wasn't the most flexible parent. I ended up spending much of the day at home, planning around Avi's schedule. I was spending too much time alone, easy to do in a Minnesota winter no matter what. It was no surprise that I was lonely.

Before I fell deep into Eden's mind-blowing medical needs, my parenting approach was *just* this side of apprehensive. The side way over there. A skipped nap was stressful, and a bout of strep throat made my heart thump with worry. I wanted everything to be just so—the organic plum oatmeal baby food, the sheets on the crib, the temperature of the nursery.

Looking back on it, it is clear I was experiencing anxiety (with some postpartum OCD symptoms thrown in for good measure), partly due to the cumulative sleep deprivation. But at the time it all seemed critical, getting things *right*.

I knew I needed to find some friends with children because I had very few. Most of my friends were queer and waited longer to have children. And some did not choose children at all.

By the spring after Avi's birth, I was ready to do something about it. I always wanted a village, whatever the life phase, and it seemed clear that I needed to build one with other mothers. I was willing to work for it, in part because of my tendency toward loneliness and other big (and generally uncomfortable) feelings.

I invited almost every new-ish mama I knew over for an outdoor potluck on a Sunday afternoon. It was an idyllic, sunny day and almost everyone I invited showed up. I wasn't the only one looking for mom friends.

It was not a BYOB (bring your own baby) event, although we made an exception for newborns—the point was to get some much-needed time *away* from those babies. It was BYOB in the traditional sense though; there were a few bottles of wine floating around. I made a lime quinoa dish that I'd been churning out on autopilot. When I emailed a casual invitation for the first gathering, my long-time friend Debra, who had a four-month-old, responded, "Would not miss it!" She arrived right on time carrying a giant container of fresh chopped salad.

She later hipped me to her more realistic personal aspiration for motherhood—be more like World's Best Dad. She had the mug to prove it. Dads could do the basic things that moms do, like push their child in a swing at the playground or take a kid out for ice cream, yet be met with sincere, encouraging nods, or even compliments. Dads could be into their careers without feeling guilty for the time spent away from their children. Dads could take their screaming toddlers on an airplane, surrounded by offers for help from strangers, while moms would receive only disapproving glares or criticism. Dads could have hobbies, passions even, without being judged for their time away from their families. Dads had reasonable standards.

Moms? Moms were tasked with everything else.

I asked all the women to sit in a circle on a patch of grass while the sun streamed over the neighbors' fence. We all dished on the best and worst parts so far in mothering.

"It's been a lot harder than I thought it would be. I've been so anxious, just about everything—especially maintaining my pumping schedule, then trying to keep up at the office," one mama confessed, her face crumpling. She gave the group a tight smile through the tears, and a pang of empathy shot through me.

I found some tissues, passed them to her, and jumped in, hoping to comfort her, "Oh, yeah, that makes so much sense to me. I am a wreck through a lot of this, too." The mama looked down at the grass, still wiping the tears away quickly. The sun caught in her highlighted hair.

My boisterous friend Carly, who nursed her newborn in a sling like a boss, also attended that first Mamas gathering. At one point, she said, "Oh my God, are you just barely able to stand the utter cuteness? I basically get nothing done whatsoever. And who cares?" She held her newborn daughter's tiny hand to her mouth and lightly nibbled on it, then laughed.

Sometimes I wanted to be a Carly, and care less yet still love full throttle.

When it was my turn I said, "Well, I think the best thing so far has probably been how much I love Avi. Everyone said oh, you're going to feel some crazy love, and I was like okay, sounds good. And then… whaaaaat . . . that part is bonkers." I recounted how getting Avi dressed was like wrestling a bear in his natural habitat.

I felt some comfort in connecting with other people going through a similar thing. And although my perfectionistic expectations were challenged by my current reality, I had no idea then, in that grassy backyard in Minneapolis, exactly how bonkers the love was going to get.

This was back when Eden was an idea, a thought, a future person who maybe, perhaps someday, I would meet. My life was filled with typical concerns back then, my marriage stuffed with typical stressors.

Becoming a caregiver was one of the farthest things from my mind.

—∿∿—

With Eden, we scheduled a C-section; we had the date on the calendar weeks ahead of time. There was no in-depth exploration of how to approach the delivery; the decision for a C-section was mostly made for me, due to an issue called placenta previa, a condition that involves a low-lying placenta. In some ways, I was relieved. I didn't want to go through anything like Avi's birth ever again.

Because of the placenta previa, I had been monitored closely throughout the pregnancy. The ultrasounds indicated a high amount of amniotic fluid. My doctor was befuddled and told me to drink more water. I didn't want to overdo it, given my medical history, but I did consume the high end of what I thought was a reasonable amount. It didn't make a difference.

We selected Fairview Southdale Hospital for the delivery, which we chose mostly for its convenient location. With another child at home now, these things mattered more. At a Sunday afternoon Mamas Group, as we lounged on Debra's plush sectional, I announced, "I'm glad I'm going to be across the street from Southdale Mall. That way I can pop in for an Orange Julius right before the baby gets taken out of me." Debra laughed the loudest. She never equated motherhood with martyrdom.

My perfectionistic expectations had already shifted. But not enough.

This time, my birth plan was the opposite of natural, choosing which day would be best for the birth based on scheduling preferences. I didn't struggle with this decision since it wasn't really a decision anyway. I tried to make light of it and mostly not think too much about the last time when the doctors removed my organs, and I could hear it. Those slippery sounds would be forever with me, but I didn't want to relive them.

I created a playlist for the occasion and packed headphones in my hospital bag so I could listen to something else. "I'm Looking Through You" by The Beatles was the first song, and it didn't strike me as ironic, as I laid there, all cut up on that surgery table, until later.

When I first held Eden in my arms, she had the look of a wayward baby bird. She was so pink and tiny, only five pounds, twelve ounces, although the doctors had projected from recent ultrasounds that she would be at least seven and a half pounds. No one could explain it. *It's a fluke,* I thought. *No need to read into it.* But there were other signs that she was not as healthy as we had hoped, including those high levels of amniotic fluid discovered earlier in my pregnancy.

I breathed in her raw sweetness and felt her body, flushed and smooth as a summer palm, as she settled onto my chest. I whispered her name to her for the very first time, and it felt like a prayer. A prayer to something, somewhere—maybe even God, I wasn't exactly sure—for a life that echoed a name like hers. *Eden*.

CHAPTER FIVE

An Electric Pulse

"I will love you, even when you are dead." When Avi stared into my eyes and said this, he was only four years old. We were deep into a giggle session, sitting on the beige carpet in the basement. I don't remember what we were even laughing about.

This struck me as possibly the kindest thing anyone had ever said to me. Later, he had *finally* gotten his pajamas on after nearly nailing bedtime avoidance strategy number thirty-four. Then he asked me, continuing back to the theme, "When are you going to die? Will it be in October or November?"

I thought, *I certainly hope not. Fall is my favorite time of year.*

I said all the things you're supposed to say when talking about death with your young child, all those "therapisty" things I had learned from my professional training. That we don't know exactly for sure when anyone will die, but that I likely would not die for a very long time. And, of course, that I was planning on being around until I could hold my grandbabies. No pressure *whatsoever.*

That last part was not exactly verbatim from my professional training.

What I was really thinking about, as I shared my even-handed response with Avi, was how we know we are going to die, often unexpectedly. And then most of the time we adults walk around pretending, of course, that it won't happen to me anytime soon. Or ever.

Some days I could manage it, and other days I felt bowled over with this knowledge, the understanding that I could lose anyone at any time.

49

This feeling was most acute when it came to Eden. I looked cool and calm on the outside, which was something I could generally pull off, but inside I was constantly trying to steady myself.

I took Avi's warm little hand in mine, and I kissed it.

Eden wasn't getting enough nourishment for her brain and body, but for almost a year, we didn't know why. I schlepped her to occupational and speech therapy to help her learn to eat. I'd pack up a bottle full of formula, the bottle warmer, baby food, an assortment of eating tools, along with a gaggle of toys—I'd balance that torrential diaper bag in one hand and hoist Eden in her bucket seat with the other. My back was a mess. And, after months of no improvement, we started to explore possible gastrointestinal causes. Not for my burgeoning sciatica; for the lack of appetite in our sweet and tiny Eden.

Eden would take an ounce or two of formula and refuse the rest. She pushed the spoon away and grimaced when I tried to give her solids, no matter what the taste and texture. While Avi gleefully chowed down on his first bites of oatmeal and opened his mouth like a little robin for more, Eden clamped her mouth shut and cried. We were baffled and alarmed. She remained in the first percentile for weight, no matter what we tried.

During this period, I did most of the housework, coordination of household activities, and was present at nearly every one of Eden's medical appointments. Before having children, I had been so convinced that, as a feminist, I would do parenthood in a lovely, egalitarian way. Yet here I was, steeped in a traditional role of mothering. It happened before I even realized it, like water freezing, eventually covering the whole lake in a thick sheet of ice. I had my career, too; I just had everything at once.

Compared to my whole *I've got this* attitude; Cedar was casual and low-key. He sat at the kitchen counter with me after a long day and looked me in the eye, even when it was late. That's one of the reasons why I fell in love with him—he asked great questions and never tired of my answers. I adored an honest, expansive conversation more than nearly anything else.

Also, at times, Cedar was forgetful and distracted, the shadow sides of his calm creativity. In the mornings, while I prepped breakfast for Avi and bolted into my to-do list, he would stare into his coffee as if he was peering into another solar system. I was overdoing it, and he was underdoing it, and that's how it was for a long time.

During that era, I juggled caring for Eden with my own job as a psychotherapist. I had been at the same Jewish nonprofit for almost a decade and used to say that we saw anyone with twenty-five dollars and a problem. Although that wasn't a precise description, we often worked with people who couldn't afford other options, who had big challenges to overcome, along with people who believed in the mission of what we were doing, providing attainable support to anyone who needed it.

I frequently worked with people in distress, with serious and persistent mental health issues. Fortunately, I was able to learn from seasoned mentors about how to do that thoughtfully. I also picked up some choice Yiddish words like *plotz* (collapse or explode with emotion) and *shvitz* (sweat). I schvitzed a whole lot during my earliest sessions. There was pressure early on as a young therapist to be more experienced, especially when I was in my baby-faced mid-twenties. Clients much older than me used to ask, "So, how old are you anyway?" For better or worse, I stopped getting that after Eden was born.

I became a psychotherapist, in part, because I knew what it was like to struggle with big feelings. I was born with an emotional weather status a lot like Minnesota's—sometimes radiant, and other times bone-chilling. Much as I'd have liked to be San Diego at all times, seventy degrees and sunny, streaming constant buoyant thoughts, I learned early on that temperamental internal weather was a part of me. My soul was not Southern California, no matter how hard I tried.

Most of all, I became a psychotherapist because there was nothing I liked to do more than talk about things that matter. What I savored most were the biggest questions, the biggest conversations about love, freedom, meaning, death, grief, and loss. You know, the light stuff.

By the time we were in the thick of Eden's health challenges, thankfully, I had my bearings; I had been in the field of psychotherapy for almost ten years. There was a place I went when I was with my clients, where I could tune in fully to what they were experiencing, where for the duration of a therapy hour, I found a break from my own challenges. It was like a switch that I could flip on, and I loved it. It was relieving for me to have that role, to be there for someone else. I had a calling beyond our little family and that made my struggles less all-consuming.

Especially because during Eden's first few years, she and I spent *a lot* of time together. Avi went full-time to a Montessori preschool surrounded by wooden materials and soft voices, while Cedar taught music at an arts high school. When I wasn't working, I ushered Eden to appointments, therapies, and in-home treatments. She did speech, OT, and PT to help strengthen her muscles and grasp large motor skills. Eden was on her own timeline for milestones like sitting up and someday, hopefully, standing on her own and walking; those appointments supported her development.

There was also Eden's feeding regimen, which took up the rest of our waking hours. I would do anything to keep her alive and fed, and I did. Breastmilk was the only source of calories that Eden seemed to enjoy and nursing the thing that soothed Eden most, so I nursed her on demand until she was around fourteen months old. When she was struggling there was nothing that she wanted more.

I wanted to be done with the desperate pumping in between nursing sessions to keep my milk flowing strong, the supplements I took to boost my supply, the hours spent trying to coax Eden to consume enough nourishment (which also included various types of formula). I lived with a constant pressure to perform and produce—if my milk dried up, then what?

She was at risk for death.

If she died, I knew I would look back and wonder, *Did I do everything I could to keep her here?* I needed that answer to be an undeniable yes.

There was a part of me that believed I was responsible for Eden's problems because I brought her into the world. She came out of my body, for this? For a series of diagnostic assessments, to be hungry, maybe even starving? To sit in waiting rooms, for a failure to thrive? The possibility of a feeding tube loomed; it had been brought up by various practitioners as a possible outcome if we couldn't get her bigger and stronger. If she wouldn't eat, we would need to do something drastic.

Then, most weekdays, just as Eden went down for her afternoon nap, I would drive out to my office in the suburbs, booked with therapy sessions in the afternoon. An older friend who lived a few blocks from us cared lovingly for Eden while I was at work. My mother helped, too, during those long, early days, even though she and my father lived about forty-five minutes away.

I used the childcare so that I could go and do my job. I married a musician and we now had two young children, one with astronomical medical expenses. And, I wanted to protect my other identity, my work outside of being a mother. It was mine.

To greet my regular one o'clock on Thursdays, I'd take a deep breath, straighten my skirt, and walk slowly over to the lobby. Sometimes, as I walked down the hall, I'd have a flash of heartache that rolled all the way through me, a static charge: *Eden*. But when I saw Michael (not his real name/identity) sitting there, hunched over an old copy of *People* magazine, I smiled a genuine smile. I thought about our last session, when he'd told me that he'd never been one for therapy, but that he had finally joined a recreational soccer league, which made his weekends less lonely. He was considering reconnecting with his sister after years of estrangement.

I'd warmly nod a greeting, and he'd followed me back through the familiar path to my office, past the front desk, and we'd settle into our comfortable, worn chairs across from one another. We were there together, and that's where I wanted to be. Present in a creative exploration of how to live a good life, despite (or including) the inevitable, unexpected plot twists.

In April, when Eden was almost one, we took her to the hospital for another test, an upper GI X-ray, a new step in the quest to figure out why she was so averse to eating. Cedar and I had ideas and theories. All kinds of theories. I even had a conspiracy theory (not really). But we had nothing conclusive.

For the test, Eden had to drink barium so the doctor could view her digestion. As Cedar and I stood in another windowless room of Children's, Eden just looked around at all the machines and took it in (literally) from a thick Avent bottle. She did not cry, she just snuggled into me. As she cooed for the technician, I wondered, *Where did this baby come from*?

If I had to drink barium, I am certain that I would be less cooperative.

Eden's upper GI X-ray came back abnormal. It showed that she had a midgut malrotation—in short, twisted up intestines. This internal abnormality was likely related to her genetic difference.

We met with a pediatric surgeon to explore the benefits and the risks of a corrective operation. The surgeon, who had impossibly good hair and impeccable posture, stood before us in turquoise scrubs in a small hospital office and laid it down: "If she doesn't get what she needs during this critical early childhood period, she will likely suffer lifelong learning problems due to malnourishment. These are problems that you could prevent with a feeding tube. And, if you don't repair the intestines, they could rupture at any moment, which could easily cost Eden her life."

Was it even a choice?

Still, we consulted about whether or not to place the feeding tube with multiple medical providers beyond the pediatric surgeon. I talked and over-talked about it with my irreverent and supportive friends, my parents, and with Cedar.

Of course, we didn't want to do the tube. What parent would want that for their child? Before we had Eden, I thought feeding tubes were only placed during a terminal illness or with the elderly. Sometimes, I would half-joke to Cedar, "We've got problems that we didn't even know were possible."

Regardless, we went ahead with the feeding tube to help Eden come through her intestinal surgery. It would get her through the recovery period, a bridge of sorts. Then the tube would be a thing of the past. *Right?* Given all that we were learning from the doctors, this seemed likely, but as they often reminded us, there was no certainty about how it would unfold.

Later that night, I stayed up until eleven hunched over the kitchen counter with only one light on and soaked my softest sweater with tears. I feared not just for this surgery but for others the doctors had told us may need to happen over time—the possible hydrocephalus, the tethered spinal cord, and her two cerebral cysts. All this medical care seemed like way too much focus on what was wrong, versus what could be right.

The next day, a cloudy winter morning in April, I got up at six, as I often did. Eden needed a feeding tube. And, I had a life to live. I put on my best pair of jeans (I only had one pair that really fit) and took Avi out for a handmade glazed doughnut. Once we were settled back in the car, I turned around to look at him. "Avi, the doctors are going to help fix Eden's stomach. She will go to the hospital for a few days and come home with something called a G-Tube, which will help her get the food that she needs. She's going to be okay."

Was she really going to be okay? I hoped this was true.

Avi seemed relatively unfazed, his face still open and bright. He was only three, and so far, for him, the world had been a safe and welcoming place.

It started snowing, like powdered sugar from the sky, even though it was supposed to be spring. Yes, I was self-soothing with a lavender cake fritter. But watching Avi grin, with possibly more chocolate on his face than whatever made it to his mouth, it helped.

During that time, I could cry every day about Eden's condition and walk around feeling bone-aching awful. By then, Eden was emaciated. Her head looked bigger than ever, almost gigantic, towering over her skeletal frame.

I also didn't want to be that person, the person in the room who couldn't see the loveliness around her. The sweet treat mornings and the way the light leapt off the flakes of snow. The everyday things with Avi like our walks around the neighborhood as he pointed out nearly every make and model of car. And kissing Eden on the forehead, her zingy eyes, and those giggly peek-a-boo games. The way she nursed like a well socialized saber-toothed tiger—sometimes nipping with that one crazy sharp tooth of hers, but all snuggled in next to me, a wondrous being.

But even through the usual moments that could have been enjoyable, the grief was with me, wherever I went, affixed to my body like a tattoo I did not choose.

This was grief, muddying the beauty. And grief laced with fatigue has an electric pulse.

This might be surprising coming from a therapist, but here's my take: there are times when feelings are actually not that helpful. At least not the all-consuming ones, not at all hours of the day and night. What can be helpful is just to live through it and keep on with everything else. Yes, of course, I had to feel it. I was wired that way. And yes, *of course*, feelings can give us information, they can help us know ourselves, they have a purpose. But this relentless guilt when I hadn't done anything wrong? It snagged me, stuck to me, and wouldn't get off me, without my consent.

I began to write, fervently, as if writing could dig me out of the heaviness. I wrote about everything, the deluge of heartache, our unorthodox family experiences, my biggest fears (there were more than a few). I hadn't written that much since I was in my twenties; I didn't feel the call until Eden's health began to deteriorate. I started a blog, *Itty Bitty Yiddies*, which distracted me, in all the best ways, toward something original, something for myself.

My family and friends were following along when Eden had a gastric feeding tube placed in mid-April, when she was almost a year old, coupled with a surgery that corrected the midgut malrotation of her intestines. It wasn't my feeding inadequacy as a mother, after all. When I realized this, I felt a flare of anger at the professionals who had insinuated it might be my fault, which had been all too common.

The surgeon, standing with us in the prep-room right before the procedure, came off as admonishing, stating bluntly, "Her weight gain has been abysmal." He shook his head disapprovingly. And added, "She may need a follow-up surgery, called a Nissen. I just want you to know. So that it's not a surprise." He went on to describe the procedure, but I stopped listening.

The surgeon discovered that Eden's bowels were tied in an actual knot, which he said he hadn't ever seen before. The lower intestine was twisted up on itself and partially obstructed. *Of course, she didn't want to eat.*

In the recovery area after the surgery, I was incredibly relieved to see Eden, tucked under cotton striped hospital blankets, her hand wrapped in white tape to secure her IV port. She was wailing and confused, and her face was all puffed up from the surgery. Yet she was right there in front of me. I placed my hand over her tiny palm and left it there as long as I could.

Right after that, when we got up to the hospital room with Eden, a peppy older nurse asked if Cedar and I were medical professionals. I liked that I was holding it together enough for someone to think that. Even amid all the tumult, I wanted to be seen as capable. But really, she probably just wondered how we knew so much about the various monitors and procedures. It was because we spent some quality time at Children's the winter before when Avi got RSV (Respiratory Syncytial Virus) and had to come in for two consecutive in-patient stints. Avi called it RSVP, which for just a few moments made me forget that it was stressful and not an actual party invitation.

We stayed in the hospital with Eden for six days. It was, in a way, the opposite of healing, with its jarring lights, constant noise, and bustle. And at the same time, I was grateful for modern medicine and the whole tireless clinical team.

We thought our daughter was finally going to get the nutrition she so desperately needed.

Clergy came to sit by Eden's bedside, which fortified me. When Rabbi Zimmerman and Cantor Abelson came to visit, they sang a healing prayer while Eden cuddled up with me in the rocker. Her tubes were touching my hoodie. She became still in my arms, staring coolly, when only a minute before she had been inconsolable from post-surgery pain. When they pivoted to a *Fiddler on the Roof* selection, her cries resumed. Otherwise translated as, *Broadway, I don't think so.*

Eventually, Eden was discharged. We headed back home, feeding tube and all. I wasn't sure if I could learn how to run it, despite an in-depth training session at the hospital. The pump involved a lot of precision and math, two things I had never excelled at. Cedar was more confident. He had a strong ability to follow a stringent protocol and embraced the need for accuracy right away. I learned just fine, if begrudgingly. I discovered that I could manage Eden's care quite well, but I did not enjoy it.

I longed for less responsibility. I longed for the life that I once imagined I would inhabit, the complaints I thought I might make like *oh these terrible twos* or *work has been really busy*. The places I thought I might go. I longed to fall asleep easy and wake up to something other than the piercing sound of a machine beeping.

CHAPTER SIX

Puke, Part I

On Mother's Day, two days after Avi had stuck a Cheddar Bunny up his nose (which sent us, after sundown, to urgent care), and three weeks after Eden had gotten the feeding tube, she was eating better than ever.

I cradled her warm body in my arms; she was the size of a large football, snug against my chest. Gazing at her cherry blossom lips, I pressed the silicone nipple against her mouth. Eden cooed and gazed up at me while slamming five ounces of formula without so much as a pause, as if she was in a frat downing a Heineken with her buddies. Eden was finally eating so well by mouth that we didn't have to run the tube at all until her bedtime bottle. It was one of the best presents I could have gotten, better than any possible permutation of breakfast in bed. We also had a family hike where nobody cried, which with two kids under four (and at that time, me), signified a successful event.

Later that evening, I nursed Eden to sleep, mostly for comfort. I held her upright in my arms for twenty minutes, as we were instructed to do to let her stomach settle. As I rocked her light little body in the faux suede glider, I gazed down at her smooth face. In response, Eden put her warm hand on my chest. She took that bitty palm of hers and rubbed it softly on my skin below my collarbone. Then she pressed it into me, as if she was smoothing a wrinkle on my shirt. She fell asleep, smelling like ripe stone fruit, with her hand above my heart. Her body was heavy, her breath right against me. I felt like everything made sense, that we were in it together for a reason. Or, even if we found out that there wasn't a reason, we would make one up.

With Eden so peaceful in my arms, I tiptoed over to the crib to avoid the creaky sections of the wood floor, an invisible obstacle course I knew all too well. Relieved by the quiet of my steps, I leaned over the crib to lay Eden down, her arms hanging down from gravity as I lowered her body onto the faded rainbow polka dot sheets. The room was dim, and my girl was finally content.

Pop.

It was just like a balloon exploding, with that same startling sound. Alarmed, I looked down and saw that Eden's tube extension had become caught between my body and the side of the crib. And at that moment, I realized I had mistakenly pulled the entire feeding tube out of her body. I instinctively rushed her close to me. And then everything that had just gone into her stomach came gushing out all over the two of us. I felt the warm, wet stomach juices soak into my shirt and down the front of my jeans.

I carried Eden, who was wailing, next door to Avi's room to let Cedar know what had happened. He was sitting beside Avi on his toddler bed, his arm tucked loosely around him, book open. Cedar located the spare tube while I phoned the neighbors to see if they could stay with Avi. We couldn't reach a soul; it was Mother's Day, after all. So, we raced downstairs, each of us carrying a child, and buckled them into their car seats in Cedar's station wagon.

While Cedar drove us down 50th Street toward the hospital, I leaned over Eden's car seat, holding a plastic piece of tubing into her stoma site to keep it from closing up. One of us put the song "Home" by Edward Sharpe and the Magnetic Zeros on repeat. Once we had traveled several blocks, Eden had stopped crying; she seemed to like the music. The plastic tubing kept popping out, so I had to keep sticking it back into her. Gastric juices were bubbling and rushing all over my hand and down her onesie.

The lyrics, "Holy moly, me oh my, you're the apple of my eye" played on a loop in my mind. "Girl I've never loved one like you."

Avi looked at me, at the plastic placeholder and the tiny hole in Eden's stomach where her tube used to be. "Is she going to be okay, Mama?" Avi asked. He was wearing his favorite firetruck jammies.

I was doing deep breathing exercises and trying not to berate myself as I answered his questions. What I *said* was, "She's going to be fine, love. We are going to the hospital because that's where they can help Eden." What I *thought* was, *I cannot fucking believe I just did that.* And then, again to myself, *Just breathe. Get through this moment.* Avi looked at me, unconvinced, his eyes almost wet. "How long will we be there?" he asked. "And when will we leave?"

After we got into the triage area, Cedar left with Avi to get him to bed. Eden and I ended up spending five hours in the ER. She screamed in pain for most of it, and I rocked and shushed and cried some, too. Feeding tubes got pulled out as a matter of course, but the timing—so soon after surgery—was a complicating factor. I held her tightly while she vomited profusely. Sometime after midnight, a technician took a set of X-rays to see what was happening with the tube site.

The next day, the doctor had to surgically put in a new tube, plus fix some of the tissue that wasn't healing well. The tissue would have had to have been repaired anyway. But it probably wouldn't have required an operation.

As we waited for Eden to get to the recovery room, I told Cedar, "Maybe we made a mistake. Doing the feeding tube. Obviously, I made a mistake by pulling out the tube, and I'm so sorry."

"I know, love. It could have happened to anyone, though. It could have been me," Cedar said.

"I can't stop hearing it . . . that loud pop. It's just echoing in my mind. Did you hear it?"

"I didn't hear it. Avi and I were in the middle of a dramatic reading of *Hug.* I know you didn't mean to."

"How did I even do it?" I continued. "On the best day that we had had in so long. Of course, it was Mother's Day. Sounds about right." I sucked a big breath in, and I could almost taste the cleaning products in the room. We sat for a few moments, and then I continued.

"Maybe we should have done more testing when I was pregnant. Especially, given everything that happened before. I just can't keep watching her go through all of this. She's not even a year old yet. And putting that mask over her face and watching her eyes roll back, again? It's horrible, doing that to a baby."

"I know it's hard. Thank you for being the one to do it. You know I get so queasy. I didn't want to go in and like, pass out in front of the surgeon," Cedar said.

"That would have added excitement. And that's what we *don't* need," I raised my eyebrows with an exasperated look. I looked back at Cedar and the clock on the wall. "Every other parent we know seems to have it so much easier. And they are so unaware of it. I swear if I have to hear another teething *horror story . . .*"

Cedar looked at me and nodded. "Part of me feels unlucky," I looked away. "Do you ever wish you had someone else's problems? I never have before. Not like this."

"Yeah, I feel that sometimes, too, babe. How could we *not* feel like that at least part of the time?"

The procedure itself went fine. In and out, day surgery. We knew the nurses and staff from our recent stint there. They reveled in how Eden had grown—an inch—in the past three weeks and told me this happened all the time with feeding tubes, which despite their best efforts, was the opposite of comforting.

After that day, the puke storm rolled in. Before the tube was in place, Eden hardly ever threw up, only a handful of times in her whole life. No one—not the surgeon, nor any doctor we consulted with—informed us beforehand that vomiting was commonplace with a feeding tube. I had also been avoiding internet searches beyond a few trusted sites; they only raised my anxiety and generally provided little factual medical information. Therefore, we had no idea any of this was coming our way.

In addition to the throwing up, Eden suffered from intense bouts of diarrhea. It was highly uncomfortable for her and cumbersome for us with laundry and diapering. It also affected her hydration and weight.

The first year that Eden had the tube, she threw up multiple times a day—sometimes upward of five or ten—and ate virtually nothing by mouth. When she was sick with a cold, even anything slight, it would increase significantly. She would spend those days nauseous, retching, and heaving. The vomiting led to aspiration, which led to chronic pneumonia. Sometimes I wondered if it was at least partially my fault, since Eden's severe vomiting kicked off following the Mother's Day incident. Several gastroenterologists reassured me that it was unrelated, but on a hard day, it still haunted me.

Eden's profuse vomiting was an unforeseen, full circle loss. It sent me right back to my own childhood, standing in the hallway outside of the bathroom, in leggings and a big t-shirt, my heart pounding. One afternoon, while downstairs, my brother and I made blanket forts. He was crouched down, leaning the biggest pillows against each other, and I took my chance. I whispered, "Mom is throwing up. Is she sick?" He didn't say much, until he saw her whisking by us, looking, as she always did, like Farrah Fawcett. He motioned to me and announced, "She said she heard you throwing up."

"No, I didn't," I insisted. "I didn't say that." My head was down, my heart trouncing like a cat. I had said the thing that we should not say.

It was never my mother's fault. We were born into this world, and soon after, given these relentless roles, these relentless standards. We were handed an impossible task in motherhood, in humanness (this far transcends gender), in a culture that leaves us alone to do so much. To figure it out on our own.

I had my share of self-criticism, which I think I've made abundantly clear by now, yet somehow, despite my mother's struggles with food, it wasn't my struggle. Perhaps, in part, because my mother never put her own battle with her body on me; she was careful not to voice her own personal rebukes and she did not offer any negative commentary about my body, not ever. If she said anything, it was a compliment. She wanted something better for me.

"You have that Nadler beauty," she would often declare, her elegant chin arching toward me, and I believed it. I'd catch her dazzling wide eyes and I'd sometimes point out how squinty and small mine became when I smiled. She would shake her head, "They are stunning, just like your grandmother's. All the Nadler women have them."

So, when we got the news that Cedar and I were having a girl, in this way, I felt ready. I was so excited to show my daughter how to savor a meal, how to feel proud of her strong body, and how to enjoy food with abandon.

How to keep it down, at a minimum.

This made it even more crushing to see my girl stuck in this cycle: nauseous, writhing, gagging, and throwing up. Those days felt like a hollow tunnel—days that turned into weeks and then months, with no end in sight to her suffering. Eden continued to refuse food altogether; she relied fully on the feeding tube formula for all her calories. The doctors called it food aversion. Apparently, this too was common in people who had feeding tubes. I didn't know any of this beforehand.

There would be no joy in food for Eden, no savoring, no pride.

There would be no eating at all.

I couldn't make it better. The doctors could not make it better either. "I'm not a magician," Eden's gastroenterologist told me once, while I was nearly begging for her help. I could only hold my daughter in my arms, take her thin hand, sing whatever I could remember the words to, and sometimes rock her back to sleep. It did not feel like much.

I did second and third and fourth guessing about why we consented to the feeding tube and every medical intervention Eden had ever had. Was it ethical? Was it fair to her to keep her on a form of life support when her quality of life was so compromised? What had we done? And what choice did we have at this point?

Eden's life got worse after the feeding tube, there was no doubt about it, although the fact that she had a life at all was not lost on me. It was hard not to consider all the ways we could have done it differently. Even though there wasn't much of a choice—malnourishment and perhaps death or the feeding tube—I still felt as if I could have done something more. Like my first experience with birth, if I could have only worked harder, I would have been able to make everything right.

What kind of a mom was I, anyway? With her own child suffering, so close to the edge. I nearly wrecked myself with the ruthless relentless whir in my mind: *what if, what if, what if.* These regrets and longings and ruminations were an attempt to get control over something that was beyond my control.

If Eden's strife was my fault, then at least there was something I could have done. It was still, in a way, within my scope. I made it personal, when so much of what happens to us is not.

So much of any life is a matter of luck. Or maybe just pure chance.

I craved control, clung to it, during a chaotic time. And who could blame me? Except for myself. I had that covered.

CHAPTER SEVEN

Game Changer

Being Eden's mother is both a spiritual calling and something like a fork stuck in my eye. She is quick to showcase a bright, toothy grin and full body hug. She doesn't care about who you are or where you've been. She is in the moment, baby, and she is all in. Which meant the rest of us were, too.

When things were especially tough for me as a caregiver, my mother would compare my daughter to Helen Keller. As in "She does remind me of Helen Keller, but, you know, she [Helen] really did turn it around." This generally added a hot ping of sadness, despite her good intentions. "We just need to find her Anne Sullivan," she said one Sunday over the phone. I leaned back in my chair and closed my eyes for a moment.

Then I sighed, which I was getting adept at doing.

Yet there was another way to look at it: Helen Keller was a total revolutionary.

It wasn't all difficult conversations; I was starting to appreciate the fluorescent, unexpected moments that dotted each day of Eden's early years. Like the moment I let out an unintentionally massive sigh in the locker room at the gym. A woman with her makeup all laid out nicely on a towel on the vanity turned to me.

"That was a big sigh," she said.

Great. My sighs were now attracting attention.

"Every time I come to the gym, I forget something. But at least it's not pants. You don't want to go outside in this weather without those." We both snickered at the thought; it was below freezing.

"What did you forget?" she asked, her eyelashes wet with mascara.

"Socks."

"Really? I have an extra pair right here, never worn. I just put them in my bag this morning, just in case." This kind stranger handed them to me.

"Really? Wow. Thank you so much. Yes, I'll take them." They were thin and rolled together in a neat little ball, the color of candy circus peanuts. "I'm actually trying to ask for help more often," I continued.

What I didn't say was that this was a long-term struggle for me, and that I found it to be one of the most difficult things to do. Even when a friend offered to bring dinner when Eden was struggling, I often declined. And/or I felt so indebted to show my appreciation afterward that accepting help became an actual stressor. I would think about the looming thank you note instead of enjoying the casserole/lasagna/roasted chicken.

As I stood there pulling on my jeans, she turned back to the mirror. We ended up getting into a deep conversation as we got ready for the day: about Eden and about her nephew who had developmental delays. She told me how his life had expanded her awareness far beyond herself. Any kind of warm, unexpected exchange like that boosted my otherwise low mood.

Since Eden's diagnosis, I locked eyes with more strangers than in all the previous decades beforehand. Thanks to that, I also had so many surprising conversations. Running out for wipes, getting gas, picking up a tub of yogurt—any of those things could turn into an instantaneous connection.

Around that time, during my annual exam, a nurse I had never met before asked me about my children. I gave her the abridged version of Eden's challenges. "It's hard, isn't it?" she said while she tightened the faded blood pressure cuff. I tried not to cry as I felt the squeeze in my upper arm, mostly because it felt so good to be taken care of. She then held up a picture of her own son who had dyspraxia. When she said, "Can I offer you a prayer?" I said, "Yes." It did include a spontaneous hands-on blessing in the name of Jesus. I declined the psalm book the nurse recommended, something along the lines of *He Has Risen*, but I generally accepted all the prayers that were offered. If I got hit with an occasional "praise the lord" like my Catholic Aunt Janice sometimes shouted, that was fine by me. I appreciated an interfaith fellowship session.

Caring for Eden made me want to live more boldly. The struggle she faced made daily life astounding. Surreal. Everything was fleeting—I already knew that, theoretically. But I began to know it in a way that was like looking in a mirror in weird, harsh lighting. I couldn't believe it was my face, my eyes, my shirt, my life staring back at me, but there it was.

Sometimes all the heaviness lifted, and when I looked at Eden's beautiful, kind-of-close-together baby blues, I saw every possibility. She was like the January night sky—cool, vast, and unbelievable. Eden would stop whatever she was doing to gaze deeply right back at me.

These moments buoyed me. And, by the time Eden was almost one, one of these moments meant we lucked into our own kind of Anne Sullivan.

I was about to quit my job as a psychotherapist; Eden was still recovering from her intestinal surgery and on the feeding tube twenty-four/seven. At barely twelve pounds, she could not yet stand up. There was so much vomit. Along with her various medical concerns and frequent therapies, it was too much for a nanny (and forget about daycare). We needed a nurse, stat. But where could we find one who had the skills and guts to take on Eden?

Cedar was teaching at the arts high school, and his job was tied to our health insurance, something we felt we couldn't change. I was holding down much of the parenting and working as a psychotherapist about thirty hours a week.

The kind-hearted older friend who had been taking care of Eden so I could work outside the home had her own health problems and needed to step down. It was too much for someone without nursing skills, even for such a seasoned caregiver.

I didn't know where to find anyone who might be able to help us. Around this time, seeing our exhaustion, my mother went online to find a few students in health-related fields who could assist on the weekends. I'd like to say that I asked for her help because of my whole thing about wanting to ask more for help. What I remember is that my mother did the hardest part, prescreening candidates, including weeding out the ones who were a definite no (like the guy who sent a barrage of aggressive emails insisting that he was absolutely the best fit without a doubt and why wouldn't we hire him already?). These two caregivers took the edge off, but it was just a few short shifts each a month. We needed someone who could be a consistent, steady presence.

I shared my predicament at the Mamas Group meeting one spring Sunday. We had been meeting monthly for four years at that point, so they all knew what was unfolding. When it was my turn to talk, I let it all out.

"I think I will end up at home, caring for Eden. But it feels like giving up a part of myself. But finding someone who is willing to wade through all that vomit? Who could manage the feeding tube? Seems impossible." Nods and uh-huhs from the Mamas. I loved this group. "You know that part-time nanny we thought we found? Right after she met Eden, she quit before she started. She told me it was because I didn't keep the basement playroom organized enough. I mean, *what*? I think she was scared to take on Eden but didn't want to say so. If any of you know *anyone* who has that medical piece, who wouldn't shy away from managing a feeding tube, please let me know." The women nodded warmly.

Debra said, "Emma, I really hope you don't have to stop being a therapist, especially at this point in your career. It's hard to get back in once you've been out."

Someone touched my shoulder and squeezed.

Tamar, all dark, tousled hair, looked at me intensely and spoke. "I'm really going to channel this. I think I might know of someone or someone who at least knows someone. I will ask her, okay? Sometimes things just suddenly change, and you just have to go with it. Do you know what I mean?" That was Tamar, an acupuncturist who considered the intangible divine. I wasn't exactly, fully sure what she meant, but I was grateful that she was willing to reach out on our behalf. I left Mamas Group feeling satiated by the caring response and the idle hours, but not especially hopeful about anything else.

The next day Tamar called me at work. I was sitting at my desk in my office with a few minutes between sessions, so I answered. "Hi Emma.

Oh, I'm so glad I caught you. I just am all of a sudden having this really strong sense. I called Julie, who I see all the time at services, and she said that she might be able to help you. Like actually *her*, and she's incredible. She's super active in the congregation, all the healing stuff. She asked, so I told her your name."

I sighed heavily, and then replied, "Tamar, thank you so much. This is so kind of you to reach out to help. I'm really not sure it will even be a possibility. It seems like too much of a boundary crossing. She knows my name?" I breathed out quickly. "Her sister-in-law Jill is my supervisor, and I don't know if she'll be comfortable with it. They are so tight knit. I don't even want to ask her. It feels like overstepping."

Tamar replied quickly, "Emma, of course, I don't want you to feel pressured. But this could be better than what I even imagined. I'm not sure you should pass up this chance." As we ended the call, I thanked her again, and told her I would be sure to follow up with her.

Tamar went to Lake Harriet and prayed on it. She told me, after everything, that she didn't try to get God involved. She said that she just wished out to the sky and the water that I would change my mind.

Later that afternoon, in my weekly supervision meeting, sitting on a stiff office chair across from Jill's desk, I explained, "Jill, I just . . . I don't know if I'm going to be able to keep working. I still don't have anyone to care for Eden, and I don't know where to go from here." I teared up as I gripped my black appointment planner tightly in my hands. I was supposed to be there to receive guidance on how to best serve my clients. Instead, I was doing my best to hold back my tears. I straightened my blazer and tried to pull it together using long, deep breaths. I resolved not to start my next session with a tear-stained face.

Jill took her own breath in, and looked at me calmly, which was always her way. I looked at her dark, steady, empathetic eyes. In all the years I had known her, I'd never once seen her frazzled.

"I think you should call my sister-in-law Julie. She's a nurse, and she's looking for something new right now." I sat up higher in my chair. "Wow, really? Are you serious? My friend called me earlier today about Julie, but I didn't know if that was too close for comfort, for you." Jill leaned in closer across the desk, her eyes the color of maple syrup, "I think that if I didn't connect you, I would always wonder, what if I did?"

—⁓—

That's how it all started with Julie, a cheery, charismatic nurse in her late fifties. At our first meeting, just days after Mamas Group met at the end of April, Julie and I sat across from one another at the flamingo pink dining room table in our arthritic Minneapolis house. Before having children, I had hand-painted the table myself.

Julie wore round copper glasses, and her straight blond hair was shiny and cropped short. Her face had a brightness to it, along with a wide, expansive smile. Her look, with straight cut jeans and a loose-fitting tee shirt, had a splash of tomboy. Somehow, she reminded me of Julie Andrews in *The Sound of Music*, but without the dresses or song sessions. Her confidence and rosiness came through just as much.

I asked Julie about what she thought a reasonable hourly rate was given her decades of experience in a hospital setting. She waved her hands around like she was swatting at a fly. "Really, just a little something. Please. I'm just going to save up for some new shoes. I do like my shoes." She laughed, and went on to explain, "I have this thing about taking on too much. Marc, my husband, made me promise not to commit long-term before talking with him first. Oy, I have to reign it in sometimes. But let's try it, a part-time schedule. I can do at least six weeks. And hopefully, Eden will be doing better by then."

I looked into Julie's eyes in the same way Eden often peered into mine, like anything was possible. "I hope you fall in love with her," I said.

—⁓—

Because of Julie, I got to keep my job, the thing that got me up and showered and out the door each workday, even when I had hardly slept. Many caregivers are forced to leave careers they love and/or need due to a lack of support, and I was fortunate to have a chance to keep going. It wasn't a trip to Tahiti or anything, but it felt good to put on my professional, non-puke-stained dresses and leave the house. And it was relieving to continue to have an identity outside of being a caregiver.

In those days, during many new medication trials, provider changes, and formula shifts for Eden, Cedar and I used the phrase *game changer*. As in, "This (fill in the blank) is totally going to be a game changer." It started out sincerely, and then after some time, when good news was sparse, we started throwing it around to each other for kicks. We used the term *game changer* for anything—new breakfast items available at the hospital cafeteria, a choice parking spot in front of the clinic, and on and on.

But Julie was a real-life game changer, a genuine one. She was a legit registered nurse, and more than that, she treated caregiving as if it was a series of prayers. She had attention to detail, just the right amount of fearlessness, and generous, unlimited affection. Eden became Eden Bobeaden, which stuck—and Eden returned the gesture with a reciprocal nickname: Juju, and later, Julie Bulie.

On one of Julie's first days caring for Eden, I crouched next to Eden, who kicked around joyfully in the bathtub while sucking on two fingers. I heard the thumps of Julie bounding up the stairs. When she appeared, she announced with a grin, "Hi dearest Eden! Boker tov. It's so good to see you this morning, darlin." Eden looked up at us, blew a raspberry, and hit the water with delight.

Julie turned to me, surveying my disheveled half ponytail and smudged glasses. "How are you, Emma? You look a bit tired."

"Well, less so now. I'm glad you're here. Are you up for taking over? I'm going to finish getting ready, and then head out to work."

"Of course," she replied and nodded knowingly. I lingered in the doorway of the bathroom for a few moments, watching as Julie gently poured a cup of warm water over Eden's hair, massaging the apricot baby shampoo with such affection and focus, as if Eden were her own.

CHAPTER EIGHT

Puke, Part XCVIII

One summer night, soon after meeting Julie, I sat shakily on the glider in Eden's sky-blue bedroom, as she retched and vomited for over two hours. We were both covered in puke, yet I held her small, soft, flushed body close to my chest.

When Eden started to choke on her own bright yellow bile, unable to breathe steadily, I dialed 911.

We went by ambulance to the ER at Children's Hospital of Minnesota. I rode with Eden on a stretcher in the back, clutching her tightly. We were both streaked highlighter yellow from her insides. Cedar took the Prius and met us there. Thankfully, our warm-hearted neighbor, who was also my dear friend Melly's mother, stayed back with Avi. It wasn't the first or the last time she had been at our side.

After a whole lot of tests (X-ray, CT scan, ultrasound, blood work), we waited around until 4:00 a.m. to be admitted to a room in the main hospital. By that point, Cedar had long gone home. I rocked Eden in a creaky green pleather chair as she alternated between wailing and napping until it was nearly time for coffee. I was surrounded by medical staff yet still afraid, in that aching, full body way.

When we returned home a week later and I sank back into our comfortable mattress, it felt akin to a stay at a luxury hotel. But even under a soft blanket, the ache persisted.

The Friday night before the Fourth of July, Cedar and I both got hit with the stomach flu. We alternated between laying on the cool tiled floor of our bathroom and parenting. Shabbat Shabarf. And then on Monday, once the holiday hit, we had to take Eden back to the ER. It wasn't clear if she had caught our bug—impossible to discern since her baseline was so vomit-stricken anyway.

We had been trying all kinds of interventions from home (gastric decompression bags, electrolyte solution, a slower rate on the tube), but we couldn't get Eden stabilized. So, we went back into the hospital to try a new intervention called the G-J tube. The J part went into her intestine and had to be surgically implanted.

In triage that Fourth of July, a medical assistant cocked her head at me and asked, "Didn't I see you here on Mother's Day?" We were regulars for holidays *and* everyday occasions.

Amazingly enough, Eden, who was a little over a year old, flapped her hands and grinned at the nursing staff, still able to find delight in their faces. She often blew a kiss or two to whoever was around, like she was living on a parade float. I kept Eden nestled up next to me as much as I could, and we paged through the same five books. I think I memorized *We're Going on a Bear Hunt*.

Every time we landed at the hospital, I texted Melly. We became close when we both were at UC-Santa Cruz, two Minnesotan Jews studying together out West, and then during the summer I was living at home recovering, we'd worked together. If I texted her on a whim, *we are at gdmn childrens again*, she would almost always come and sit with me, even late into the night.

One night around ten, tucked down the hall from the ER near the elevator, we perched together on top of a stretcher. Melly asked, "Eems, are you sure we should sit here?" I replied, "Yeah, definitely. This is just overflow seating."

"We do love a good gurney," Melly said. She matched me step for step in the gloomiest humor, which was the only kind I could get behind some days.

Over that ominous stretch of months, we had frequent visitors. Their presence made hospital life, with all its beeps and relentless probing, feel bearable. Julie and her husband Marc began to come by often, even on Julie's days off, to soothe and entertain Eden, who had become increasingly fussy and fed up with the hospital. Marc was tall and sturdy, with a full mustache and beard. A baseball hat covered his salt and pepper hair, and his brown eyes lit up easily. He reminded me a little bit of a teddy bear; one who liked iced tea far more than honey.

Marc discovered early on that he could get a smile on Eden's face in roughly three seconds flat. He had an instinctive way with her with an endless collection of silly faces, funny songs, and slapstick antics. He cracked Eden up, and vice versa.

During our longer stays, Julie sometimes slept on the pull-out pleather cot, which really meant staying up most of the night comforting Eden, who roused nearly every hour. Cedar and I would then both get to sleep at home for a precious break, which could also be called a hospital honeymoon.

Not only did they show up, but Julie and Marc were also cheerful and relaxed in a way that was foreign in a hospital setting. When they were around it felt like things might be okay after all.

We were lucky enough to have friends drop by, as well. One weekday morning, Kate brought me a soft knit plaid wrap to keep me warm. Her nurturing presence was palpable as she explained, "I got this for you at Tao Foods. I thought you might get cold here." She handed it to me gently, wrapped in plain brown paper, along with my favorite green smoothie.

It was always easy with Kate, even when easy was hard to come by. When we first met, the year before, I was struck by her style, which was something close to elegance, looking like an everyday Kate Middleton at preschool pick-up. She was a seasoned psychotherapist in private practice; she exuded a cool confidence bordering on what I initially thought was indifference. She had lustrous dark brown hair, which she always wore down, and was tall, with a distinctive, regal nose. How was she so put together? And with all these children? I was also struck by how I didn't feel envious of this at all. I was inspired, and curious. And could she teach me how to round brush the hell out of my hair, too?

Our mutual friend Carly, an original Mamas Group member who reminded me of Sarah Silverman (the same type of heart and mouth and hope for the world), had set us up as friends.

Carly's molasses brown ponytail was perched like a crown as she declared with her trademark megawatt smile, "You *need* to be friends. You remind me so much of each other . . . such similar energy." Carly invited us both over for bagels one Sunday morning soon after. Not too long after that, Kate and her partner had both Carly's and my families over for dinner. Avi only ate the cookies, and of course Eden ate nothing, but the adults were able to talk around the candlelit table—or at least take turns sitting and supervising while the young kids ran around outside in the backyard.

After we hugged everyone goodbye, on the drive back to our neighborhood, I gushed to Cedar, "I really want to be close with Kate. She has this seriousness, but she doesn't take herself too seriously. And, also, *wow*, she's so smart."

Common between us was a deep commitment to nurturance. As a child, she could have been described like my third-grade teacher described me, with three "verys." As in very very *very* responsible. If we had met back then, I think we would have been close. Years later, it was so refreshing to be dear friends with another overly accountable psychotherapist. In some ways, it was better than being one myself.

When Eden wasn't in the hospital, Kate and I began to meet in the middle of the day at Lake Harriet, a city lake with a popular walking path. We would stride around that blustery body of water together in whatever clothes we happened to be wearing that day, hugging each other hello and goodbye and never stopping to sit for several miles, until we got all the way around again. We didn't wear high tech workout fabrics. That would require changing and then changing again, and who had the time or energy for that? Outfit changes seemed reserved for stay-at-home moms and perhaps ladies who lunch.

Nothing against stay-at-home moms. I never bought into the so-called mommy wars; we are all doing the best we can within the imperfect cultural landscape of the United States, where childcare often costs nearly as much as our paychecks.

Every mom is a working (her ass off) mom.

In our real clothes we always talked about real things—our small, spirited children (five between the two of us), our work lives, our parents, partners, and, sometimes—more than you might think—who we were before we were mothers. We would often ask each other for an opinion on something: how to deal with tantrums, the best place to get an office couch. I told her about everything going on with Eden, and Kate got it. Fully. In a way that few people could with something so atypical and terrifying. She didn't pepper me with question after question, like some people did when they didn't know what else to say. She also offered up her own stories, and wasn't afraid to share her problems with me, either. Sometimes we talked about painful things but, somehow, it never felt as painful when we were together.

The other Mamas showed up during this hard stretch, too. Debra, World's Best Dad, arrived one afternoon with a giant tub of pesto pasta because carbs are her love language. She lived for (and mastered) acts of service, rather than feelings-oriented conversations, which set her apart from most of my other friends. As we sat together on an extra bed in Eden's hospital room on the sixth floor, somehow it kept springing forward and folding up on itself. The attending medical assistant offered a few unsuccessful tries at getting it straightened out (and also nearly got folded up in it). She gave up and rolled it into the hall. By this point, Debra asked, "What's with this place?" and then we were unable to stop laughing, which was partly stress-related and partly that the whole situation was slapstick comedy gold. When the medical assistant graciously came back with a new bed, we were still trying to pull it together.

Then Eden hoisted herself up for the first time to her knees. When we looked over at the crib, she was casually having a developmental milestone. I hollered, "Eden! You did it! Nice job pulling yourself up, baby!"

Eden beamed and flapped her hands. It was a moment of glee amid pain, which was becoming our family specialty.

All the hospital visits started to blend together in a strange and disorienting way. We had been roomed all over the sixth floor, so that nearly every corner held previous memories, to the point where if I stepped out to refill my water or take a phone call while Eden slept, I would head back to the room that we stayed in the last time, only to find that the sign on the door now said *Marcus* or *Kiara*.

I kept writing during this stretch. It gave me something to do beyond medical monitoring. I spent hours chronicling our experiences, banging too hard on my keyboard while typing, and Cedar would inevitably crack that I must be trying to injure my laptop.

It was the most satisfying kind of escape, one that didn't require any avoidance. Writing about my grief was infinitely easier than living it.

My parents hosted Avi whenever we were in the hospital with Eden. They engaged him in all kinds of fun diversions at their lakeside home: fishing, swimming, boat rides on my dad's 1988 wood-paneled Winsor Craft speedboat. They generally snuggled in for the night by reading an entire chapter book to Avi before bed. In this way, our little village sheltered him from some, but not all, of the stress of caring for a chronically ill child. They also helped us pay for copious medical expenses. Financially, we were incredibly fortunate with them in our corner.

My folks taught Avi some of the things we should have as parents, but didn't have time for, like how to swim. They also helped Avi learn to ride a bike, in age-old fashion, by keeping one hand on the back and running alongside him. They stuffed in him in a snowsuit and taught him how to ski, just like they taught me when I was a child. And, because we couldn't travel much as a family due to Eden's health issues, my parents took Avi to see the Golden Gate Bridge, and, later, to glide down a Colorado mountain on those skis. They were *those* grandparents: engaged, affectionate, and probably a lot more fun than Cedar and I were during that time. Avi was spared from endless hours at the hospital.

But as Eden's parents, Cedar and I could not be spared from it. I was riddled with a bout of pneumonia that I could not shake. The coughing became an incessant bark. One evening, while reading in bed with Avi, I hit a serious hacking jag. My son, in those fire truck pajamas, put his small, smooth hand on mine and whispered, "You are welcome to cough in my bed anytime."

That moment reminded me why I became a parent in the first place. No, not to have an interminable respiratory infection and little time for self-care. To witness these young humans becoming themselves. For better or worse, Avi was used to being around illness. He was kinder because of it.

When we weren't in the hospital, we visited doctors all over the Twin Cities searching for answers, frantic for a way to ease Eden's symptoms. No one was able to give us a definitive diagnosis for her gastrointestinal issues, let alone an effective treatment. Freeing her from near-constant distress was an impulse with no resolution.

Eden's frail and fading health wasn't something that I or Cedar or anyone else could control, although of course, I tried.

Still, Eden looked sick and sunken; her onesies hung loosely off her small frame. Her head looked even bigger than it used to, compared to her emaciated body. Her intestines were now repaired, so why was she still struggling so intensely?

CHAPTER NINE

Every Gorgeous Living Being

One morning, as I sipped from a cold cup of coffee, I turned to Eden's in-home special education teacher and began to speak. I finally had mustered the courage to ask the question I had been turning around and around in my mind.

Months before, after we had first gotten Eden's diagnosis, I enrolled Eden in Minnesota's Help Me Grow program for infants and toddlers with developmental differences. Educators (including physical and occupational therapists) made regular home visits to promote learning. When Eden was out of the hospital yet too sick to do much, I really looked forward to those sessions. With such pragmatic and skilled teachers at my side, I felt less isolated.

This special education teacher, standing before me with sincere eyes and cropped brown hair, was my absolute favorite.

I finally spilled the question that had gnawed at me for months. "Do you think she looks . . . different?" I held my breath, along with Eden in my arms as we stood in the tiled kitchen together. I looked at Eden, and then back again at the teacher. She had previously shared with me that she had a sister who was disabled, which is what led her to this work.

"Everyone looks different," she said matter-of-factly.

I think the subtext was that, yes, Eden didn't look typical. And, who the fuck cares. But the teacher didn't say that part because she wasn't the swearing type. I knew what she meant.

Here's the thing: even very young children—toddlers, children who had only been in this world for basically a matter of minutes—gawked at Eden on the playground. And sometimes, when I looked at her heavy-lidded eyes, elfin-like features, and witnessed her vigorous hand flapping, muscle contractions, and signature guttural squeal, I felt a heaviness in my chest. I worried she would be judged for it.

And then I realized that whenever I worried about others judging her, I was judging her myself.

It reminded me, in a way, of when I reluctantly came out to my mother after I went to a Low concert in Loring Park with a nice Jewish girl. She was cute and even more enthusiastic than me, which is saying a lot.

The next day she had left a breathy message on our family's answering machine, the one on the shelf of the family room that looked old even when it was new.

"Hi. I had so much fun with you, and I'd really like to see you again."

You know who heard it first: my mom.

Later that day, my mother and I were transplanting a cluster of hostas under the back deck. We were both kneeling, our hands in the cool dirt. My mother turned to me and asked, "Who is this girl who left you that message? She said she would like to *see you again*?" My mother always had soft eyes, but I felt them sharpen in that moment.

I looked back at her, our faces close together, our bodies crouched down tightly. "I like her." I explained.

"Like?" she prodded. "Like *like*. You know." I confessed; my palms wet against the metal of the garden trowel. The light filtered strangely around us, as if it was already dusk, but it was not. I was seventeen years old, and I wanted to be anywhere but there.

She paused, and then I saw tears running down her cheeks. Shame bubbled around in my stomach, burst into my chest. It covered me like the sunscreen I had vigorously rubbed into my skin earlier that morning.

"I think this is a harder road. A harder life. I don't want things to be harder for you," she said. We looked down for a few minutes, digging silently. I thought about how waxy and fake the hostas looked, and at that moment I was struck by how much I hated them.

I wanted to shake off her comments, but I couldn't. Not then. I felt her disappointment as firmly as a hand on my shoulder.

"Well, you know, I like both. I'm not, like, a *lesbian*."

She looked back at me and sighed. And then she said, "I should have sent you to Jewish camp."

I wanted to get fully sucked up into the garden bed we had dug together. I longed to sink into the earth, far away from this conversation.

And the truth is, I did go to Jewish camp for many years throughout my childhood.

Of course, her instinct was to protect me, especially during a time when most of the world did not embrace the LBGTQ+ community. This was in the mid-1990s, a different era in terms of civil rights and social norms. She did, eventually, become much more open-minded, supportive, and even outspoken. She did, at the time, what she could, based on society at large.

But my mother's insistence then that it would be harder made it more difficult. All I wanted her to do was accept me as I was, fully and completely. To say that it was okay for me to be myself, to cheer me on, even when I didn't match her expectations of who I was going to be.

But now, as I considered my own daughter as she entered toddlerhood, I realized how hard that can be when loving someone, no matter what. I understood, now, what it meant to grapple with a culture that tells you there's one right way to be and to internalize it. Even against my better judgment.

People would often say to me—countless checkout clerks and strangers in parking lots—"She looks sleepy." But no, those were just her eyes. Her gorgeous, unflinching eyes. Eden turned heads, just not in the way I had imagined.

I'm not proud of this, not even close, but I thought, too often, about the child I thought I was *going to have*. Every time those thoughts flashed inside of me, I felt one of those big, sweeping gusts of shame. I want to say that from day one, I accepted my child unequivocally. I would love to share that I never once wavered, compared, seethed with envy for another parent's seemingly mild-mannered average-seeming kid, a kid who never saw the inside of a hospital except to be born, that I was *not* struck with a sense of utter unfairness (as if the world was ever fair). That I never looked over at a typical healthy family and thought, *Why do they have to rub it in my face? Those horribly happy people.* It would be great to report that from the beginning it was Zen and the art of disability. So Zen.

The truth was more complex. I did think Eden was beautiful, amazingly beautiful. And that bonkers love I felt with Avi? Equally bonkers with my girl. It was as clear as her name or the way that we gazed at each other, as if there was nothing left to do in a day, as if we could both see something that could never be explained.

I wanted to end my nagging, perfectionistic thoughts immediately, but there was no shortcut out from under them. There was no easy, singular moment of acceptance regarding all of who she was and what she would confront. But I knew that embracing all of Eden—perhaps, even her lack of desire to eat (the Mount Everest of mothering)—was the key to love, or at least to the kind of love I wanted.

I was not sure I could get there, to that place of acceptance.

I wanted to, though. Badly.

I yearned to feel it then, to breathe in a higher wisdom, perspective, and most of all acceptance for every gorgeous living being, especially my own. I wanted so much to take it and live it and make that pride a part of me. I didn't want to be a product of a messed up, ableist culture, where "healthy" was synonymous with "better."

Yet often when I saw someone else's stocky, healthy two-year-old stomping around town, her belly round and balance steady and sure, throwing back handfuls of Cheerios like it was nothing, I had a flash, a thought that came without my knowing or wanting it. A whole cascade of other thoughts could easily come rushing in. What if Eden had been born healthy? What if she could eat like that? What else would I be doing other than this? I wanted to spend most of my time having experiences that did not require a copay. I wanted a less complicated life.

And I wanted my child to have it easier. So much easier.

CHAPTER TEN

Live a Little

Cedar and I sat up in bed on top of our soft sheets, the worst place to argue in any house. In my blue pajamas, my hair in a slapdash ponytail, I cried, "I have given up so much for this child. Why am I the one who has to give up what I love? You get to do what you want."

As soon as I said it, I knew I sounded like a child myself.

"You should do more of what you want to do. I can't do that for you." Cedar said, flustered, sick of the same conversation over and over again.

I am not proud of that argument. The whole *he got to do it* (and by *it* I meant *anything*) more than me. It was easy to become angry in our marriage, and then twist that anger around and around, like what I did with a lock of my hair when I worried. *You did this or you didn't, but you said that you would. I didn't get to do this, but you did. I did it more, you did it less.* Technically, this is called scorekeeping. And it was one of the biggest pitfalls Cedar and I encountered when we were worn down and stressed. We weren't going to blame Eden, all tiny and innocent; in our worst moments, we were going to blame each other.

For the record, Cedar absolutely did *not* always get to do what he wanted. We both had to change to make room to care for Eden. At the beginning, we gave up too much. Things like taking care of ourselves physically—exercise, leisurely meals, down time, and whole weeks of sleep, if you strung the lost hours together. Even child-centric activities that other families did, like attend school plays or events together, were limited. Public vomiting is not generally embraced.

Cedar didn't perform much locally or see his friends perform very often either, and that was his community. Similarly, I hardly went out to do anything on my own. Giving up too much of ourselves in a competitive, self-sacrificing way was what we called in our house *the race to the bottom*. When Eden was sick, especially in those early puke-soaked days, we played that game like a sport.

Those conversations (technically, arguments) eventually turned into a plan. I needed to start spending more time doing what I wanted to do and less time complaining about it. "I need a vacation," I told Cedar. I was in a hole and not a good one.

Luckily, with Eden now around fifteen months old, we had secured more nursing support during the day. Julie was still caring for Eden part-time, and then a home healthcare agency that we had signed on with sent a few additional nurses, each who picked up one shift a week. It was strange; there was often a person in our home who sort of knew our daughter, but really did not. I felt guilty and torn, having these new people around, especially when Eden would cry and cling to me because of the unfamiliar new faces. I wasn't sure how much to step in and help, and how much to let go.

But generally, it was more helpful than not because Eden was still hooked up to her feeding tube twenty-four/seven, therefore she needed constant monitoring. And with her newfound mobility—she was now scooting around the floor in a sort of half-crab walk—the pole that hung her feeding pump and a gastric relief bag had to be rolled closely behind her. Overall, nurses were our people. They never even flinched when Eden puked.

—⚬—

Cedar was gone for almost two weeks to rehearse and play at the Eaux Claires Music and Arts Festival with the indie-rock act Bon Iver. He had been asked to be a part of a saxophone choir, in part because of his long friendships with a few of the band members—the Minneapolis music community was tight-knit—and because, I knew, he played the saxophone like he was claiming his place in the world. The year before, he had been a part of the horn section on the Bon Iver album *22, A Million*.

On the Friday of the festival, I hemmed and hawed about whether or not to go to see him play that night in Wisconsin. When Cedar and I talked beforehand about whether I would go, we agreed that both being out of town at the same time was logistically impossible. But, as the afternoon of the concert wore on, I couldn't stop thinking about how badly I wanted to be there with him.

I paced around my parents' house, where I had decamped with the kids, weighing the pros and cons, until my mother said, "Emma, you should go. Live a little."

Somehow, we figured out a solid childcare plan and, like any *good enough* mother, I canceled Eden's occupational therapy, packed an overnight bag, and didn't stop driving until I got to the Eaux Claires festival grounds.

I wore the non-mommiest outfit I could find from what I had brought to my parents' house (this did include, for some reason, a pair of mauve embroidered short shorts), and borrowed my mother's bright red lipstick.

As Cedar got ready to play, I found myself alone near the stage in the pouring rain, shoulder to shoulder with strangers. When the music started, the face of the woman standing beside me changed into something I'll never forget—she looked like she was on the best drug, dancing as if she were alone in her bedroom. Her hand gripped her chest, right over her heart. She held it there, singing, swaying, lost in the moment.

James Blake crooned with his distinctive, stark rawness. I could smell the wet grass and smoke wafting around me in sheets. I planted my feet in the mud, barely noticing that my sandals had completely soaked through. For those hours at the festival, I was lost in sound, my face touching the sky.

It had been so long since I experienced this kind of pleasure. The deprivation of joy that I had experienced over the past months led to, paradoxically, a wave of bliss. The music was searing, swaying, almost surreal. I was sturdy and vast, nowhere, and everywhere. I was myself again, and not at all. I felt the way my fellow concertgoer looked.

I didn't feel the way that woman looked the next day because I didn't get much sleep that night—if any—for all kinds of reasons, most of which did not include debauchery of any kind. Since we couldn't find an open hotel room in the packed small town surrounding the festival grounds, I joined Cedar's hotel room, which he had been sharing with one of the other musicians. The roommate's snoring was about on par with the festival sound system—I truly had never heard anything like it. It was so sonically robust that the walls may have even quivered. It was its own performance. Regardless, I had to hit the road before breakfast to get back to Avi and Eden.

I was only gone for about eighteen hours total. I returned home even more exhausted but inspired.

It was now clear: I needed more space, more time, more breaks. I needed connection, revelry, the chance to be an autonomous person—at least some of the time. I needed to do the enjoyable things I used to do. I also needed more rest.

Going all in on caregiving wasn't fixing anything. I couldn't fix Eden anyway, no matter how hard I tried. I couldn't make her struggles disappear, couldn't relieve her suffering, no matter how much I suffered.

The only person I could fix was me.

—⁓—

While I was away, Eden had caught a bad cold and started the hacking and throwing up routine again, so right as I walked in the door, I was all the way back in it again. When I looked around, I noticed that my mother was tired, too; she coped with this by downing umpteen shiny silver cans of Diet Cherry Coke. After she'd spend time at my house caring for Eden, I'd routinely find one sitting on top of the dryer by the door. As if she took one last sip, slammed down the can, and then walked away satisfied. The lipstick on the straw inside the can was always stained a deep crimson.

My mother left those Coke cans scattered around like an alcoholic might abandon a cloudy highball after bar close—each one entirely drained. Back when I burned incense on a regular basis and wrote in a journal, I used to try to get my mother to quit those Diet Cokes. "They cause cancer," I'd say, head high. "And besides, you shouldn't have five of anything per day."

I thought I knew a lot back when I was a teenager. But later, after having my own children, I finally knew enough to understand that I shouldn't tell my mother what to do.

It had become clear by that point that I wouldn't have the typical mother-daughter trajectory with Eden. I wondered if someday she would find my gone-cold coffee cups around or whatever I would be drinking in thirty years and miss me a little, even when I was still there. I knew my mother inside and out—what a single word meant, what happened to her eyes when I said something that she believed in. I wanted that desperately with Eden. I wanted all of it, even those headstrong teenage years.

It seemed improbable, given her prognosis, that my daughter would know me like that, like I knew my mother, with all her astonishing acts of kindness, her busyness, her caffeine—and of course, like any other life, her unfinished business.

My mother gave me so much love and comfort during this time of uncertainty. I called her, probably too often, to talk about the latest with Eden. She picked up the phone, always with a short and steady, "Hi," which was reassuring in its simplicity. She showed up regularly, on the phone and in person, much like the days of my own recovery and unstable gait after the TBI. Sometimes we talked quietly about how if Eden had been a typical child, we never would have had all this time together. The truth is, I wouldn't have needed her as much.

My mother's responses, to most any concern I would bring to her, were rife with creative problem-solving, ideas, suggestions. My mother was the master of the push-through-it strategy of life, the never-give-up-persuasion.

But there are things, I discovered, that I could not make happen. Things that I could not change. No matter how hard I tried, no matter how many resources I explored, no matter my approach, my attitude, my work ethic, my motivation behind it, I could not always make it better. And that realization distanced me from the can-do attitude by which I was raised.

We had our differences, but I knew (eventually) enough not to scold her about the Diet Cokes, I also knew (eventually) enough to understand that our connection was uncommon and that it wouldn't last forever.

So, when I decided I needed a reprieve in the form of a vacation, my mother was who I wanted to be with most. In late August of that year, we traveled together for a two-night trip Up North (how Minnesotans describe traveling to Northern Minnesota). It was on that trip that I discovered the power of the weekend retreat.

We rented a cabin outside of Nisswa, about two hours away. On the way up, I navigated us through the scenic route—we really avoided that rush hour, extensively, to the point where we found idyllic country backroads so remote that I don't think they were classified as actual roads. It ended up adding an hour to our drive, a picturesque anti-short cut. Out the window, I saw faded, falling down barns and Holsteins and as the drive wore on, the full moon.

We hadn't done a trip like that, just my mother and me, since we had gone to Colonial Williamsburg for the American Girl convention when I was eight. That weekend had brimmed with sightseeing and historic reenactments, including teatime with my doll Kirsten.

Up North had a slower place; I could do whatever I wanted. I reenacted nothing but relaxation (one of my old pastimes), sprawled out on a worn-out couch in front of the gas fireplace, even though it was high summer. I wrote for hours and finished a Rainbow Rowell novel. The air smelled like birch trees and woodsmoke and dew and Earl Grey tea.

My mother and I wandered over to the beach, then took selfies near the azure lake. I convinced her to get a massage, even though she always claimed that it felt weird and tickled, and then afterward she said, "Okay, you're right. That was good." I loved being right about something like that. My mother was right about almost everything yet didn't flaunt it.

We went out for a leisurely dinner, one of my favorite activities. The restaurant was a cellar of a place, but on purpose. She drank red and I drank white. In between deliberate bites, I looked around the quiet, candlelit restaurant feeling pure relief. We sat at the table for well over an hour, chatting and eating soup *and* salad like adults sometimes do. There was not a feeding tube or syringe in sight.

Throughout the trip, my mother kept saying things like, "You know, this isn't so bad here." As if it was going to be horrible. I was like, "Isn't so bad? This is one of the best weekends of my life!" I guess she thought she might be bored (*thanks Mom*). She also had a thing about not wanting to travel to a lakeside resort. "If I wanted a lake, I could have stayed home," summed up her overall feelings (she said this twice). Still I felt, in many ways, revived.

But though I could get away, I couldn't totally *get away*. There was always something pulling my thoughts back home, no matter where I went. Around two in the morning, I started doing something extremely ill advised—consulting Dr. Google about the effects of long-term steroid use on children. Both of our children used daily inhalers to manage their asthma, and for some reason, it felt imperative that I clock in research on this at that particular middle-of-the-night moment. I was breaking my own rule about resisting panic-filled internet searches. At 2:29 a.m., I sent an email to Cedar that included nothing but a link to "Moon Faces: Causes and Treatments." The source: WebMD. Later, I called Cedar to check in.

He picked up the phone and I could hear a half-grin in his voice.

"Hello, Emma? Are you okay?"

"Yeah, I'm okay. I'm just about to take a run on the trail."

"When I got that middle of the night email, at first, I thought your computer had been hacked. But then, after I thought about it, it seemed like it was you."

I cracked a smile against the phone. Cedar knew, and I mean *knew*, all the best and worst of me. He was used to my sleepless antics and related concerns, which often got stirred up in new surroundings. I was sleep *high maintenance*. We chatted warmly for a few minutes about how it was going for him back at home.

He said, "It's been okay. The usual. Not terrible, I guess," he offered in a sort of cryptic way.

"Not terrible is the new good," I responded. I knew he didn't want to get into it if there were problems, that he was trying to spare me of it, knowing that information wouldn't help either of us while I was away. His generosity was so clear to me then.

"I love you, Cedar," I added gently, my eyes set on the rustling leaves up ahead.

"I love you, too, babe," he replied. "I'm glad you get to have this time." We hung up, and I missed him, in the way that it feels almost good to miss someone when you're apart for only a few days.

I went home, of course, back to the nights where I sometimes laid on the floor next to the crib and held hands with Eden, while the whole barfing/crying/nebulizing loop continued. Or she'd just wake up with an ear-splitting cry, needing nothing more than a short burst of soothing. "Shhh," I'd say, popping up quickly to place my palm on her warm back, and she'd roll back to sleep as if nothing had happened. Yet my heart would thunk while my thoughts raced. I'd lay there, wondering how long it would be until the next cry. Would it be seconds, minutes, hours? I was ready just in case she needed me.

Sometimes Cedar or I would have to set an alarm to turn off the feeding pump or to refill the bag with formula. Sometimes I'd just lie there, cursing myself for squandering those precious hours of sleep. Sometimes—too often—Eden would be raring to start the day around four in the morning, which felt especially inhumane after an already eventful night.

Regardless, the sun rose each day, doing what it always did, brightening the sky and everything else. And no matter what happened within those dark, bleary hours beforehand, Cedar and I rose also.

It took months before we were able to get consistent overnight nursing care for Eden. Unfortunately, the home-care company claimed they couldn't staff most night shifts because of a nursing shortage. Like many home health agencies, they also didn't pay competitive rates to attract and retain nurses.

Julie was a steady presence, still covering a few key shifts a week (generally my workdays), along with a few nights each month. She would also come over to help when Eden became acutely ill, checking in frequently to provide unparalleled sensitive care. She would almost always pick up a phone call or respond to a harried text. We had back up, and we felt it.

Our best efforts to boost all support put a dent in the fatigue, and it was progress, no question. Yet I continued to feel worn down. Each day, I went to do therapy with clients in community mental health, and then came home to my caregiving/parenting work.

Eden was not getting any better, and we had no reason to expect that she would make a startling recovery. Together with all that possibly lay ahead for her, it didn't seem likely the caregiving path was going to ease up. It seemed that it would likely continue this way for a long time, maybe even for the rest of our lives.

CHAPTER ELEVEN

The Cuburbs

That fall, when Eden was eighteen months old, Cedar was invited to go on a year-long tour with Bon Iver, again as part of the saxophone choir. The show had gone well at Eaux Claires. Now these touring legs would require longer stretches away, for weeks at a time.

Although the timing was terrible, neither of us felt like Cedar should decline the opportunity. It was the kind of endeavor that when refused, may never come again. I knew that parenting without Cedar would be difficult, possibly brutal. But it also felt like him staying around, knowing that instead of a vomit-filled day he could be on stage somewhere in Ireland or Paris or another heavenly location with one of his favorite bands—this would surely lead to a torrent of resentment. It seemed that no matter what he chose, there would be fallout.

I saw with open eyes what I was getting into, and I said yes anyway.

In October, just as the first two-week leg of the tour was kicking off, Eden was back in the hospital for pneumonia and on oxygen intermittently. There was an incredible amount of sleeplessness, of crying, of dinging and pinging and measuring at all hours of the day and night.

This was Eden's fifth inpatient stay since April, since she was almost one, and there were many more ER visits beyond the actual hospital admissions.

I pined to be back in the world, beyond the hospital walls. But I was often solo, and therefore unable to leave. I had caught another respiratory illness, so Eden and I were cohabitating together in one persistent coughing symphony.

During those long days, when I wasn't soothing Eden, I began to discover the art of distraction. Before Eden, I had generally faced problems head on, right away. But hospital stays were often about passing time.

I spent a lot of time watching Eden sleep. Her bright face was reassuring. While she snoozed, I simmered while eating more cold hospital room service quesadillas than I could count. I looked at photos on my phone and messaged with Cedar. We would go through periods of texting like teenagers—back and forth about almost everything: memories, complaints, logistics, along with corresponding emojis. It made me feel less alone, but sometimes it stung, too. Cedar tried not to give too many details about the fabulous life he was living, which may have reduced my envy, but made him seem more distant, in a way. We had a shared past and a future. But we didn't have a shared present.

Sometimes, when Eden was awake, I would climb in her little crib to spoon her. We would watch Teen Beach Movie (her favorite) with our bodies squished together, while Eden twirled my hair. My mother also clocked in hours at the hospital, as well, although she was more focused on educational content than Disney heartthrobs.

Our village rallied: my parents continued to care for Avi whenever Eden was in the hospital. He didn't seem phased by the arrangement. Occasionally, my mother asked him if he wanted to go to the hospital for a visit. He never did. We all felt it was in Avi's best interest to keep his usual routines afloat, especially because he was still young enough for preschool.

Julie spent more nights at the hospital, giving me a chance to sleep in my own bed, and/or to spend a morning with Avi. She asked not to be paid whenever Eden was inpatient. She knew I was sick and had expressed numerous times that she wanted to do it. I relented, accepting her magnanimous gift, and so Julie took on a notable amount of those epic, sleepless stretches.

On the nights that Julie stayed, Marc joined her early in the morning to dote on Eden. He played songs off his phone or wholehearted games of peek-a-boo, crib side. Eden was enraptured.

Marc, in his uniform of a baseball hat with a MN graphic on the front, polo shirt, and jeans, was a Minnesota guy through and through. Even though he had recently retired from a highly successful career in finance, he and Julie rarely took vacations. "I just like to be home," he would often remark. And, undeniably, he also could also find a way to be at home in the hospital.

Instead of jet setting, Marc spent many hours with Eden while she was in-patient; one afternoon he brought Eden a zoo's worth of stuffed animals. Or at least he wanted to.

He held up the hippo and then a rabbit the size of a football. "Are you sure you don't need a few more of these for Eden?" he asked with a grin. "Julie had to rein me in."

"You do generally like to overdo it," Julie said.

"Only the best for Eden. This kid has been through so much, she should get ten of these guys if she wants them. Twenty!" he said, his eyes lighting up. "Whatever she wants. Look at her," he motioned to the hospital crib where Eden was rubbing a bunny ear between her thumb and her forefinger contentedly.

"Thanks Marc. You and Julie are so generous. And I think one or two is good. But whatever works. I'm not getting in the middle of this. I'm just happy you are here."

I would tag in the next morning with bagels and black coffee in tow, and then Julie would go home to sleep. Sometimes Marc would stay. One day as nurses filed in and out, Marc held on to her hand.

"Don't you worry about it, Eden," he said. "I'm putting on your favorite album, *Baby Beluga*. Let's find your favorite song on here."

Eden squealed and shook her muscles in approval, tightening her legs and flapping her arms, her long hands fluttering quickly while Marc cued up the music on his phone. Marc paid attention to each and every like and dislike that Eden had, and in that process, honored her in small yet meaningful ways.

Even so, I sometimes hit despair hard. Eden's vomiting continued and we still did not have a diagnosis or a treatment.

Cedar had just played a show at the vast, iconic Hollywood Bowl, and then rolled into a splashy afterparty where he spent a good chunk of time talking with Lizzo. She wasn't quite famous yet but was already a pioneering bad ass.

One morning, before heading back to the hospital, I emptied the expired food from the fridge at the same time as I was cooking breakfast. I had hardly slept, and I had caught some type of flu. I was in that high-intensity mode, pushing through exhaustion with no time to take care of myself.

Our sink clogged while I was scrambling eggs. I pulled the eggshells out of the drain with my hand, threw the wet, crackly mess in the garbage and started some coffee. I sobbed, in the kitchen, my body pressed up against the hard edge of the sink. Another thing breaking? Somehow this was what did me in.

Later, I called Cedar and told him how angry I was with him for being gone on tour for weeks, right in the middle of all of this. I said I couldn't stand it anymore. I told him there could be no redemption now, not even if he got on a plane this minute. "Eden's been in the hospital for days. And where are you? In some beautiful fucking hotel," I howled. Cedar listened, like he almost always does.

He said, "You have every right to be angry, I would be, too. And how could you be doing well under these circumstances? That would be weird." And then, after we talked for a few minutes, his non-defensiveness, his kindness, his total empathy was all that I heard.

"I can't be mad anymore, at least for today," I said from the kitchen floor, my grip on the cell phone loosening. "You get it. You always get it. And . . . I really still can't make any promises about being mad or not mad tomorrow."

Marriage didn't feel exactly like it first did, not anymore. No one was hoisting me up in the air, for starters, or dancing the hora in circles around us. When you have a child who is missing DNA, the honeymoon is over.

What did I know then at our luminous wedding? About love, about what it was like to stick around? About what happened after the limerence and fanfare, in the everyday moments that made up a real life with someone. I knew how to love well when life was easy-ish. And it *was* easier at the beginning. There was no denying it.

I don't exactly know how I got from home haircuts inspired by Ani DiFranco all the way to a ranch-style home in the suburbs. Bit by bit, I suppose, through a series of steps, including the choice to marry a man when I could have married anyone.

But mostly, it was Eden. It was always Eden.

We weren't planning on moving. The suburbs found us when it was winter in every sense of the word. My previous flu had evolved into another bout of pneumonia that lasted for months; I had broken a rib during a bout of intense hacking, which sent shards of pain through me each time I coughed. Cedar was about to leave again for two weeks to stay at a boutique hotel in the Lower East Side of Manhattan in a bedroom with floor to ceiling windows.

Was I supportive? It depended on the day.

I was happy for Cedar, who was able to do what he was born to do. I didn't want him to miss the opportunity to play with this incredible band. It was, in many ways, a chance that might never come again.

But there were times when I wanted to actually *be* him.

I wanted the crisp, cool hotel sheets and the breezy, sleep-laden layover days where there was no agenda beyond the camaraderie of the road.

Our village wasn't fully formed yet. Without it, I longed for a different life. It was time to do something, anything, to make it better.

I had again departed to stay at my parents' house with the kids while he was gone, just as I did during each leg that he was away. The packing strategy I used was illustrative: laundry baskets shoved in the trunk of my hatchback, spilling over with syringes and nebulizers.

In my old childhood bedroom, I stared up at the ceiling where there used to be glow-in-the-dark stars. Next to me was a crib and an IV pole with a feeding pump with a Farrell gastric relief bag hooked up to it. When Eden woke crying, about five times a night, I would sing from the bed, hoping it was enough. It usually wasn't. Inevitably, I would get up to snuggle her tiny body against me, hypervigilantly tracking the two tubes to be sure they wouldn't get tangled or yanked out unexpectedly, reciting prayers I half-remembered from childhood. On many nights, there would be puke. If Eden hit a certain number of emeses per day, she was at risk for dehydration, so we would switch her over to Pedialyte or some Arnie Palmer concoction (part formula, part clear fluids). If that didn't help, we would call the gastroenterologist, and sometimes we would head back to the hospital.

This was not the kind of nightlife I imagined my husband was enjoying.

During those years, vomit became nearly as familiar as dirt or a spray of water from the garden hose. I would sometimes rub it into whatever I was wearing and move on; it was the best I could do.

Cedar was juggling his nearly full-time music teaching job at a performing arts high school along with the touring schedule. When he came back from stretches away, he was already behind on his lesson plans, stressed about catching up on grading and searching for a substitute teacher for the next leg. He would get home late from the airport from somewhere amazing in a completely different time zone, and then the next morning, head out again to teach a sea of teenagers with green and pink hair.

One very December day that year, I was walking with my mother on a trail in the woods a few miles from their home. Former lake cabins dotted the maple-lined path. Cedar was with Avi and Eden, still in town yet preparing to leave the next day.

I had on my long down coat, the kind you wear in Minnesota for approximately five months straight, so that by March it's so full of schmutz that it looks like a garbage can. I was sobbing. My nose was running, and I wiped it on my fleece glove.

As we walked down the path toward the beach, I told my mother the things I had said many times before. "Watching Eden suffer like this . . . I can't describe what it is like, watching her going through this pain. It's my baby, my girl. I brought her here, for this? And there's no end in sight for any of it." My voice wavered, and I sighed. I looked at her, trying to read her face like I did when I was a child. Our feet crunched the leaves below on the path.

"I thought it was going to be easier. That I would be a regular parent, with regular problems." I took a breath. I felt that familiar sinking feeling;

I wasn't sure this was helping me to say this out loud, but I didn't know how *not* to say it, either.

"I need something to change. I'm totally exhausted. Beyond it, actually. I don't know if I can keep going as it is." By this time, Eden had been in and out of the hospital for eight months. "What if this never ends, and I'm just stuck here, doing this, for the rest of my life?"

"Honestly, Emma, I never wanted this life for you," my mother replied, her voice cracking. The big down hood was up on her coat, but I could still see her eyes, wide and glossy. My mother had said that to me before, too.

I wanted her to tell me that this could be a good life. That Eden was just as good, as great even, as any other child.

And I wanted her to be able to declare, definitively, that this too would pass, change, get better someday. That Eden would heal, and so would I. But there was no certainty in what lay ahead, and we both knew it. There was no certainty anywhere; it had never been clearer. I looked into my mother's eyes for a sign that things would improve, but she could not free me from an unknown future.

She could not free me from anything. It was not up to her. And I was no longer a child; I was a mother now.

Here she was, anyway, walking next to me again. I let my tears roll down my cold cheeks and left them there.

If they froze, so be it.

So be anything, so be it all. I wasn't in charge of how this would go.

My mother continued, her voice both strained and smooth, "You can do it, though. I mean, you're doing it now." I thought about this. Yes, I was doing it, but I felt so trapped.

My life was, in many ways, no longer mine.

She looked at my wet cheeks and said, "I'll do whatever I can for you. Sometimes I feel like I can't do enough to help. I have to take care of myself, too. You know I need my workout. And I have to have time with your father. But, of course, I'll help in whatever ways that I can. You know that, Emma."

Yes, I did. I felt it suddenly, all over. *I want to live out here, near my parents. Close to these thick woods.* And there it was after we walked up the hill, a house for sale, right underneath those towery trees, just a quick stroll to the beach. I'd never pictured myself in a mostly one-story rambler, but I felt more open than ever to what I'd hadn't pictured yet.

Cedar and I toured it together first thing the next morning, right before I drove him to the airport. He liked it, and I loved it. Even though it was built in the 1960s, it made things feel *new* again. Almost.

Cedar and I went back and forth about the decision during a series of harried phone conversations while he was in New York. He didn't want to leave Minneapolis. I said it was the cuburbs after all (the country plus suburbs), and wouldn't it be freeing to have all this fresh air? I had already heard that the special education for the school district was stellar, which was a major motivation for the change. I discovered that an excellent public special education preschool was only a mile away.

We knew that leaving the city for "good schools" was fraught in terms of equity. We would be leaving behind our friends, and maybe even the parts of ourselves that believed in urban life and its higher levels of diversity. It was very white in this cuburb and very straight.

We would be entering into a whole different community, a different life. But weren't we already in a different life? I didn't know anyone else doing what we were doing each day.

I toured more homes in the area alongside my father. Afterward, the rambler seemed more fitting than I had thought. Eden couldn't walk then, and we didn't know if she ever would. Our two-story house in Minneapolis, with the bedrooms upstairs, was less and less practical.

One night while Cedar was still away, I sat in the well-lit living room at my parents' house and swiveled around on one of their oversized plush chairs. I called Kate; she was an ideal person to talk this through with, since we had so much in common. We had resonating values, similar career paths, and even compatible vices, including a pre-Kondo fixation on domestic order. Kate lived in South Minneapolis. Before that she had a small apartment in Manhattan, and earlier in Boston. She was not a voice for the suburban experience.

"Kate, is this crazy? Moving out here on a whim?" I looked down at the thick rug, staring intently. It had been only a few days since I'd had the idea to move and now we were getting ready to draw up an offer. "Do you think

I'll regret it?" She replied steadily, in her slightly East Coast accent, "Well, I think you've always made good decisions, Emma. I get why you want to do this, especially now. Given everything, it makes sense. I really don't think that you will regret it." After we ended the call, I was still torn, especially considering the common wisdom to delay major life changes during an acute period of grief. But this acute period of grief had no end in sight. It was an ambiguous loss, a term coined by researcher and educator Dr. Pauline Boss, a loss that lacks certainty in some form. A loss with no form of closure.

A few days later, I went for a long weekend to see Cedar. We needed to see each other in person. I flew during a snowstorm with a name on a small jet that bounced and swayed and had me praying like it was Yom Kippur. The flight reminded me just how much I wanted to be alive.

In New York, I stayed in Cedar's posh hotel room with an unobstructed view of the Manhattan skyline. The night I got in, Cedar and I went to a sushi bar together. My flight landed after midnight, and I loved being out in those dim hours together for the pleasure of staying awake, not for the purpose of taking care of anyone else. We sat at a booth until almost sunrise talking.

A few days later, I went to the Bon Iver show at Kings Theater in Brooklyn. In a room full of thousands of people, it was musical stargazing in a collective cosmic experience. The songs, ripe with heartache, hurt in all the best ways.

In the three days that I was gone, Avi spiked a high fever and Eden came down with another respiratory virus. Again, with Eden throwing up alongside her coughing, which was so dramatic that it seemed unrealistic. If that kind of coughing was depicted by a character in a play, I would say that it was heavy handed. Bad acting, baby.

I didn't go home early. I knew the kids were getting the best care possible by my diligent parents and several other caregivers who took shifts with Eden, including Julie. The care was arguably better than mine, given my chronic sleep deprivation. I kept in close touch over the phone. I knew I would be back within a day or so, returning to my caregiver status.

So, instead of nursing duty, I went out gallivanting around the city with the love of my life, eating slices of veggie pizza in a packed little restaurant at 1:00 a.m. on the Lower East Side. Wearing brassy lipstick and a dress with a little shimmer to it, I felt far away from my caregiving duties. I even felt a bit sexy. I felt like me.

That felt great, possibly even better than great. I wasn't a martyr kind of mom. And because I didn't want to give up myself—it was against my own values—this led to a constant struggle during those early days and years.

The next day, Cedar and I dozed until noon and then went searching for a breakfast spot around the time we usually put Eden down for a nap. We looked around in little shops in Soho eyeing cashmere and woolen clothing that we did not buy. We strolled, without a stroller. We did very little, really.

Cedar and I walked around smiling at each other as if we were on a second date. As if it was still that more carefree era before we had children. We were, in some ways, happier back then. Bright eyed, idealistic. The studies may be right about happiness, how it often decreases with each child born. And especially having a child with so many intense medical needs.

But, of course, just like those studies also report, parenting was the most meaningful, otherworldly thing I had ever done. Although during that trip, I wondered, in the ways that a mother is never supposed to wonder, if I had chosen not to have children, if my life would have been better. Freer? Happier?

The day I left to go back to Minnesota, I slept in until 8:30 in the morning, which felt teenager-ish to me. When I woke up, Cedar presented me with a salty bagel sandwich from Russ and Daughters along with a still-hot latte. I ate it sitting on top of a fluffy comforter on the bed that someone else would eventually make. The sesame seeds fell all over me. It was fleeting and terrific.

We agreed to move. Cedar didn't want to leave Minneapolis, but he understood how much I wanted this change. We knew our decision to move out of the city was flawed in some ways, but it seemed like our best shot at having a more manageable life.

I wondered if it would ever feel manageable enough.

CHAPTER TWELVE

Caregiver Meets Coachella

When Cedar came home from New York, the vacation feeling we had experienced together felt like the distant past. We made it through the winter, through our move out to the cuburbs in early February, through the months that ticked by. I cleaned out everything we owned, organized us to the nines, gave away anything unnecessary. The closets looked almost as good as the end of an episode of *The Home Edit*. And my insides were more like the front seat of my car. Cluttered with so many things.

I did most of the move myself, which didn't help. My rib had finally healed from my epic bout of pneumonia, but Cedar and I had not.

I wanted us to start over. Was that even possible?

Quickly, due to my slightly (ranging to not so slightly) obsessive tendencies, we settled into our new house. When Debra stopped over the first weekend with a full sandwich spread in tow, including mustard, she looked up and down at the color-coded bookshelves and said, "It looks like you've been living here for years."

It was a little bit country—we could see the sunrise in the morning through the windows of the family room and the sunset from the kitchen between the branches of maple trees. On most days, after grasping for coffee, I roamed down the trail to watch the light reflect off the lake.

No matter how tired I was, I began to exercise regularly again at the local gym (another thing I could not have predicted). The routine of leaving the house *and* taking care of myself buoyed me. When people—a close or not so close friend or my parents, Marc, and Julie or really, nearly anyone—offered to help, I consistently said *yes*. I relied on other people now. I began to feel less guilty about it, less consumed with regret.

There were sweet moments and new developments, and we celebrated them. On most days, Eden learned at least one new word. Then, promptly after saying it, Eden would vigorously clap for herself, looking around for us to notice. We did, and we clapped alongside her.

On one bright day when the snow had melted, I rigged up a bubble machine that blew a stream of glossy rainbow-tinged bubbles around the yard. They launched into the wind and burst in our hands and in our hair. With the help of her ankle braces, Eden, almost age two, cruised tentatively around the deck furniture, a new development, the bubbles pouring out next to her. My mother kneeled nearby, and she and Avi cheered with us, "Go Eden! Looking good!"

I started to get to know the neighbors that very first spring. Just as there was no one else like Eden, there was no one else like our neighbor Kitty either, who created pastel landscapes in her quaint backyard art studio that overlooked her garden. Even when we didn't know each other well, we were drawn to each other. We later said that we both felt it right away, even from the first time we spoke. I had called her to ask her a few questions about the neighborhood, and she gave me an upbeat earful. One of the first times I met her in person, she handed me a multi-colored, hand-drawn map of each house in the neighborhood, with names of each resident. It was very precisely drawn.

Kitty had a small, sprightly build with a pixie-ish silver bob. She was flushed and weathered from her time in the sun and generally decked out in an earthy color scheme. Before she retired, Kitty was a cardiology nurse at Abbott Northwestern Hospital in Minneapolis and worked in the ICU. She knew the world of caregiving, and she knew how hearts and bodies sometimes fell apart. Also, her younger sister had cerebral palsy.

Kitty updated me with the latest news of her sister, who lived in a group home near their hometown, a few hours away.

I called Kitty's yard the little arboretum. It had a pond she made herself, and a double lot where she grew rows of vegetables and groves of bright native and tropical flowers, which spilled out of planters. Deep green grapevines cascaded over her carefully constructed trellis archways. Orange trumpet vines and hydrangea climbed over the teal garage. It smelled like lush, green earth, with a hint of mothballs.

The kids discovered early on that Kitty's yard was full-on enchanting, and most days they begged to go over there. I almost always let them. We'd run over to check out what was growing and try to catch frogs in the pond. Eden liked the rickety porch swing, so we'd rock together while Avi circled the paths. I kept asking Kitty, "Are you sure it's okay that we come by nearly *every day*? Please tell me if we are intruding on your peace and quiet or if you need a little space. I would get it. If I could take the space *I* would," I said.

"You know I like it when you visit," she reassured me with her bright smile. Her boundless energy and smallish frame gave her a fairy-like energy, if you caught her at the right angle.

"It gives some activity to this place—oh, they are sure busy, Emma. And it's nice to have you all here, appreciating the garden."

Kitty taught Avi about growing plants from seed in her greenhouse and shared the names of all the different varieties of blossoms. She took Avi by the hand to point out the blooming crocuses and to spot shoots of green emerging from the earth.

One day Avi came back hauling a giant, smooth river stone that Kitty found in Lake Superior, almost too big to carry. When I said, "Hey, that should live outdoors." Avi tilted his head and replied, "It's a really special rock, Mom. Kitty gave it to *me* and she's trusting me with it." I relented. Who could argue with trust? It sat among his favorite things on his bookshelf.

If we were in the front yard, Kitty would often stroll across the street with a few plants she'd picked up while at the nearby nursery. "I thought of you!" she'd exclaim, as she wheeled her rusty red wheelbarrow over. We gardened side by side; Kitty could plow through the earth and dig a hole like *wham*. She grew up on a farm, that much was clear. And I did not, although being out there with her made me feel like maybe I could have.

My parents were able to help more often since we were now a short drive away from them. Their gym, the same one I joined, was a few blocks from us. Because the gym was, in certain ways, their form of synagogue, they were often right around the corner, so I would see them almost every time I went to work out. They brought chicken from Kowalski's, along with other meals more times than I could count. They came over to entertain Eden—and although my dad was skittish around her, cautious of her frail health, he came up with a fake crying bit that she begged him to repeat. They came often to pick up Avi, and hosted him for frequent overnights, which involved thousands of LEGO pieces.

My mother started spending each Saturday morning with Eden and set up a little school in the front yard, complete with a rocking chair, books, and a blanket. She would bring a tote bag filled with educational activities for Eden crafted out of items she found around the house. Before DIY was a trend, my mother scrounged for supplies. She'd whip out some stencils from 1985 or thick cardstock that I remember from my own childhood. When I held the materials that I used way back when, it transported me back in time.

Later that month, Cedar left again for two weeks at Coachella. When he wasn't at the iconic, desert sand-swept weekend festival, he was staying with the band in Palm Springs in a rented-out property with full meal service and a pool. Bon Iver was second billed that year, with Lady Gaga as the headliner.

I flew out to join him between the first and second weekend and stayed through until the next Monday. The night before I left, I frantically stuffed a carry-on filled with vacation-y things, including a new lip gloss and a featherweight scarf. I brought a handful of short dresses and three books. Eden would be cared for by Julie and Marc, and Avi went to my parents' house. Julie and Marc had started to feel like another set of (young-ish) grandparents by this point, doting on her lovingly and stepping in to help whenever we needed it most.

I got off the almost four-hour plane ride in a jean skirt and comfy gold flats. In the big bustling bathroom of the Palm Springs airport, I did my best to smooth my frizzed-up hair and put on a dab of eye concealer and a sweep of blush, which was my general way of trying to look rested.

After my ride dropped me off in front of the property, I walked into the courtyard pulling my carry-on bag behind me. The first person I saw, beside Cedar, was Justin Vernon, the inspired founder and lead singer of Bon Iver. He sauntered over in swim trunks and a white tank top, grinning, and gave me a burly, welcoming hug. This wasn't our first meeting; I had had some warmhearted conversations with him over the years. Still, my heart raced.

Almost a decade before, I had spent countless hours listening to *For Emma, Forever Ago* when I lived alone. I used to play the album on repeat in my bright yellow kitchen as I cooked up veggies from the Kingfield Farmers Market. I was heartbroken then in a very different way, sun kissed, and in my twenties. I felt like that album was made for me.

There were maybe fifteen or so people lounging in the sun or swimming in the bright blue pool. I worried about what I was wearing, and later how I looked in my floral one-piece halter swimsuit. I had the sense that I didn't belong, which hadn't been generally my issue (although, of course, I had others). It was partly because Cedar was playing in the saxophone section; he wasn't in Bon Iver proper, in the core band. The Bon Iver guys had been playing together for many years, some for almost a decade. The touring started out in the way that most bands start out—sleeping in a van together, sharing a hotel room, hoping that people would love the music but not really knowing which way it would go. And then, over time they had ascended to international recognition. They had that inexplicable bond that comes from thousands of hours together, a shared early history. Even though Cedar was not on that level, we were treated extremely well, regardless. For example, every musician and crew member got private hotel rooms at each tour stop, which was above and beyond the industry standard.

Entering this band's space, surrounded by famous musicians whose lives were so entirely different from mine—a few days later I had lunch next to singer-songwriter Bruce Hornsby—it was a lot. I was used to being at home and getting thrown up on or, alternately, cramming in client sessions in a community mental health setting. My life, at that point, was not exactly a freewheeling artist scene. I had barely even seen free time in several years; I had no idea how to handle myself.

I really didn't want to be some anonymous wife—that felt too small, too domestic. I wanted to be a person, not a partner. Ideally, a person doing something creative (and my distinctive carpet stain removal strategy did not count, at least for my own fulfillment). This lingered in my mind and clouded what were sunny days.

Cedar and I went out for dinner together and hunted down a hard-to-find tiki bar. We swam and napped and showered without any children needing us. I could have been calculating Eden's caloric count for the day, but instead I had a mild sunburn and nowhere that I had to be.

When we were with the group, I tried to be open and friendly. But hanging out with musicians was not like hanging out with therapists. When therapists get together, we ask each other all kinds of questions—and then follow up questions—and we want to hear every single detail. Here, the language was music, and I didn't even play an instrument. Also, nearly everyone was prepping for a major show. It may have been hanging out for me but this was a work trip, and they were gearing up to play in front of 250,000 people.

No pressure.

Amelia Meath and Nick Sanborn, who made up the electronic pop duo Sylvan Esso, were among the people there. At the time, I wasn't yet familiar with Sylvan Esso's music—this was right before their sophomore album launched. After that trip I discovered how much I loved their music; they became one of my all-time favorite bands. Back home, following Coachella, we had at least twenty kitchen dance-offs featuring their album, *What Now*. We would put it on before dinner when one or both kids were on the edge of a meltdown. Suddenly their heads would be bobbing back and forth like little teenagers, with Eden singing, "Oh, ohhh." Not a tear in sight. At one point, Eden showcased a brief but respectable air drum solo. She already had her own signature style.

One day during that trip, as we sat around on uncomfortable poolside furniture, I asked Amelia and Jenny Lewis, another indie rock maven, "So, what do you do?" and "Do you have any children?" These were not great rockstar questions, whatever that means. They were not great questions, in general.

There was a clear plastic table between us, and I was wearing my swimsuit. I had a novel with me, but I wasn't reading it. Some band members were splashing around together in the water nearby, and I heard EDM coming from a nearby cabana. Underneath an umbrella, some people were sharing a spliff. I didn't smoke that weed, but it wafted around like drawn out sun-soaked days and fleeting idle time.

They were warm toward me, which made my discomfort somehow worse. I don't remember if they asked me anything about myself. They probably did. I might have said that I had a few little ones at home. I don't think we talked about therapy or writing or anything beyond my roles as wife and mother. I felt surprisingly self-conscious.

I no longer felt like I had much in common with other mothers either, at least the ones I knew who had typical children, and this weekend getaway was a visit to another planet entirely. If I was going to be forthcoming, I could announce, "I mostly stay home to try to keep my child alive; she's on a feeding tube but isn't tolerating food." Even for me, that felt like too much to share with people I had met only minutes before.

The next morning, Amelia offered to bring me back a coffee from a run that she and Nick were making to a shop a few blocks away. I waved it off but admired her willingness to include me.

The best part of Coachella was the music. The weather was painfully hot. On Saturday, the day I was at the festival from mid-morning until around midnight, it was nearly 100 degrees. I wore a navy-blue striped romper, which I got right before the trip. It was thin and light with a wide open back, and the shorts were very short. Still, walking around the grounds, I was wearing more fabric than most, at least compared to the other women. The uniform was, essentially, lacey negligees. There were various sexy iterations of that and the occasional bold outfit, like a clear plastic mini skirt. I was like, *Wow, okay, this is definitely not the Midwest. And, go girl, whatever works, do it.*

A few hours before night fell, I exchanged smiles with a woman as we passed each other backstage. I took in her blond hair and her friendly eyes; we had a brief, bright moment as we walked in opposite directions. I didn't know it was Lady Gaga until Cedar said, "Whoa, Lady Gaga just totally smiled at you."

Years later, when *Chromatica* first came out, I told Eden about that moment as we were strolling near the beach. The song "Stupid Love" came on our outdoor portable speaker (we tried not to leave home without it) and it reminded me of that Coachella moment. I gave Eden every detail, which wasn't that many. Despite the nonstory-story, Eden kept bringing it up afterward. She would scrunch up her face into a tight smile and then announce, "Lady Gaga smiled at you. She did it!" A few weeks after that, when we were listening to our family playlist, Eden brought it up again, shaking her body with delight, "Lady Gaga smiled. At Mommy! She did. Live in concert." *Live in concert* was one of her favorite phrases. I tried to incorporate it into sentences as much as possible, just to watch her eyes shine like river stones.

The Bon Iver show was gorgeous, mystical, and somehow, unexpected. I had seen the band play many times over the years, too many to count, and yet each time felt like the very first. The song "715-Creeks" sent me back to scenes from the hospital, watching Eden's oxygen levels rise and fall on the monitor. When Vernon sang/pleaded those haunting, harmonized lyrics, the words seared into me.

Under a dark sky and a string of lights outside of his trailer one night, I approached Justin. Most people who knew him well called him Vern, but I didn't know him that well.

"Hey buddy," he greeted me.

I wasn't sure if he called me buddy because he couldn't remember my name, but I suspected he knew it.

"The show was amazing!" I felt a flush of fan-girl energy, which I tried to brush off. I continued, "*Creeks* reminds me of some of the most desperate moments I've had with Eden. My daughter. The one who has been in the hospital so much."

He looked me straight in the eyes and replied, "I hope it helps."

There was a pause. I didn't know if it helped, and I didn't know what to say. How could I explain anything about what it was like to listen to a song like that, so many miles away from her? The ache that I lived with, that never went away, that sometimes I forgot about, but never for more than a few hours at a time. How could I explain anything about what we'd been through, what living with this kind of unresolved grief felt like, especially over good beer with this particularly charming person, in the middle of the desert? How could I express what it was like to be a mother to a child who I thought I might lose at any moment?

"It's as beautiful as can be, that song of yours," is all that I could muster. Justin continued, "If there's anything that I can do, for your family, anything, really, please let me know. I'm sure that it's been a lot for all of you."

He was gracious, as always. But I couldn't find the words to share my own experience, not on that trip, and hardly at all during that time. There was a stiff loneliness in not being able to share what it was like, yet of course, ambiguous loss wasn't small talk, and didn't fit into the rhythms of everyday conversation, let alone backstage banter. I didn't want to lead with searing pain—it wasn't exactly after-party material—yet the grief dripped off me, and I had no words to explain myself.

Still, I loved being at those Bon Iver shows, especially during that tender time. Standing near the stage, too close to the person next to me, escaping into the sound. Being surrounded by so many others sharing in the collective experience—feeling together at the exact same time and place. Sometimes I saw a rare, fantastic glimmer beyond the confines of myself. Sometimes I did forget about Eden, about vomit, about worrying about whether she would live to see age twelve or even six. I needed that more than anything, a break from the frightening, repetitive chatter of my own mind.

I forgot and then always, I remembered with a sudden little jolt, almost like remembering where I put my keys, but without the relief of finding them.

Oh, there, there was that thing, the grim uncertainty.

It was always somewhere.

CHAPTER THIRTEEN

Family-ish

When I was twenty-four years old, after a stint in Vermont, I moved back to Minneapolis. I craved being back near my family and the lakes and landscape of home. I also wanted to be near Solvay and Quinn. I had originally met them ten years earlier at summer camp, now they were both hunkered down happily in Minneapolis. We had stayed connected through the years, even when we were in different places through frequent visits, weekly calls, and handwritten letters. Quinn and Solvay showed me how to be close in a way that wasn't biological family but was family-ish.

I spent nearly every weekend with Solvay and Quinn. We had our own language that consisted of hyperbole mixed with genuine enthusiasm; it felt like I didn't need to explain myself.

They were queer in a very particular, committed way. They didn't come out because they were never *in*. I didn't have to come out either, at least not to Solvay or Quinn. We were open about our sexuality from the beginning, back when we were in our teenage years. It wasn't a big to-do. We had a common understanding of these things, informed in part by Kinsey's work, that most everyone is on a fluid spectrum of attraction. I don't exactly know how we even knew about Kinsey or had these types of ideas, especially back in high school. Yet somehow, that was that, and none of it was fraught or difficult. I did date cisgender men—lots of them—and this set me apart from the group.

Sometimes we biked to our favorite neighborhood spot a few blocks away from my apartment with its sturdy built-in breakfast nook, for tiny theater shows and to gulp Two Hearted Ale. We also took the Greenway bike trail to rambling performances put on by punk rock types who were big on creative expression and small on showering.

As I got close with Cedar, we started to shift in different directions. One night, over roasted chicken at our place on Upton Avenue, Quinn opened a conversation with Cedar with a serious look, and asked, "So, what is it like to be a straight white man?" I stiffened in my chair and glanced at Cedar, almost cracking a smile. I mean, he *was* a straight white man, but the question came off as fairly confrontational. He paused for a few seconds, looked at her, and said, "Well, huh. I mean, it's weird."

Looking back on it, it was the kind of awesome, bold stance Quinn was known for. She wasn't apologizing for anything, and she generally pulled it off.

We drifted over a series of years. Ever-loyal Solvay relocated a few months before Cedar and I got married. Quinn and I began to have less overlap in our lives; we didn't see each other as often.

Back when we lived in Minneapolis, when Eden was boomeranging in and out of the hospital, I tried to get in touch with Quinn periodically, but mostly couldn't reach her. I even called her and left a voicemail during an afternoon at the hospital that seemed to drag on forever, thinking, *She'll definitely call me back while I'm here.* But there was nothing.

One night, as I was sitting in the dark in Eden's room, holding her upright against my chest after a tube feeding, I finally got a text back from Quinn. *I love you from afar, but I just don't know how to be in your life anymore.* I replied, *I don't understand. Can we grab a coffee or at least talk about this over the phone?* We'd talked through so many things over the years—roommate issues (when we'd lived together) and various tensions and transitions along the way. This seemed no different. But she did not respond.

At first, I was gutted. I sat in that room with Eden and rocked her for a long time, feeling her steady, rhythmic breath, considering the precariousness of everything. I went over and over it in my mind, trying desperately to figure out a puzzle that lacked many clues—there was no argument, no clear, conspicuous conflict.

I rehearsed, too often, what I would say to Quinn when she finally called to apologize. She didn't. I was more than stung by the timing of the text while Eden was so sick.

There's no way our rift was because I had a child who was disabled— Quinn was not that type of person, far from it—but it may have been that Quinn felt she wasn't doing enough for me *since I did* have a child who was struggling so critically. I don't know for sure; I never found out why from her directly.

I know there were things I did that made staying connected difficult. I didn't reach out as much, and when I did, I didn't have the flexibility that would be conducive to us staying close. I often was particular, rigid even, about scheduling plans—where and when and how I could meet. I sensed she judged me for the mainstream choices that I'd made— most especially, marrying a man.

Maybe she *did* judge me. Yet, maybe I judged myself even more, sensitive to any possible slight. Or maybe by believing that she judged me, I'd closed myself off.

I missed her big, loud laugh and the way she would greet everyone, so thrilled, jumping around a little even, like you hadn't seen each other in months, even if it had been a day. I also missed her full-on utopian vision for life, her belief that anything was possible. She was an original, a lover of life, a daring soul.

I took that sense of possibility with me, but Quinn was the original source.

I talked this through with Cedar, probably too many times. Solvay and I sometimes lamented it softly during her occasional visits back home, neither one of us wanting to overstep. They were still close, and I was the odd one out. Yet whenever Solvay was in town, it was mostly the same between us as it was in high school, although back then we kissed in a bunk bed while listening to *Rent* (but only for a spell, until we realized we were better off as friends). We weren't kissing now and hadn't for many years. Cedar and I would host her and her partner for a veggie-laden summer dinner in the kitchen, or there was the time we met at the library, Solvay's sweet-cheeked daughter in tow. We left our kids with our partners so that Solvay and I could stay in the stacks together for a long time. We meandered through the rows of books, reminiscing about how we used to borrow feminist erotica stories from her parents' bookshelf as if it was our personal lending library.

Many months later, as Kate and I wound around on foot near Minnehaha Creek, pushing our strollers, weaving awkwardly around the paved city paths, we talked about our oldest friends. It was a mild day, and we had a narrow window together, as we generally did, before our other children had to get picked up from somewhere. I wasn't planning on it, but I told her about Quinn. I did my best to explain our history together, although attachment between people is hard to explain in words.

When I said, "It hurt as much as any breakup," as I tried to navigate a curb with Eden's stroller, she understood what I meant.

It became clear to me—more than ever—that in friendships, I have been left and I have also been the one who leaves. I have been a stellar friend, and I have been unavailable and preoccupied. I am, in many ways, no different than Quinn. I have drifted apart from friends, found distance where there used to be connection, moved or graduated and lost touch, or ended things too abruptly. There are many people I have called friends, who I no longer know anymore. For reasons we sometimes understand, and sometimes do not, we cannot maintain all connections to all people throughout time.

Even so, as a mother, I needed help; I needed a village. Just like any mother anywhere. We need a village to loosen the burden of all that ends up falling to us, over us, on us. Mothers cannot do it alone, and of course, we shouldn't be expected to. Yet the cultural message we get is you are not worthy unless you have it all, which means *do it all,* ideally on your own. Who is that message serving? And where is the systemic support for families when we need it most?

What if I asked for help? What if I got it? What if I was in control of very little, really (frighteningly so), yet I could reach out to make my way through it?

If a village connection lasts two decades, isn't that still stunning? Quinn and I were villagers together at a particular and formative time in our lives. Sometimes, we grow with our villages, and sometimes we must adjust the boundaries of the villages as we grow. Or they adjust for us, despite our best plans. When my friendship ended with Quinn, I felt it burn all over, a difficult, unresolved ending during an unresolved season of loss. This was not the way life was supposed to turn out, in all kinds of ways. But suddenly, somewhere deep inside me, I felt a door to acceptance creaking open.

CHAPTER FOURTEEN

The Eden

wanted to let go of a lot of things, like my friendship with Quinn, but I often felt stuck in how my life was *supposed* to turn out, as if that would somehow serve me. Eden's self-injurious behavior (especially, her head banging) was one of those things that shocked and disturbed me from the beginning. This reaction may have been wired into my humanity, due to the safety concerns and the need for immediate intervention. How does one let go while simultaneously being right there, trying to minimize permanent brain damage?

Agonizingly, Eden lacked the skills to express what was going on inside of her, so she would show us her frustration or pain by hitting herself above her eyebrows with her tiny, clenched fist or slamming her head against whatever hard surface was immediately available. If she hurt herself, she would keep on going, undeterred. It ramped up when she was sick and uncomfortable. Witnessing this was a fast track to heartbreak.

Despair was never very far away. I stumbled into it like a patch of uneven pavement suddenly underneath me, which sparked tears and harried phone calls and shaky neighborhood walks. I did what I could to move through it—which was sometimes what I thought other people might do to cope, people who were less prone to sensitivity and more prone to matter-of-factness. People like my mother.

And if there was one thing my mom taught me, it was to celebrate the good stuff, preferably with some dancing. And Eden loved to dance morning, noon, or night.

On the good days, Eden was a tiny bit of magic in everyday life. Magic that knew how to shimmy. She did with her neck what Shakira did with her hips. My daughter's neck didn't lie.

So, for Eden's second birthday, we did something that always made me feel more hopeful about everything.

We hosted a dance party.

Because of her mobility challenges, Eden created her own version of twerking, adapting it to something that could have, and should have, swept the nation. The Eden involved a fast head bobble, and later a backward shuffle plus arm motions ideally accompanied by the song "Push It" by Salt-N-Pepa.

When Eden started to transcend way beyond The Eden with '80s inspired flair, I knew my mother had gotten to her. I was right; she owned up to it proudly. Nana was a wild dancer with zero shame, her moves the opposite of despair. The one where Eden put her hands up to her ears with her elbows out to the side, and then pumped her body? That one was all my mother, with a subtle pelvic thrust involved, too.

Eden came by her love of dancing honestly. This part was transferred through her DNA, and it was not the part that got lost. Nadlers are always the first to get on the dance floor at any event or wedding (although, thankfully, not before the couple do their own dance). We are also apt, and highly motivated, to create a makeshift dance floor whenever possible.

I had never been the kind of mother who throws big birthday bashes for toddlers. I don't have the drive or the interest to organize bags of party favors or peruse Pinterest. For Avi's second birthday, we had our immediate family over for barbecue chicken, threw around a few water balloons on the patio, and overdid it with a top shelf chocolate cake that was meant for at least twice the crowd. It was an easy, connected evening, and no one went home with a swag bag.

But for this birthday, we went all in. Our girl had a lot of reasons not to make it to age two, but somehow, she did. Marc and Julie were all in with us, as evidenced by their arrival for the party: a gaggle of balloons trailed behind them. Silver mylar versions of Wonder Woman, Minnie Mouse, and Cookie Monster swayed and pinged off one another. When Marc let go of the strings, they floated dreamily toward the ceiling, bounced a little and then settled in.

"There's even more out in the car," Julie announced, her eyebrows raised. Marc looked over at Eden, rosy as ever, perched in her clip-on highchair at the kitchen island. He motioned to her and nodded, repeating one of his favorite phrases, "Anything for my best friend."

Eden, in a leopard print outfit, flapped her hands with delight. Her white-blond hair was gosling short. Her cheeks, which were often flushed, were even pinker than usual. "Hi hiiii," she shouted, beaming. Marc picked up the Elmo balloon and handed it to her. "I know you like this guy. I'll be right back! I gotta bring in the next load." And with that, he spun around back toward his SUV. It must have looked like a clown car on the road, stuffed full of floating mylar.

"You always bring the party," I said to Julie, who was leaning down to kiss Eden. "I think you're one of the best celebrators I know. Besides Eden, obviously," I continued. Eden, chewing on a pacifier, looked over and gurgled, "Juju!"

We had invited about fifty people, including nearly anyone who had helped us along the way—Eden's former physical therapist and in-home special education teacher from Minneapolis; Jill, Julie's sister-in-law and her family. Kate brought her girls, and Debra was joined by her whole crew. Sara brought not just her immediate family, but also her in-laws who were visiting from out of town. Even Melly's parents, our former Minneapolis neighbors who had bolstered us with their reassuring presence, made it in time for the cake cutting.

Kitty came by, too, sauntering over to wish Eden a happy birthday, gleaming.

We featured a drink named after the birthday girl, a grapefruit sage tonic. *The Eden.* She now had a dance and a drink in her namesake, which wasn't bad for age two. The kids had juice, but on the day my daughter officially transcended babyhood, I added a healthy glug of tequila to the grown-up version.

Before Avi helped blow out the candles on the giant vanilla sheet cake, the light flickering off our faces, I stood next to Cedar, who had turned toward me, holding Eden in his arms. I made an impromptu speech to the people who had helped us live through the past two years.

"Thank you for being here, today and, well, a lot of days. You've helped us, well, make this as great as it could be."

Immediately after I spoke, my face flushed, and I thought, *That sounded awkward. Did I just announce that this has been great?*

Relationships can be awkward (and so can I, especially when riffing in front of a large group).

After we passed out slices of cake, I cued up the thirty-seven-song playlist Cedar and I had made for the occasion. Near the stairs, on the dark hardwood floor, a small dance circle formed, which, of course, included my mother, shimmying in mint green skinny jeans. I pulled Cedar in for "Shotgun" by Junior Walker & the All Stars and we rollicked together nearly as hard as we had on our wedding night. I kicked up my feet; he twisted low. Toward the end of the song, we twirled each other around. It was like old times, sort of. And it was still daylight, the sunlight spilling in the front windows.

Eden pulled a sparkling rainbow balloon around from room to room, and the other kids lobbed the other ones back and forth like volleyballs. We offered each child their choice of balloon to take home as a party favor, as if we'd planned it. Our gratitude to Marc and Julie, as usual, was boundless.

My mother later told me that the party had made her proud and not just because her daughter was gyrating in semi-public. She was proud because we were savoring the moment, because we were looking on the bright side (something I generally tried to do, but with mixed success). She was proud because we had taken a moment that could have been labeled *a reason to grieve* and we had decided that it was *a reason to celebrate*.

The grief was not gone. How could it be? Grief, the ambiguous kind we knew, had sunk into our skin, plunged into our daily routine. It lived among our unlikely village, and it could not be siphoned out. But there was also more than mourning. I was starting to understand that we could do more than mourn—we could gather, and we could dance.

CHAPTER FIFTEEN

Years

One month after Eden's second birthday, Cedar, Julie, and I sat around a sturdy four-top at a wine bar in Terminal 2. Avi stayed back with my parents. Eden, content in a highchair by my side, looked around at all the travelers, cooing and clapping her hands.

"Cheers to this wayward adventure," I said as I held my glass high. I felt as good as anyone could before a trip like this. Julie brought an undeniable excitement with her; she had a joy of being alive that was contagious, a loud and generous laugh no matter what. I felt safer with her, in part because we likely were. The only thing better than having a trained nurse in our corner was having one who made each day feel a little bit like a party.

"To Boston," Julie added with a grin, sweeping her bright blond hair out of her eyes. "And to Eden, may we help her find her way." We leaned in and smiled at each other while clinking our glasses. I felt at home, even in the middle of this arid concourse.

We were beyond lucky to have Julie traveling with us. She agreed, offered even, to do an overnight shift starting each evening so that we could sleep through the night and have some downtime, too. This trip would be the solar eclipse of parenting a child with disabilities—uncommon, immaculately timed, and totally stunning.

We were making the trek to Massachusetts to meet with a world-class pediatric gastroenterologist who specialized in motility disorders. We needed to find answers for Eden. And that meant doing something that was definitely not on my bucket list: flying halfway across the country with a toddler going through a full-blown colonoscopy prep. Before the three-hour flight, per the hospital's advice, we administered a laxative through Eden's feeding tube to prepare for an elaborate diagnostic test.

By the time we were soaring above Wisconsin, I had already changed more than a handful of diapers with Eden lying across my lap. Yes, I had poop on my Levi's. But when her diarrhea somehow flew onto the carpeted aisle of the plane and landed with a plop, I could not stop laughing. I considered making a formal apology to all the other passengers.

"This ALL stinks terribly," I wanted to grab the PA system and announce. "Most especially, me." I had brought several outfit changes for Eden in the carry-on backpack, but I had forgotten to include anything for myself.

—✺—

Two days later, Cedar and I were sitting together in a windowless space in a children's hospital in Boston. In order for the doctor to capture a more precise picture of her internal workings, Eden would need to spend about six hours with a thick tube, sensors attached, winding down through her nose, throat, and into her intestines.

While Eden was sedated (to prep for the test), Cedar and I wandered down the hospital corridors. We passed a tiny, colorful chapel with no one inside. *Where is God in all of this*, I wondered. I considered it a Jewish question because of my Jewish upbringing; the term Israelite literally means "to wrestle with God." But really—of course—wondering about God in difficult times is ecumenical, for anyone. Equal opportunity struggling.

When Eden came to, she was hooked up to motility tracking machines from the inside out. She cried and fussed, and we did our best to soothe her through it in another windowless room.

But seriously: where was God, anyway? I had never been a believer in an all-knowing superpower, but I had always believed in goodness, in connection, in something bigger than my own small self.

When the digestive study was finally finished, the doctor told us, "We can sedate her again to get this tubing out. Or I can just yank it out quick, which may be the easiest." Cedar turned his head as he tugged the apparatus, snaked inside her little body, out through her nasal cavity. I cannot remember if I watched it or if I also averted my eyes.

But I do remember wondering, *Where was mercy, where was so-called peace?* I couldn't find it, not in that hospital. Not in sleep, not in waking, not in any moment when I walked around knowing the thing that I could not unknow: my baby is suffering, and there's almost nothing I can do for her.

I carried that with me. I could not put it down.

—⁂—

"The good news is that she has all of her organs," the doctor gushed after Eden's gastrointestinal testing was complete. We were standing on the cold tile of an observation room.

That is good news! I thought, then caught myself—isn't having a child with all their inner organs present more or less a given? Yet, I already understood—nothing was a given.

We finally got a name for her condition: *foregut neuropathy.* This meant her intestines weren't contracting as they should, slowing the digestive process (another term for this is slow motility). And although there were hundreds of times when I worried otherwise, it was no one's fault, not even mine. She was born this way.

There was also no cure. But the doctor told us he'd seen every child he's treated eventually grow out of these particular digestive problems. There would come a day—if the doctor was right—when she wouldn't just eye everything edible and exclaim, definitively, "No." Eden pronounced it *nohh,* shaking her head vigorously.

It would likely be years until she could get off the feeding tube, although there was no exact timeline. *Years,* a heavy, hopeful thing. She would need to get bigger and stronger. Maybe around age ten, maybe twelve or older. And until then, we would try various drugs and interventions to get her through it.

Eventually, maybe, Eden would eat. Perhaps she'd bite into a ripe sungold tomato right off the vine in the summertime; she might steal French fries from her brother's plate. Some Friday night we would sit down for Shabbat dinner and maybe she'd yell for ice cream before the meal started.

But as I knew so well by now, when it came to Eden, the only thing certain was uncertainty.

—⁂—

The night after her testing, when the appointments were finished, Cedar, Julie, Eden, and I stopped to get donuts for what was probably the fourth time on the trip. As I folded a hunk of glazed old fashioned cake donut into my mouth, it felt good to really enjoy something. Maybe that's where God was, in these moments of being fully present.

After we chowed down, Julie said, "You two should really go out tonight. Boston is the best! I'll take Eden, get her down for the night. Go! Have a nice dinner." After some real Midwest-type questions, in various shades of "Are you sure this is okay with you?" Cedar and I left Eden with Julie at the swing set near our Brookline hotel.

We walked almost two hours to an old Italian restaurant in the North End, one where Cedar had enjoyed a leisurely, decadent meal just a few months before while on tour with Bon Iver. We walked for miles, just because we could, passing fountains and bus stops, bakeries and buskers. It felt freeing to use our bodies in that way after days of sitting around, not one overhead fluorescent light in sight. We finally found the restaurant we'd been looking for, which smelled terrific, like just-baked bread, even from outside. We sipped a dry rosé, dug into fresh handmade mushroom ravioli and then, afterward, wandered down the street in hot pursuit of authentic tiramisu.

Accessing pleasure, especially amid a struggle, was a form of resistance. I ate, even though my daughter could not. And in that moment, I savored it.

During dinner, I was reclaiming my own life.

When our plane touched down back in Minneapolis, Marc was there waiting at the airport, ready to push Eden's stroller or help carry something heavy, in the very same way that he had dropped us off right there before our flight. At our driveway, Avi ran from Nana and Saba's sedan straight into our arms. And on the front deck, we were greeted with a lush, sprawling bouquet of bright pink peonies, a gift from Kitty.

More likely than in donuts, maybe *that's* where God and mercy existed—in this unlikely village.

—⟨⟨⟩⟩—

After our trip to Boston, there were some unfortunate firsts. As Cedar and I often said when referring to these events—in an attempt to add some levity—*baby's first*. Things like *baby's first barfing streak in the middle of a dinner party!*

Right around this time, Eden got baby's first walker. A real walker, not a toy that lights up or plays electronic children's music. It was a red metal one identical to the kind a grandma might have, except a whole lot smaller. It was at once very cute and very sobering. We would coax Eden into the walker, and sometimes she'd get a few slow steps forward. Then she'd plunge into our arms, depleted.

One Wednesday afternoon, as I was getting ready to leave my office for the day, Julie texted me a video. In it, Eden is standing at her walker in a polka dot dress with rainbow-striped leggings, her orthotic braces layered over them. Eden's face is tan and focused, her light hair barely visible. You can see her feeding tube poking out the back.

Julie leans over next to Eden gently urging her forward, her hand on Eden's tiny arm, "Take a step, there you go sweetheart." Eden, vigorously smacking on a pacifier, pushes the walker in front of her slowly, and takes a cautious step forward. "You got it, Eden," Julie coos. A jarring version of the children's song "Down by the Bay" blares in the background. Eden looks up at Julie and reaches for her hair. Julie laughs. Eden begins to concentrate deeply on the floor in front of her, pulling forward, producing four more steps. "There you go," Julie affirms.

Our girl was going.

—⟨⟨⟩⟩—

In early July, Eden had *baby's first Botox procedure*, injected into her intestines. The same Botox pinning back the faces of models and movie stars, initially developed as a remedy for misaligned eyes, is also an experimental treatment to reduce vomiting recommended by the gastroenterologist from Boston.

We had to put Eden through another round of anesthesia. I stood next to her in the OR again, stroking her cheek while the doctors sedated her. A tiny clear mask covered her nose and mouth. She cried and cried while I tried to soothe her, and I did my usual pretending matter-of-factly that it was fine. And then after her eyes, eventually, rolled all the way back, I walked back to the OR waiting area as I pushed my own tears away. I thought about those first tender years of her life, sucked away by near-constant medical intervention. And then I thought of all the other children who had even more invasive medical treatments or much worse, the children who had no treatment or care whatsoever.

At the children's hospital, this all became glaringly clear. I had a formal education, no language barriers, and whiteness (which, until we dismantle racism, will remain a key factor in privilege), along with financial wherewithal, and still found it intensely difficult. There were many families like ours who couldn't, for myriad reasons, navigate the system to get services and treatments in place.

Also, I was born into a supportive family that had resources to help us, another enormous privilege. My family—the original village—was a safety net that helped us make it through. Without that net, we may have been destroyed.

The Botox worked, at least somewhat. Eden came through the procedure in the way she usually did, with the most emphatic grin I ever saw. That smile: she just kept flashing it, even at strangers, despite her frequent bouts of nausea. Those eyes: they would light up again approximately fifteen seconds after she had been stuck retching and gagging and sweating.

A few weeks after the procedure, she played on the floor with her brother, and scooted around squealing, moving from place to place with a freewheeling crab-crawl, dragging her feeding tube wherever she went. Sometimes there was no puke in sight. And sometimes the carpet was covered in vomit, just like old times.

We periodically called the Boston gastroenterologist, who had turned out to be the kind of doctor who generously took his time answering our follow-up questions. After spending so many hours zig-zagging the medical system, we knew how unique it was to have someone responsive on our side. Even if he didn't have all the answers for us, at least he understood our questions.

Mostly, we lived with the word *maybe*. Maybe Eden would thrive, maybe she would learn to walk on her own. Maybe we would frequent the ER again this coming winter. Maybe the vomiting would subside completely.

Maybe, Eden would do so well that my vision of having *three* children could become reality. Cedar and I sometimes talked about having another child, but Cedar, and nearly everyone else I knew, thought this was a lot to take on. What if the new baby also had a genetic condition or other significant disability? How would we manage those additional needs? Regardless, did we have enough time and energy to dedicate to another child? More sleep deprivation felt like too much to overcome. I loved the idea of having one more child, but the practicalities of it—financially and emotionally—seemed more than we could muster.

Even as Eden's gastrointestinal health slowly stabilized, the uncertainty would sometimes still permeate. I knew sometimes Cedar still felt it, too. One night, before heading to bed, when I stepped into Eden's room to check on her, I let my eyes adjust to the darkness. With my bare feet on the carpet next to the crib, I could hear her balanced breathing, see her teeny toddler body all stretched out with one arm up, as if she fell asleep cheering. Her face was serene, her mouth still making periodic sucking motions, even though her pacifier lay on the mattress next to her. *Eden*, my daughter—so intensely mine, and yet, not mine at all—her own person entirely. And then it hit me hard, as it often did. Maybe someday we would have just one child instead of two. Maybe someday she would be lost to me completely.

CHAPTER SIXTEEN

Calling It

The months after that hard winter didn't get any easier for Cedar and me. The daily difficulties of parenting without his physical presence were over, yet we were still strained, like a relationship hangover.

One particularly harrowing discussion started while we walked near the beach. I was crying. A fat tear rolled into my ear in that weird, uncomfortable way. I let it. We had been talking about all the things that might have been different *if* this or *if* that. This sometimes plagued me, the things that might have been. On my best days, I could see the way it happened was the only way that it could be, because that's how it went.

It wasn't always my best day.

Cedar pointed out, "If I never would have done the tour, then maybe we wouldn't have moved here to this place you love so much."

I looked down at the paved path. "I know I said I was okay with it, but I didn't know how hard it was going to be. When you were home, you were so worried about catching up on work, so preoccupied, not wanting to take more time off from teaching. I wanted you to come home, and really be there. I felt alone, for a long time." I sighed, one of my big ones. "It's been a year, Cedar."

"Well, technically not a whole year," Cedar corrected.

"That's not helping," I said, nearly rolling my eyes. We often sparred about the details of time: I rounded up in weeks, while Cedar rounded down.

"I'm sorry, Emma. I get it. I wasn't here, and you were left with this super sick kid and Avi and work. It was a lot on you. Too much."

"I'm just not sure if we can go back to the way that it was. I want to forgive you, but I don't know. It's been a lot between us. I have felt so trapped with the caregiving." I continued. "I need you here, doing more for us. The daily things, so I don't have so much on me."

"I just wonder, is it too late?" Cedar asked. "Will it matter what I do now? Or is there no coming back from this. Will you just be done? Do you want to just call it?"

Wait. Divorce?

I felt that familiar, acute ache. I didn't want any of this. Not the ever-present grief that was affixed to my chest, not this conversation. Not a divorce.

We walked, and I heard the dirt grind loosely underneath my sneakers. "Maybe you should have been with a woman," Cedar said. "A woman might have been better for you, for your expectations. Just, honestly, for what you deserve. An equal partner. I feel like I have to work so hard."

I didn't want it to be true. I wanted to hold back, but that wouldn't save us.

"Cedar, sometimes I think that, too," I said. Now it felt like someone was taking a small stick and scraping out my insides.

Would we lose each other? Had we already?

"But I love you." I hoped my honesty might redeem this moment somehow. I continued.

"And here we are, we have this life together. There's no one else I could think of doing this with. I mean, really. We are tied together forever now, regardless. Until the day we die, whether we are married or not. But I need you to step up. How this goes depends, in part, on what you do."

"I hear you," Cedar said. "I'm here now."

"I hope so. I can't keep going like this." We walked a minute or so in silence.

"I know. Which is one of the reasons I want to do everything I can to figure out how to make this better with you." He sighed. "I really love you, Emma. I never even thought I would even get married until I met you."

"Right back at you, Ceed. I love you so much. And you helped me see that I deserve love. You did. Before we met, I wasn't so sure. No matter what happens, you gave me that." I was full-on publicly sobbing now.

As Cedar and I passed the lifeguard stand, something new occurred to me. "She's changed me, too," I said, my feet heavy on the sidewalk. "Sometimes it's so much stress, so much worry, so much to hold. But I also think that her fragility, her joy, and all of the intensity—it's made me better. Well, better and worse. I mean, I'm not saying I feel better *today*, but just, in general. You know, the love part."

"I get it, what you're saying. And then I want to put that into my music." Cedar added, looking out at the lake. "But I don't have the time to actually get to it." I studied him for a moment while he was looking away. His eyes were as opaque as pond water on a cloudy day. He shook his head a little.

As we walked, I slid my hand in his, an invitation.

We would not be calling it.

Not today.

"It's strange, though, because I remember when we had all the time we needed, and then some. We could have made anything. I could have written volumes, and I didn't. It was just us, back then. What did we even *do* then? We both used to have so much free time, so much space. I don't think you had the same drive to create either."

"I know," whispered Cedar, looking straight at me. "It's her. She's got this magic."

"Until she doesn't," we laughed, a little gravely. I looked down at the ground, noticing the reddish dirt now that we were back on the path. "Also, I do think we're less . . . I don't know, less self-focused. Not as worried about the things we probably would have been worried about."

"I might have been terribly obsessive," I said, unable to hide a smile.

We both knew it was true. I was already obsessive enough.

CHAPTER SEVENTEEN

No Pity, Just Pizza

On one warm night when Avi was only four, he and I stayed up late huddled together in his bed. It was almost 9:30, but there was a grand finale of fireworks happening too close to our house. I wasn't even trying to get him to sleep. His golden face turned serious between what sounded like rocket ship blasts. "I have a surprise for you," he whispered in my ear. "Tomorrow is your birthday. I'm going to go with Daddy to get you flowers." He followed this declaration with a peck on my cheek. He didn't quite close his mouth when he kissed me, just pressed his open mouth to the side of my face briefly, his breath smelling like powdered sugar.

It was very much *not* my birthday when I woke up; my birthday wasn't until the next month, and even then, I did not get any flowers (I had not exactly been holding my breath). Avi, who often surprised me with his sage-like spirit, did not know my actual date of birth. But what he did know was how to live hopefully, to pretend as if something lovely would take place tomorrow.

I wished that I could automatically do what both of my children could do naturally, what most children do—enjoy the now and make up some good stuff about the future. That did not come easily to me, not since the coma, and even less so since Eden's diagnosis.

There were days when I needed a soak in the tub and a candle that smelled like woodsmoke and my lavender hot pack that I heated up two to three times an evening, no matter the season. Healing prayers sometimes helped. I often read them out of a little handmade book held together by staples that Rabbi Zimmerman gave to me when I came to see her one morning bawling so hard that I was tempted to wear sunglasses on the way out of the synagogue.

I chased hope like some people chase true love online.

During this period, especially with the tension between Cedar and me, I thought more about God than ever before. Praying felt good, even though it seemed predictable. It wasn't that I believed God would cure Eden's digestive tract or my marriage or that God should be responsible for making anything better for me personally. Some days, I could draw strength from God, or at least from the God that made sense to me—the unknown forces of interconnection and goodness. Some days I could embrace the mystery of it all.

And some days, I could not.

Regardless, the vastness of the woods around our new house gave my questions somewhere to go, to breathe beyond our lives. The universe is constantly expanding, far beyond all humans, let alone our little family. I knew this, and it felt reassuring—none of this mattered. Equally as true and reasonable was the fact that *of course* it mattered— desperately. To us.

Sometimes I would say, "It could be worse." At one point a friend responded to this over the phone with "Emma, could it?" *Yes, it could.* It could be much worse. This is not toxic positivity; I think it's extremely clear that I willingly acknowledge the difficulties (and sometimes drone on about the specifics). But I saw a lot in our hospital stays. And I was aware of what was happening around the globe—yes it could be worse, in so many ways.

But having a village made this perspective easier, at least some of the time. Julie and Marc were right there with us, along with the ever-present backbone of my parents. And even if she had only a few hours, Kate would make the thirty-minute drive out from her house so that we could usher the kids down to the beach or take a walk together.

"I'm happy to drive—I *like* driving. And I like that jacket," she told me matter-of-factly one afternoon as we set out to tromp around the neighborhood. I was wearing a black pleather jacket for some impractical reason.

I don't know if she knew how much that one sentence meant to me. Not the pleather jacket part; the part about being together. I had been worried that I wouldn't see my city friends as much after moving, and largely, I was right. But Kate showed up, despite being one of the busiest people I knew.

As summer waned, together with our crew, we made our home feel more like a summer camp, not just a medical outpost. Bear hugs and more high fives than we could count. Bonfires and s'mores in the backyard when we could get our act together enough to have all three ingredients in the house at the same time, and when someone could make sure Eden didn't rush into the flames, which was its own designated job. I tried to be easier on Cedar, with less critical commentary about what he wasn't doing and more acknowledgment of all his contributions. When I aimed for fellow camp counselor energy, rather than disgruntled spouse, it became easier between us.

We often played two on two soccer, which really meant that Eden wandered around the front yard singing and every few minutes fell into the goal and got an arm or a leg stuck in the net. Someone would pull her out, and then we began again.

People who could handle how demolished I sometimes felt—and yet also access some levity—were everything to me during the early years of Eden's life. I didn't see Melly as often once we moved from Minneapolis, but every time I did it revived me.

One humid day, she and I decided to take Eden out together to a nearby lakeside town. Going anywhere was not easy, but Melly, in a bright pink paisley dress that matched her flushed cheeks, was up for it. We ended up referring to the outing evermore as *baby's first brewery*. Melly got a homemade cherry soda, and I got a crisp, cool lager. We sat outside on the patio of a local taproom together with Eden, who was decked out in a fox-themed onesie and white pants—one of her best seasonal looks. Her feeding tube streamed calories into her while we took turns holding her in our laps. Eden shook with joy as she held up a finger toward a nearby fire pit and declared, "Fire." Melly gave Eden a squeeze and remarked, "Eden, you're such an old pro. You really do know your way around a brew pub, thank you very much."

After we finished our drinks, we carried Eden and all her gear to a pizza place around the corner. "Remember the days of grabbing slices at Pizza My Heart in Santa Cruz? And the night we ran into each other there?" I asked Melly. In that moment I felt keenly aware of how different, and the same, we were back then.

Melly was able to ride the line between *yes*, there is something wrong, my baby definitely has a feeding tube, and it is largely horrible, and yet somehow, none of that overshadows the moment. This wasn't a graveside visit, after all. We were alive, right here, sitting outside next to one another on a sunny, breezeless night. We could still sit down over a veggie extra cheese pizza, try to make a makeshift fan out of a napkin, chug ice water, and crack each other up.

At one point, Melly exclaimed, "Eems, I have cute aggression right now with Eden. Look at her just sitting here with us, taking everything in. But I won't bite her, *swear*. That, she doesn't need." I just sat there, too, tilting my head, but in a good way. Then I reached in for another slice. There was no pity, just pizza.

———✺———

All cute aggression aside, at two and a half, Eden looked bone-thin in her leggings and her tall, stiff silicone orthotic braces. Marc held her hand near the swing set in our neighborhood near the beach. "You want to go swinging? Let's go swinging," he sang, and she stepped forward with him.

This was her first series of steps without a walker.

Eden took a few more choppy steps, leading with her left foot, dragging the other one behind, which made a scraping sound on the gravel. She reached out with her free hand for balance, swung it around, then held it like a cartoon sleepwalker, straight out in front of her. She stopped and stumbled back into Marc's leg with a soft thud. He caught her.

"I got ya. Come on," he said, breezily reassuring. They continued forward for almost twenty more steps, her trudging along, determined. Marc was still holding Eden's hand, when he turned to look at her slowing. "Getting tired?

He then leaned over and opened his arms to scoop her up.

Julie caught the whole thing on video, one we watched on repeat way too many times, cheering those steps like they were a last-second touchdown at the Super Bowl.

My baby—the one they said may never ever walk—was making serious strides.

It was now clear: Eden will walk.

Walking wasn't essential for Eden to have a good life. Not even close. Yet it was one less barrier she'd have to traverse.

As the months went on, Marc became increasingly involved in Eden's life. As a former CEO, Marc was more used to the heavy-hitting world of wealth management than the heavy-hitting world of getting thrown up on.

He began by helping Julie out, back when Eden was a squirmy toddler hooked up to a continuously running feeding pump almost all the time. Marc was in his fifties, and when he started caring for Eden alongside Julie, had recently retired, and was looking for something new. He thought he might get back into the business realm; he attended meetings and explored options. But soon, Eden's magic hit him hard, and he told me later, something in him softened. Bit by bit, he and Eden got attached to one another. He became the kind of person who would show her picture to his mother—maybe not just one, but several, kvelling over Eden's every new word.

That spring, just before Eden turned three, Julie tore her meniscus in her knee, needed surgery, and was suddenly facing a long and uncertain recovery. She remained present in Eden's life as a beloved friend but couldn't do her regular nursing work anymore.

She and I remained close; most months, we had a girls' night out just the two of us, always full of bouncy conversation (and often a stiff drink or two). Her laugh was easy, and her perspective was a mix between wise and refreshing. I still called her for nursing-related advice on occasion, like when Avi hit his head on the corner of a cabinet after slipping in his socks. She had a knack for reacting just enough, for knowing when to seek help and when to rely on home remedies.

In Julie's caregiving absence, her daughter Rachel stepped in as Eden's personal care attendant. In her mid-twenties, in-between jobs, Rachel was warmhearted and capable. We had a special connection with her, in part because of her parents and the familial feeling that our arrangement elicited but also because of what she brought to the work. Eden lit up whenever she saw Rachel.

Rachel was yet another lucky-break addition to the village. And, in Julie's absence, so was Marc, who began to help with Eden about five times a week. He saw the need and stepped in to give us two-hour chunks of respite every weekday afternoon. It was volunteer work. We offered to pay him, but he refused.

"She's my best friend. I don't need money for that," he told us. "And she deserves to have fun, just like any other child." Everyone who loved Eden was painfully aware of the uncertainty around her life trajectory; Marc responded to it by bringing as much joy as possible into each minute he spent with Eden.

Marc didn't dispense medications or manage her feeding tube. He didn't even do diapers (if Eden needed a change, he would bring her to one of us who was comfortable with that sort of thing). I admired his boundaries.

Somehow, despite no previous experience with children with disabilities, Marc was a complete natural. He knew how to make Eden laugh and how to engage with her, despite—or maybe because of—her idiosyncrasies. When Eden misbehaved, he didn't take it personally or get worked up about it. I never even saw him mildly irritated. Marc accepted Eden as is, and she felt it. His strong build helped; if Eden started to fuss or grabbed at his glasses, he'd playfully toss her over his shoulder with a "Whee!" and she'd forget what she was upset about. They had a blast together, this unlikely pair.

Marc schlepped our daughter to Ridgedale mall on countless snowy afternoons, to most of the playgrounds and parks within a ten-mile radius of our home, and even farther, like all the way to the ladybug ride at

Nickelodeon Universe. Marc and Julie also took Eden to special events on the weekends, shows like Disney on Ice (Eden lasted two minutes), Annie Jr. (got through a third of it, standing over to the side of the stage), and Sesame Street Live (Eden made it through the entire thing). Baby Shark also was a huge hit, despite my personal opinions about the soundtrack.

Marc took Eden anywhere that she might enjoy. She had a phase when she would say, repeatedly, "I want to go in" to each and every store we passed while driving. Her favorites were gas stations, men's clothing stores, realty offices—real standard kid fare. "I want to. Right now." She would hold down the sound of "n," so it sounded like *I want to go innnnnn*. It was quite convincing. Eden wanted IN.

Marc took her into all the places that she wanted. She was thrilled to go inside to say hi to anyone who would engage with her. In fact, she'd say "hi" again and again until it was beyond what you could classify as friendly. Marc understood what Eden asked for—he listened—and took her desires seriously.

For close to two years, each afternoon around five thirty, Marc dropped Eden back at our house. He would inevitably be wearing his faded maroon MN cap and a look of amusement. I always asked, "How did it go?" and, almost unerringly, Marc would shrug, laugh, and say, "Of course, it was fabulous."

Marc often said that Eden saved him. She came into his life at a time when he needed purpose, that he didn't know what he would have done without her.

I don't know how it happened or why. It was entirely implausible.

It is possible that Marc saved me as well. His respite care offered me the freedom to do things like hike in the woods on a Wednesday. And Julie is a bona fide Jewish saint, if there ever was such a thing. Through her nursing duties over the previous years—washing Eden's wound site or administering her antibiotic through the feeding tube, she sent a message of pure hope—she saved me, too. And Rachel. This family, this neighborhood of our village, was as close to God as I could find.

A few months before Eden's third birthday, I got a text from Marc: *what do you think about us getting a few ponies for the party?*

Real live ponies? For our girl to see and ride for the very first time? It was extravagant but sounded amazing—like an informal Make-A-Wish situation.

Absolutely we texted back. *Now that's a party.*

Birthdays were becoming Eden's best days.

I dressed Eden in a shimmery, sleeveless dress for the occasion. She still didn't have much hair, and her cheeks were flushed bright pink. All morning, I half-held my breath, hoping that she would not be too afraid of the Shetlands circling the backyard. Friends arrived in a trickle, rushing to the backyard to watch the ponies graze on forest shrubbery.

With some encouragement from Marc, Eden eventually agreed to ride a chocolate brown pony. Marc stayed at her side, making sure that she was safe and steady on that horse. She shrieked and clapped and shook with delight as they circled near the ferns. She adored it so much that she didn't want to get down off the pony.

When I urged her to give someone else a turn, Mark shook his head. "It's her party," he insisted.

—⁣m⁣—

Shortly after the pony rides, Eden, once a cuddly, amicable, portable little thing, became a girl on the go. She hardly ever stopped moving, except to sleep, not even for television. In her hot pink orthotic ankle braces and blond ducky mess of hair, she reclaimed that tiny roller girl look that she had when she was a baby. But with even more darting energy.

We later discover that this irrepressible energy has a diagnosis: hyperkinesia.

Her signature expressions were more noticeable now. The vigorous hand flapping, tensing of her legs and arms, and a guttural yet high pitched sound, which could morph into something akin to blowing raspberries, ramped up when she was excited. It was highly enthusiastic; it was unconventional. It was Eden.

Harder to navigate was Eden's repetitive speech that looped throughout each day, along with an increase in her hitting and hair pulling. I would ask her about how her day went, and she would tell me all about her favorite *Austin & Ally* episode, then tell me again. And then she would tell me again. She was still stuck on that inseparable feeding tube with no end in sight, and found everyday things—crowded places, baths, errands, routine trips to Minneapolis—terrifying. I wondered what this was like for her, and I wished I could get into her mind so that I could better understand. With her limited communication it was hard to fully comprehend it all from her perspective.

Eden got a lot of comments when we were out in the world. Curious looks and questions: "Why does she do that with her hands?" "What are those things on her feet?" "What is she saying?" "What makes her walk like that, talk like that?" The questions were sometimes helpful, as an invitation for connection. But I didn't always want to host a Q and A session. And Eden knew that people were talking about her while she was right there. She could understand what was being asked, at least partly, yet didn't have the expressive language required to answer. Occasionally, Eden would take her little fist and bop that stranger.

She wanted some dignity and sometimes that came out in an undignified way.

It made sense that she wouldn't want that kind of attention, that she was tremendously frustrated with other people's expectations of what was typical, with what was labeled okay (or so-called normal), and what was not.

Eden stood out, yet not in the ways I had envisioned that she might before she was born. At times because of the feeding tube, her uncommon strut, her crescent moon eyes, it struck me, as I watched her grow into this new, bolder version of herself that my daughter was a badass iconoclast without even trying to be. Which has always been my favorite type of person. She was entirely her own being.

I began to embrace Eden's badass charm more effortlessly—her bantam, one-of-a-kind presence. Watching Julie and Marc love her so categorically certainly gave me a map. It was never a one-and-done type of clarity. There were layers and layers to sort through, including one of the biggest realizations of all: why did I envision having a docile little girl in the first place? What was that about, thinking that my daughter would be *easy*?

That she should be easy? Or that any of this would be.

CHAPTER EIGHTEEN

Just Because We Are Alive

Back when she was not yet three, Eden took one look at the new neurologist, started wailing, and then threw up on the clean gray carpet of his office floor. It was projectile style, shooting out in an arc, a gastronomical Roadrunner stunt. The doctor paused and watched, then said, "Wow."

I jumped up quickly, pulling a gaggle of paper towels from the dispenser on the wall. Dropping to my knees, I pressed them to the floor hurriedly, as if there was a ten second rule when it came to bodily fluids.

"It's okay," the neurologist said, waving his hand in the air. "We will get that cleaned up after your visit, no problem." He was completely unfazed, which I had come to understand as a top quality in a medical provider.

After I had tossed the wad in the trash and sat back in my chair, the doctor completed his assessment. I texted Marc, who had been waiting in the lobby. He often tagged in so that Eden didn't have to stay for the full in-depth consultations, in order to make it easier on her.

When Marc knocked, Eden ran outside the exam room to greet him, squealing while jumping up and down. "Are you ready to go to Rainbow Park, Eden?" he asked with a grin. She flapped her hands and bolted down the hall, which meant *I was born ready.*

Cedar and I turned back to the conversation in the office. The neurologist confirmed amicably that Eden had significant cognitive impairment. "Eden probably won't be any less happy. People adjust to their own circumstances," he said quietly, leaning forward. "The real impact will be on you, your happiness, as her parents. If you let it."

As we drove home together, Cedar said from the driver's seat, "I think that the neurologist was probably right, about our role in all of this."

"Yeah, he seems spot on. I sometimes don't know how to reconcile what our lives have become. You know, the caregiving. I think I don't know how to be happy here or content. But then sometimes, I am."

I looked over at him loosely gripping the steering wheel, "It's not the surface stuff, not usually. I mean, she's ridiculously cute. The cognitive impairment is hard. Not having a conversation together. Just . . . we may never have that."

Cedar looked over for a minute, and then back to the road, "I guess it's a long-term project, figuring out how to be okay with what is."

"You don't seem as sad, though," I remarked as we blazed down Highway 494.

"I just didn't have the expectations you did. I don't need our life to be any certain way. You know me, I never even thought I would even *have* children. And my brother is deaf. I'm sort of used to this world," he responded.

"You do it well, Cedar. The acceptance part. Sometimes I don't give you enough credit. More than sometimes," I added as I watched the trees scroll past the window.

"Thanks, babe," he replied and reached for me. Then he offered, "But, you know, you've always been better with the action end of things." This was true, although now I saw it more clearly.

Acceptance was an action, too.

—◎—

Over time, Eden's cognitive impairment became more pronounced. Coupled with her physical challenges, especially her vastly compromised fine motor skills, it seemed likely that she would need support and assistance with daily tasks for as long as she lived. This loomed, yet still was not certain. We would probably know more when she was five or six years old.

I had always imagined that my daughter would have the capacity to reason, to analyze. It didn't look like that was going to happen. I could not shake the sinking feeling of loss.

Picture seventh grade me: after family dinner in the kitchen—early and mandatory—I would lug my textbooks over to the long, beige dining room table, and sit for hours at the head, studying. I studied three or four hours at a stretch, or more, until my parents—who held four graduate degrees between them—urged me to stop.

But I knew that underneath their insistence on a more balanced approach, they secretly approved. After all, it was what they had done. I had heard the stories of study benders and sacrifice—they lined my childhood like trophies on an old shelf.

I attended a tony K-12 private school the whole way through, the same one my father attended. The school was elite, and everyone knew it, with admittance granted only upon an entrance exam, including IQ testing and a thorough interview process. The environment was rigorous, with National Merit Scholars popping up like roadside buckthorn. Each year was an intensive preparation for the next, and for college (ideally an Ivy), and eventually a robust career to follow. There wasn't anyone like Eden.

I thought of myself as a nonconformist—yes, I took school seriously, but in an attempt to find some balance, the only AP syllabus in my backpack was AP Art (my favorite class in which to make some real mediocre earthenware). With my gushing appreciation of the natural world and carefully curated thrift-store wardrobe, I thought I was open-minded and free from rigid, stratified norms. But although I never longed for the Ivy League or an overflowing bank account, I was still a product of my environment.

Reflecting on what the neurologist had said about Eden's cognitive challenges, I struggled. Coupled with her physical fine-motor disabilities, would Eden ever be able to care for herself, cook a meal (or eat one), or hold a job? It seemed less and less likely with each passing year.

What was a person, anyway, beyond their own contributions and capacity? Who was my daughter, if she did not know her place in the world and could not explore it? Who was I, as a parent, if I couldn't fully understand her?

It all came down to one question, really—where do we get our worth? Are we good enough as humans just because we are alive, for no other reason than the basic act of our existence? I believed that wholeheartedly on paper, and yet embracing it in daily life with Eden was like navigating the subway system in a foreign country where you know, of course, what a train *is* but can't quite decipher which way it is headed and where and when you will, eventually, arrive.

I wasn't from this place, but I wanted to make it mine.

—⁓—

Some medical appointments flared my internal discord more than others. Against my better judgment, we went back to the geneticist again, the one we had seen to get Eden's initial diagnosis. This time, she sat on that swivel stool, looked straight at us, and announced, "Your child will not attend college. She doesn't have the cognitive abilities."

I flashed red. What was the purpose of such a decree, so early on, with Eden not yet in preschool? How was that helpful to anyone involved? And then, as I felt her words seep into me, a heavy sting permeated my gut.

Theoretically, I understood there are all kinds of ways to have a meaningful life. Many people do not go to college and still have fulfilling lives. Yet, I wanted Eden to have every choice available for her future, to chart her own path.

I didn't care about sports or Eden's physical prowess or even her ability to fit in with her peers. Fitting in was never the goal; I hoped instead that she would have friends and loved ones who understood and embraced her. I hoped she would find her own village someday.

Yet Eden's cognitive disability was harder for me to hold because of the expectations I had. Expectations I never even saw clearly, until they were out of reach.

I hated that it was harder. Placing a hierarchy on intelligence could lead to dangerous thinking, and that type of thinking has justified many horrors done to people with disabilities over history. Even if my thoughts were just pretentious—ugly enough—still, I didn't want to embrace that perspective. My sense of loss was human and understandable. But I wasn't proud of those pieces that I still carried around with me—the fact I even saw Eden's cognitive disability as a loss in the first place pointed to a hierarchical narrative.

This was supported by many medical providers. It was nuanced because Eden also suffered from relentless gastrointestinal distress that I wouldn't wish on anyone, along with her other impactful health concerns. But was my sadness and longing further shaped by the rhetoric of eugenics? Maybe I was not beyond these insidious influences.

When I later relayed the geneticist's declaration to my Aunt Janice, one of the Californians who we regularly visited, she responded, "College! Don't worry about that. You can *die* in college. Or get addicted to drugs."

And she has a PhD.

Oddly, I found that helpful. Probably because it made me laugh, and it also changed the script from something grave to something outrageous.

College was, in some respects, the least of our concerns, given Eden's ongoing struggles, including her inability and disinterest in eating by mouth. But it didn't feel that way to me. Periodically, that thunderbolt of grief in my stomach still raged into a full-on storm.

—⁓⁓—

My new pink Nikes were caked with mud and my hair was doing what it did best: frizzing up in the rain. The maple leaves above us were gushing wet and golden. I couldn't see or hear anyone else, just our footsteps and the black-capped chickadees calling out to one another. Sara, my friend from religious school way back when, leaned over and put her face near the sweetgrass.

"I love the way this smells, I just love it," she sighed, breathing it all in.

As we hiked through the open prairie, I thought about how rare a moment like this was for me, walking in the woods alongside a dear friend with no timeline at all. We had all day. We could do anything. And then I felt the tears, warm and automatic, because even as it happened, I missed it already.

"Baby," she replied, automatically, seeing my tears. She was the kind of person who could call anyone *baby*, without it getting weird. "I know it fucking sucks right now."

And Sara looked at me deeply with her doe eyes, eyes I had known since I was nine. We stood there together, just looking. Between that and those beloved, glittering f-bombs, I cracked open.

"Eden isn't going to launch, not like I thought. What will happen to her when I'm not around anymore to care for her, when Cedar and I are gone?" I tripped over a rock and caught myself. Sara and I kept walking. My insides felt blistered.

We walked over a floating plastic dock which sat on top of the water. "And will I be okay, even if she isn't?"

"I think so," she said. "And I also think you should go back to therapy."

"Well, I mean I'm not against it, obviously," I replied, smiling a little. "And I've already done *a lot* of my own therapy. But therapy isn't going to be able to help Eden. It won't change anything. I'll still be living this. I'll still be a caregiver, probably for my whole life."

She looked at me again. "Maybe it isn't about changing it," she offered lightly.

—⁂—

Soon after, I did start again with a new therapist and continued each week. My therapist had a genuine, active approach to clinical work. He could be lighthearted along with his wisdom, and he handled my despair deftly. Shortly after we began our work together, he told me he thought I could have a good life, despite Eden's challenges, despite nearly anything that came our way. He thought Eden could have a good life, too, exactly as she was. And he wanted me to fight for it.

It was all I'd ever wanted to hear. God, I love therapy.

We stopped going to so many appointments for Eden. Anything that Cedar and I thought she could safely get out of, we decided to drop. I didn't want to think any more than we had to about what might happen someday. I didn't want to live our lives in a clinical setting, musing about what may or may not occur in Eden's lifetime. I didn't want to spend her whole childhood thinking about how her cognitive impairment would affect her when she was an adult.

We had this time together *now*, and that was more than enough to think about.

And I wanted to *know* Eden, outside of all the appointments and goals and future planning. I wanted to make memories that weren't about changing things, about getting better. I wanted to enjoy the time I had with my child in the present.

This made it easier to be kinder to myself, not just in theory, but in practice. Dr. Kristin Neff's writing and abundant research on self-compassion, along with Dr. Chris Germer, added a framework that softened my own self-criticism around Eden's challenges. Dr. Neff once struggled with her own child's autism-related meltdowns, which ultimately led her to pioneer the framework on self-compassion that has helped countless people. I was a part of a common humanity, after all, even though I had sometimes felt so alone.

Meanwhile, I had my own appointments to facilitate. Even though my work as a psychotherapist was also centered around giving, it also preserved a core part of myself. It was who I was, long before I was a caregiver.

CHAPTER NINETEEN

The Village of Therapy

If it wasn't for you, I'd be dead by now.

This is one of many excruciating things clients have shared with me in the confines of my office. It can be heavy work. I've sat with people in countless dire situations: the twentysomething who learned of an accidental pregnancy minutes before sitting down on my couch, the teenager who lay in bed under a thick blanket for most of the day, the middle-aged scientist who threw up into the garbage can of my office because he was going through acute withdrawal from alcohol but still found a way to show up for his session.

Yet despite the weight of therapy, it is amazing to build such strong relationships with people, sometimes over many years. I help clients become more aware of what they want and how they can get it. I listen. I give feedback, resources, and support. I point out patterns of relating and encourage a new way toward connection. And when it comes down to it, I am just a person who sits with other people. Truly, I feel like I hit the jackpot; I get paid to have deep conversations when that has always been one of my favorite things to do. But working at a nonprofit, like I had been for the past decade, I wasn't getting paid much.

One winter day while Kate and I walked vigorous laps around the mall from Claire's to PacSun, I brought up an idea I'd been kicking around.

"I think I'm ready to start my own practice."

"Really?" Kate's eyes were already lit up. She had been running a successful private practice for almost a decade and even owned the building that housed her office.

"I want the flexibility, partly because of Eden's needs, and I want to see the types of clients who I actually work with best."

"It *will* give you more freedom. More say about who you take on. Well, all of it."

"And, of course, it would be helpful to make more money. We are probably going to be paying for Eden's care for the rest of our lives. But it seems like a lot—you know, to make a change *right now*."

Kate looked over at me reassuringly. Her dark auburn hair, as usual, cascaded past her shoulders as if she was in a shampoo commercial. She said, "Emma, you can totally do this. No question."

"I don't know," I continued, "it seems like the billing is so complicated. Plus managing the insurance. I don't know how you do it. Well, I kind of don't know how you do a lot of things."

She grinned, acknowledging the compliment. "Seriously, you've got this. It seems tough at first, but once you have your process down, it's not difficult. It's totally doable." she said.

We kept on with our quick strides, past fluorescent signage, our coats tied haphazardly around our waists so that we didn't have to carry them. "Also, you can decide how to structure your practice. It will be yours. And I can help you figure it out." I heard her East Coast accent peek through at the vowels, which reminded me of the pure chance involved in our friendship, including that we ever met in the first place.

Not long after that walk, I went for it.

Kate helped me set my rates and create my forms and policies. I may not have made the move to private practice without her support and guidance, perhaps not ever. It would have been much more difficult, anyway.

I was scared to go out on my own, and I had my typical reaction of sleeping less, and working longer hours to set up my business. But I did things I'd never done before, like designing a website and decorating an office, which energized me. It felt powerful to be building something of my very own from the ground up.

Once I got going, when Eden was three, running my practice gave me the chance to shape my days the way I wanted. I could squeeze in walks with friends and lunch with my dad, along with the necessary tasks of Eden's care.

My clients were, in a way, village adjacent. They didn't know Eden, but my experiences with Eden informed nearly everything I did and said. I didn't go into the gritty details of my life; my clients weren't coming for my problems. But what I had been through deepened my empathy for other people far beyond what I could have trained for, read about, or studied. Eden made me a heartier therapist because I knew about struggle in a way I could have never predicted. I was not afraid of pain, yours or mine.

And so, I used myself—and the relationship I had with my clients—every day. It's what made the therapy strong. I wanted to help my clients feel less alone. Isn't that the best thing we've got to offer each other?

—◊◊◊—

It has, at times, been difficult to have so much going on in our little family, and then feel put together enough (on the inside and the outside) to fully show up. Sometimes Eden clung to me while I was leaving the house or sometimes she was laid up with one of her bouts of respiratory illness. There were times when I went straight from the hospital to work and then back again at the end of my day. That was hard. But it was also a chance to feel a surge of meaning. I was able to draw from a well of understanding that lived within me. Consulting with a mentor regularly, a psychotherapist who is also an ethics professor, helped me sort through these questions and concerns thoughtfully.

To be clear on something important: I have never believed (or pretended) that I have it all figured out. I have bed head at breakfast just like the rest of humanity, and yes, every so often that *is* my child melting down in the checkout line at Trader Joe's from his overwhelming desire to eat peanut butter cups for breakfast.

But during those first years of my private practice, during a session, I felt a unique kind of *all there*. I did everything I could to understand the subtext underneath what my clients were and were not saying. I offered my focused, whole self. And then, when I was out of the office, I was out. I lived my life through my other roles: partner, writer, mother, citizen. And as always, a caregiver. Some days, of course, I carried concern for a desperate client or the stress of a difficult session. Yet doing therapy felt like a chance to be my whole self, to put my sensitivity to use.

Maybe it was, in part, because I had back up. I often sat in my sun-filled office with the view of a swampy marsh with my feet up on the windowsill and stared out at the mallards while Kate and I consulted over the phone. We reached out to each other for feedback and ideas surrounding the toughest pieces of the work. I was on my own, and yet I wasn't. On top of my file cabinet I had a small but thriving Hoya plant that Kate gave me, which used to sit on her desk.

When I looked at that bright, delicate plant in my new office, it was like she was there with me.

People are like library books: only ours for a certain amount of time. Except that the library provides a clear and certain interval, right from the moment of checkout, of how long the book will stay with us (or at least *should* stay, based on when it becomes overdue). With people, we get no exact timeline, no receipt that serves as an easy reminder to tuck into the fold of the pages for later. With people, we have no firm sense of what the future holds.

We are all, invariably, on loan.

—〰—

My friendship with Kate was a refuge, and as it turns out, sometimes our sources of refuge have to move halfway across the country.

I hadn't thought Kate was going anywhere. Even the winters didn't bother her. She lived in Minneapolis for a full decade of snowstorms without much complaining, so it seemed like she was here to stay. She was devoted like she had been living here all her life or maybe even more so. When she told me that her family had just two months left in Minnesota before permanently relocating to North Carolina, my reaction was: surprise-happiness-sadness-excitement-denial-full-heartedness. I can only imagine what my face looked like in that moment, trying to embody so many feelings.

In July of Eden's third year, the Sunday before Kate moved, we sat on the edge of Lake Harriet, which I had come to think of as our lake, right behind the bandshell. Before I met Kate, I had spent a decade swimming and strolling and sometimes even—after my worst break-up deep into my twenties—sobbing publicly while wandering haphazardly near its shores. Still, by association and pure enjoyment, it became our spot.

Our feet dangled over the edge above the seaweed, facing the daysailers. The sun was heavy, the air was still, and my electric green peppermint bon bon ice-cream dripped all the way down my hand onto the pavement. I could smell the damp breeze off the muddy lake.

"You are as good a friend as anyone could ask for," I said, my voice wavering. I was doing that thing with my brow that I do too often: furrowing. What I had said was vague and smaller than what I meant to say, which was more like, *I can't imagine this life without you.*

Kate wiped her face with a crumpled sleeve. "You look kind of like a child right now," she said as she motioned to the fluorescent puddle of melted ice cream between us. She didn't laugh. Instead, she looked at me with it's-going-to-be-okay eyes. That look said the thing I wanted to hear. *You are not alone.*

The wind kicked up without warning and my big straw hat flew right into the lake. We both stared as it began to sink under the murky emerald water. After only a few seconds, it was clear to me: I would jump. I ripped off my sandals and went for it. The water was colder than I expected. I grabbed the hat, now submerged, and lifted it up high, as if I was accepting an award. We laughed as I pulled myself back up on shore, the water dripping off me onto the concrete.

Later, Kate told me that when she saw it fly off, she thought it was gone forever. Then she said, knowing me, she should have known better.

We said it wasn't goodbye, of course, that we would write and visit soon, text and call. But it was a goodbye of sorts, and we knew that, too. It was the end of an era, of living in the same place at the same time. Of celebrating Passover together, our kids' elbow-to-elbow at the too-small kids' table at my house, of meeting in the morning for sticky, pull-apart cinnamon rolls at Triangle Park. There wouldn't be any more last-minute lake strolls, rainy, rowdy walks to the beach with two strollers and a wagon, or dropping off fresh pink tulips just because.

We had the time that we had, and that's all we ever get. I knew that as much as anyone.

That *knowing* was one of the many reasons I needed a friend like Kate—someone who was very much like a sister, but only the best parts. That *knowing* was why I woke up sometimes at three or five in the morning, still surprised, thinking, how did it all turn out like this? This was life, loving people and then losing them, or at least losing their physical, face-to-face presence. Losing what we thought would be and replacing it with something new.

In many ways, we didn't lose each other at all when Kate left. We texted and wrote and called each other. In fact, we were in touch more days than not. We consulted with each other in between clients about things like business strategy and neighborhood politics. We sent countless late-night texts filled with hearts and stars and mountain top emojis, signaling support from afar. And I even made it to Durham, with Debra, for a too-short, long weekend where we ate our way through the city, and doubled up laughing over Kate's massive, ever-increasing succulent collection (about seven for each room and counting).

We all have our ways of coping.

I sometimes wondered, when Kate asked about my opinion about whether she should move to North Carolina, if I should have said what I was thinking. *I don't want you to go.* What I said was what I thought I should say, the most right thing in service to this person who I loved. It was equally as true.

I think you'll be great anywhere.

Ultimately, I was glad I said what I said. Kate's decision about whether to move was not about me. Her partner got a plum job offer, and they agreed that this was the best move for them. Our lives had to keep moving.

—♏—

Eden had started at the nearby preschool in Teacher Maggie's general education classroom with one-on-one para support, including one morning a week that was to be solely with her tribe of children with disabilities.

As it turned out, there was only one other child in Eden's special education class—not much of a tribe. So, after some easy chit chat during drop off and pick up, I invited the other mother whose child was in the class to meet up. That didn't materialize, even after a few attempts (friendships can be just as—if not more—confusing than dating).

I had my people, but I still coveted connection with people who could understand this kind of life first-hand. It wasn't easy to find. Most of the mothers I met who had children with any sort of disability were spectacularly overstretched, booked with therapeutic appointments and caregiving duties and possibly their own careers on top of it all, with few free hours to congregate. But those moments we could connect? Worth continuing to try.

Every day, halfway across the country, Kate began her day an hour earlier, ushering her three daughters out the door into our ever-surprising world. She hadn't left the village. She'd expanded it Southeast by 1,212 miles.

CHAPTER TWENTY

Kitty and the Bold Days

Kitty was like a neighbor in a movie: disarmingly quirky, unselfish, and often available for conversation. She also had the requisite cats. Over time, we grew into the habit of exchanging things that made us feel more alive—pieces of writing, roasted squash soup, and bouquets of zinnias the colors of Fruit Loops.

During the summer when Eden was four, we spent a lot of time in my front yard leaning against the brand-new cedar fence, gazing out into the flower bed that we finally finished in July. Kitty did most of the digging, although she wouldn't rub it in. She was nearly seventy years old, and yet, she could excavate that garden as if she was decades younger.

One evening as the sun settled and the mosquitos swarmed, she planted two lavender plants as a surprise. I walked outside the next morning to water the window boxes and there they were, smelling like a deep sigh.

Those pale green plants with the unexpected lilac tips didn't make it through the winter. They lacked that certain heartiness that was required. There were times I thought that I might lack it, too.

A few days later, I dropped off half a loaf of still-warm chocolate chip banana bread on her back steps, wrapped up tight so her cats wouldn't get into it. Avi and I scooped the other half out of the Pyrex baking pan while it was still hot. The sticky chocolate chips oozed into our palms, scalding us just slightly. Kitty texted me after dinner, *Emma, it's out of this world.*

In mid-August of that year, we suddenly found ourselves with a day that I'd longed for all year but didn't even know it—sunny yet crisp with the light hitting the ruby red dahlias just so. "Could it be more beautiful? I don't even think it could, just as it is," I spouted, knowing she would understand. "I could stand here all day, watching these bloom." And for about twenty minutes we did—mud drying under our fingernails, aware of our shared awe. I had some time to stand there; Eden continued two mornings a week in Teacher Maggie's classroom, which she loved, along with her small special education class on Fridays.

When October came, with its blustery breath and darkening days, Kitty left her thin copy of Mary Oliver's *West Wind* face up on our front porch.

She had told me earlier that morning to watch for it. "I picked out a poem for you" she said softly, her weathered brown boots covered in fresh dirt, her smooth silver hair ruffled and wispy from the breeze. We had been in the driveway talking through when to take up the bulbs for the winter and what we might plant next year.

She handed me a thick, glossy magazine-like book, cracked open to a page featuring tulips in every shade, shape, and size. "And I have this very seductive catalog that you can flip through. I want you to circle what you'd like. I'm planning to order tulips, daffodils, lilies, allium, and grape hyacinth for you. Let me know which ones you want to try."

Later in the evening, resting on a stack of thick pillows in bed, I read the poem. It was flagged by a pink Art in Bloom bookmark and titled "Have You Ever Tried to Enter the Long Black Branches."

The branches are other people's lives, and the poem is about understanding someone else's world—among other things—including what it feels like to be fully alive.

I had heard it said that every Mary Oliver poem is a similar beautiful, crushing, nature-loving thing; like others, this one sang to me. Yet when Kitty gave me the poem, I was younger, too. I had no idea what was ahead, how simple things such as sloppily sharing banana bread and huddling close near the dahlias would no longer be possible. None of us did.

Eden, meanwhile, was becoming more and more like a wind-up doll who spun in circles and got stuck on a circuit. She would run into traffic if you let her, dashing around without awareness of her own safety. She was cute as hell, yet as she got older and stronger, she became rowdier than a pack of kittens.

Eden had been more like a stuffed animal for her first few years—a stuffed animal with a lot of medical problems—but with a temperament closer to a plush cat than an actual lion. At some point around age three and a half or four, that shifted. And it continued to intensify throughout her fourth year, with meltdowns as common as children at a playground. That is when we began to wonder, *Is this autism?*

Eden started to do a lot of things, many of which we had not been sure if she would ever be able to do. She talked, for one thing, sometimes in five-word sentences. It was not your typical speech, but we understood her. If she wondered if I was going to leave, she would say, "Are you not going? Are you not?" She was able to get her point across, and that was exciting.

Even more intriguingly, my girl showed savant-like qualities when it came to memory. In each of her favorite movies, like *Mary Poppins*, she knew the entire cast lists from reading them herself—both first and last names of each actor—including those in minor roles, like Admiral Boom. She could also recognize a familiar pop song within only a few seconds. She called it out loud, both the artist and the exact song title. And she could remember lyrics in a striking way.

At one point, she became especially enamored with Pink's entire catalog of songs; she carried around a laminated picture of the pop star for comfort. If we showed her a Pink video she would melt down at the end because it was so hard to say goodbye to her. Because of this, we had to limit that practice, even though Eden ran around the house asking, "*Alecia Moore*, we gonna see her? Are we? Are we gonna see her *right now*?"

Toward the end of that year, when she was four and a half, Eden's cognitive impairment continued to present in bold and surprising ways.

Often, on a walk, she would ask, "Is that where Kelly Clarkson lives?" or "There's Avi's school" (sometimes it was not a school). She repeated questions on a loop, likely due to anxiety or confusion or both. Her physical and fine motor skills were affected by her hypotonia (low muscle tone); she was not ready for many of the independent living skills standard for neurotypical children around her age, such as toilet training and dressing herself. It was unclear if and when these milestones would emerge for Eden. We weren't rushing her. Respecting her meant that things unfolded on her timeline.

The vomiting became much better as Eden grew. This was huge. But the constant puke was replaced by an even more disturbing habit: without warning or provocation, Eden could become aggressive. The targets were anyone, and sometimes everyone—me, Cedar, unsuspecting children at the public library or the park. A strike to the forehead or a surprising bout of hair pulling became everyday events. She'd tear my glasses off my face or claw at my mouth.

Obviously, we worked on the whole not-attacking-others thing. We started Eden in Applied Behavioral Analysis (ABA), a frontline behavioral therapy for children who have autism spectrum disorder and related conditions, along with medications, occupational therapy, and special education services.

As an ongoing response to all this intensity, Cedar and I built up more support to reduce the strain of caregiving on each of us and our marriage. In short, our house became a semi-public space. It was a mixed experience. I couldn't walk around my house in my underwear. (Even though I do believe in nice underwear.)

By this point we had consistent night nursing for Eden, which helped tremendously to manage the twenty-four/seven care she required. I was grateful for the support, but there were also costs.

There were often people around—the warm-hearted RNs with their charting and precision, or a less meticulous (yet often adept) PCA. Or my dad picking up Avi, my mom doing a sticker project with Eden, even Kitty stopping by to clip the dahlias. The ABA providers walked around with clipboards and constantly jotted down information.

Whoever it was, it was usually someone who did not need to see me in my drawers.

Generally, we were fortunate to have some of the kindest people I had ever met present in our home. And sometimes, it was a real bust. Like the PCA who shadowed me for a day and then told me that evening, as she quit over the phone, that she was "mentally, physically, and emotionally exhausted" by how much work it was to care for Eden. I was like *You are aware that's my child, right?*

After adding spiritually to the list, Cedar and I reclaimed that phrase and used it whenever possible. We were mentally, physically, emotionally, and spiritually over it (it being whatever the problem was that day). MPES for short.

———✺———

Having people around constantly, being observed and monitored, could also be unsettling. There was the time when Eden fell and hit her head at Marc and Julie's house; she tripped and fell for no apparent reason, like thousands of kids do every day, and bumped right into a table. Eden was not very steady physically, and so, along with her general high enthusiasm, she often fell. She still needed assistance with stairs yet did not understand that she needed safety assistance. So, with no one at fault, she came home with a blossoming bruise on her forehead. It was wince-worthy; it was a doozy.

The nursing company started investigating. Because the bruise wasn't officially reported, it began a series of questions from the company. They inquired with Eden's nurses to suss out any potential abuse. They called to question us about the incident and asked pointed questions in a highly serious tone. I was rocked to my core by the whole thing, terrified of a false accusation. This was one of my biggest fears, given stories from other parents of children with disabilities who were the subjects of comprehensive investigations involving untrue allegations. Thankfully, the company found no one at fault.

Privacy was elusive, a repercussion of the extra set of hands. When the village is that close, there are tradeoffs. But Cedar and I would give up nearly anything to have that support, to catch a break. We surely gave up some of our own pleasure. Having an RN within earshot, stationed on the couch outside our bedroom door, was not conducive to bringing sexy back.

This is what we chose, given the circumstances. Eventually, we moved Eden down to a bedroom in the finished basement to have more personal space. Once we relocated the hospital downstairs, the main level became civilian quarters. It was almost typical, except for the scores of syringes drying on the counter. And the full-on swing indoors, right in the middle of our main level open floor plan. You could sit at the dining room table and push the swing. That's how fancy we were. Does feng shui have an opposite? Because that would pretty well describe the layout, even before we added the sky blue sensory-friendly trampoline.

There was also the sheer coordination of it all. Instead of spending time with Eden or anyone else, there were many times when I needed to attend an intake meeting, arrange an appointment, review, and sign a treatment plan, or fill out forms, of which there were endless stacks. Eden had no idea the work I was doing was for her. Sometimes I longed for her to understand, just so that she could see how much she meant to me.

As a person, not a patient. As my daughter.

But my caregiving work, and Cedar's too, was often invisible.

— ∾ —

Eden enjoyed preschool, and with the help of a well-crafted plan from the district's behavioral consultant, mostly did quite well. She landed a few hits but was usually able to be redirected. During her second year in Teacher Maggie's classroom, she thrived with the structure and one-on-one support she received in the program. And she lived for the song sessions.

One day at pickup, I watched Eden through the small glass window in the door as she traipsed into the middle of the circle during *Five Little Ducks*. She got in there, right in front of everyone, as if it was a dance-off. Her sprigs of pigtails bobbed in the air as she shook her little body to the music fully, without any thought to anything else.

Eden's superpower was delight.

But then seemingly out of nowhere, Eden's mood would change. You could read it in her face; when she flattened the lines of her mouth into a grimace, it was time to watch out. Maybe it was that I was sitting too close to her. Or maybe it was that a child was melting down nearby or the noises in the room were too loud. Sometimes it was clear what set her off, and sometimes it was not clear to anyone but Eden, and, unfortunately, she didn't yet have the skills to share that information in words.

Eden's table manners followed suit. One Friday night, out at my father's favorite restaurant, she tried to push everything off the table with one sudden sweep of her hands: glasses of water, an entire breadbasket.

My reflexes became other-worldly.

One morning, she looked so darling in a hand-me-down apron-like dress with red piping. Sunlight reflected off her blond frizzing curls. Avi sat calmly next to her, quietly munching on raisin brioche. For a moment, I felt a burst of awe, standing in the middle of the family room gazing at my children. *Just look at those sweethearts,* I thought. I didn't even notice that Eden's eyes had become narrow and focused. Suddenly, she looked up at my face and zinged Avi's small white plate—as if it were a frisbee—straight at me.

Without any conscious thought, I caught the plate like a snap between my thumb and my pointer finger. When I looked down, I'd also managed to simultaneously dig my fingers into the slice of raisin brioche with one bite out of it that had just moments before been on top of the plate.

"I caught it!" I shouted triumphantly.

No one had even known that a plate was air bound except Eden and me. Avi was engrossed in an episode of *Peg + Cat*, unaware that his plate had become a nunchuck. Cedar said nothing from over in the kitchen.

"Unbelievable! I got it! Ceed, did you see that?"

"All right," he finally gave me a half-hearted reply as he looked down to prime the feeding pump.

Did I improvise a victory dance and pump my fist in the air? No one would ever know for sure, except for Eden, who was now running laps across the room.

Maybe we were getting used to the intensity. My miracle catch had happened just a few minutes after Eden had slipped off the safety straps while buckled into her indoor swing and somehow propelled herself upside down, screaming. She was hanging like a bat (a loud one). Cedar got her upright before she could do any damage. I probably didn't give a standing ovation for that, either.

These are the kind of things that went on in our home before seven-thirty in the morning.

Communication could be elusive. We took Eden to a psychologist for a neuropsychological evaluation. Unfortunately, she opened by refusing to touch the blocks, attempted to round kick the psychologist, progressed to not doing most of the puzzles, and grand finale-d by trying to knock a lamp off the desk (not to brag, but again, I caught it). In short, Eden was unable to complete the assessment. It generally took two multi-hour sessions at the office to finish, but after about an hour or so the psychologist stopped us.

"I think I have gotten everything I can get," she said. And then, "I don't think you need to bring her back for further testing."

—ᗰ—

The neuropsychological evaluation results were somewhat unexpected. Eden didn't get the autism spectrum disorder (ASD) diagnosis we had anticipated. Instead, she got a diagnosis of neurodevelopmental disorder not otherwise specified. Although Eden had most of the symptoms of ASD, the psychologist felt that her strong interest and engagement in relationships didn't support the ASD diagnosis. I challenged her on this, since ASD in girls can look differently, but she stuck to her belief that Eden didn't fit the diagnosis. I ended up referring to the neurodevelopmental disorder NOS diagnosis as the artist formerly known as autism. Or nautism.

The psychologist acknowledged that with another provider, Eden might receive an autism diagnosis, but she didn't see it that way. Diagnoses are fickle, and they are open to interpretation. Sometimes, they change. Regardless, I knew Eden was far more than any diagnosis she may or may not receive.

During that evaluation Eden also got the additional diagnoses of attention deficit hyperactivity disorder (ADHD), and stereotypic movement disorder, related to her hand flapping and muscle tensing. Her movement didn't seem like any kind of impairment or disorder to me—Eden's hand flapping was one of the most joyful things I had ever witnessed. It was different from a typical muscle presentation, yet disorder implied there was a problem. But I wasn't surprised.

There were some things we actually saw coming, unlike that plate.

—◊◊◊—

With each passing month it became clearer that we couldn't do this on our own. And, that we didn't have to. I made it my mission to show up for our village as hard as it showed up for us.

So, when Kitty's cat Mimi died, I tried to rally the kids to make a nice homemade card. Avi said, "You can't make me. I'm not making a card for some dead cat that I wasn't even friends with." I explained about neighbors, about showing up during hard times. That the card was for Kitty, not Mimi. "Ohhhh," he said, appearing relieved. We left a little care package for Kitty in a brown paper bag on her back steps. In it was a pair of forest green wool socks, a roll-on aromatherapy stick, and the card, which was mostly white space with a few faint scribbles.

Kitty still had two cats, Woodworth and Fanny, and she still had us.

CHAPTER TWENTY-ONE

Walking in the Moonlight

Fall of that year, I took Avi to get a haircut. I started dragging him to a salon when I discovered that the sports barber charged just as much. "Dragging" is not much of an exaggeration. The comb was always too sharp, the hairs tickling down his shirt, the twenty minutes of sitting in the smooth black chair oppressively long.

I hope that he will pick up a cause to protest someday, like reversing climate change or abolishing the death penalty. He will move mountains.

It was our first time with Sam the stylist, whom we had selected discerningly (he was free at 10:00 a.m. on a Saturday). He emphatically listened as Avi shared a litany of concerns as the routine haircut turned into, as Sam described it, "hairapy." Somehow, after the shampoo with volumizing formula, all kinds of big topics came up.

Sam made small talk as he clipped the curly wisps off the sides. "Do you have any siblings?"

"Well, my sister, and then the baby who died," Avi replied matter-of-factly. Sam just stood there, scissors still for a moment.

Avi turned to me. "Did you ever meet her, my twin? Maybe she would have been a nicer sister."

I decided to go there, right in the middle of this routine trim. "I did not meet her, but your twin also had a genetic condition, sweetheart. And I know it's hard sometimes, but Eden is our family," I replied.

"How do you know?" Avi pressed.

I sighed, "There are tests you can do to find out. Your twin wasn't growing well." I attempted to explain the difference between a fetus and a baby to my first grader as Sam cleaned up the hairs behind Avi's neck.

All of this was true. I was pregnant with twins before Eden. One of them was Avi and one of them was his twin, who the doctors believed had Turner's Syndrome. That fetus wasn't on track in her development and would likely not make it to term. What I didn't go into was that I had a selective reduction (a form of abortion for multiples) because the other twin's condition was likely putting Avi's life at risk. With twins, if one does not make it to term, it can induce premature labor and other dire complications.

What can I even say about it? Loss is never what we imagine it will be. And yet, we got Avi. Along with a letter from the hospital that arrived shortly after we arrived home from his birth, which asked us what we wanted to do with the human remains. Did we want a burial?

This may have complicated my initial postpartum experience.

Somehow, even though we had just met him fifteen minutes beforehand, Sam was on our team. He said, "You have to talk about these things. You can't stuff it down, it's not healthy."

After the cut was finished, I settled up at the counter while Avi sniffed the haircare products. I thanked Sam. "You are so kind. And clearly you know how to make people feel at ease."

"Don't even worry about it. And bring your other child in, I bet I can help her get a nice cut. We'll help her feel comfortable," he offered.

The first thing I thought was *Comfortable? Sitting with a stranger holding a pair of sharp shears? The library has too much stimulation.*

Eden had never gotten a professional haircut before. I did it myself for years until Julie assumed the role of Eden's stylist, cutting her bangs swiftly anytime they needed a trim, and occasionally shaping up her whole look. With Julie's steady nurse hands, Eden had no need for a salon—as Eden's hair grew in, Julie gave her a style reminiscent of a hipster Pat Benatar. But I appreciated Sam's can-do spirit and general inclusiveness. Sam had great energy.

Avi took my hand, and we strolled down the sunlit sidewalk toward Red Bench Bakery, our favorite place to get chocolate chip cookies for brunch. And then, as if he remembered all the sudden that we were actually holding hands, he quickly let go.

"Is he drag?" Avi asked, his brow furrowed, just like mine when I was pensive/worried/sometimes content. He was a new seven-year-old. I knew what he was asking, even though he wasn't asking it in a socially acceptable way. "He seemed like a woman," Avi said, as we approached the bakery entryway.

"There's so many ways to be a man. Or a woman. Or anyone, really," I answered, trying to stifle a smile. "Sam is probably more on the feminine side, and that's cool. But I guess we don't know; you can't know a person just by looking at them. I really liked him," I continued. I knew that Avi liked him, too.

I don't know why my child thought that drag was a noun; surely, I should have done something to prevent this. It may have been because he saw a bit on NBC's *The Voice* with a drag queen, and then Eden said, "Is it not scary? Is it not?" She was in a long phase where she thought nearly everything was scary, including everyday things like TV commercials. And then I gave a speech about how drag is fun and overall awesome. I'm sure it went on too long.

Once, when he was younger, maybe three years old, little Avi started catapulting himself off his favorite yellow chair. Again and again, he launched his little body, landing in awkward positions on our semi-shag carpet. When I asked him what he was up to, he replied, "I'm walking in the moonlight." It was 8:15 a.m.

I hoped that my children would always feel like walking in the moonlight is possible, that they would dream big dreams and love big love. Even that early in the morning. I wanted them to feel free to be exactly themselves, to revel in the occasion, whatever the occasion happened to be.

And to stay curious, just like Sam, our new favorite hairapist.

But how could I expect them to do this when I was showing them the opposite? I had to become freer myself. I had to keep making a life for myself beyond caregiving, out in the world, despite all that was happening for us.

Or maybe because of it.

CHAPTER TWENTY-TWO

The Opposite of Boring

By the time Eden was four and a half, I finally had made some friends who had children with disabilities. It wasn't easy to get there.

Cedar and I connected deeply, early on, with a radiant couple who spent stretches of time at Children's when we were there so often with Eden. We had at least one hospital stay that overlapped, and we were on the same floor. And a handful of times we visited each other (we were all home or hospital bound in those days) to sit and share quiet stories.

Their beaming, beautiful daughter Yaya, who had 4H Leukodystrophy, a degenerative disease of the central nervous system, continued to decline. She died snugly enveloped in her parents' arms shortly after her first birthday. I went alone to the funeral and seeing that tiny white coffin carried up to the bimah was more than haunting. She was a joyful, adorable, light of a baby, and then we said the Mourner's Kaddish for her.

"Please don't rush through it," her father said wistfully at the crowded shiva. I looked in his eyes, heavy and yet still brimming with love, and knew that it could have easily been us. That maybe one day I would be saying something similar.

Yaya. I will never forget her particular type of glow.

And so, I couldn't help it; I cried every time I thought of her, and even when I wished I hadn't, like when I ran into her father outside of Rustica bakery months later. He seemed well and composed (and tall as ever), and

I had barely made it out the door to meet Julie for a walk. I lost it on the sidewalk when he knelt to give me a hug.

It was also difficult to connect with parents of typical children, since Eden was less and less able to participate in group experiences. One quiet Sunday in September, we took the kids to play mini golf at Can Can Wonderland, an artsy indoor venue with another couple. This started innocently enough; I took a photo of Eden grinning and bow-legged near the sign. Right after the photo op, Eden smacked my friend's daughter in the face, and that was just the hello. She followed up by trying to use a golf club as a jousting sword, like this was a duel, not a playdate. Cedar caught up with Eden—she had flung herself into the crowd, a trail of flouncy denim—and eventually lured her to the car with the promise of her favorite song, while Avi and I finished the round. Not exactly a wonderland for us.

The other mom was a good sport, as gracious as could be, and posted a picture from the event of her own children on social media extolling their loveliness. I, on the other hand, did not. I wondered if she understood all the feelings I had around comparing our situations. I don't know how she would have; I only said something quick as we headed out the door like "Good to see you all, I'm so sorry, including for the actual battle scene, and I think we should go?"

The quip was a way to soothe the familiar heaviness that there were certain things we just couldn't do (many), and places that were too over stimulating for Eden. This was something I really didn't *want* to learn; it was inherently isolating.

There were also moms who didn't have children who were disabled, but instinctively understood what might be helpful. One Saturday morning, many months before, we had tried to find Kate's daughter's birthday party at a place called Triangle Park. In all that we were juggling, I had lost the invitation. I assumed that we could just look it up online because that seemed like a reasonable option at the time.

Fast forward to the point where we'd driven to two different Triangle Parks, neither of which was the birthday party site. Avi was melting down because he didn't get the cupcake that he was expecting, moaning in the back seat as if we were doing experimental torture treatments on his soul.

I offered to drive him, along with Eden, who had remained relatively calm, to the next park, the real one, the site of the party, to give some birthday wishes to his friend and yes, get the coveted cupcake. "No, Mama," he groaned. No way. He was done, hungry, tired. He only wanted a cupcake at home where there were no cupcakes.

We got home and got the kids down for their naps. I got on my comfiest pair of sneakers and stepped out into the light of the afternoon. My plan was to walk it off. That was my basic stress management routine for many years; it sure beat having a drinking problem.

Kate texted me. She was on her way over with a quick delivery: three vanilla and red velvet cupcakes, two goody bags, and a hug. She had carted her whole family back to our house after the party just to bring us those treats.

"I'm so sorry that we didn't make it," I told her, my face a little red.

"So, you missed the party! We brought a little of it to you," she explained on our front steps as she handed me the goods.

It was around this time that I reconnected with a childhood family friend who we used to call "Sarbear." She now had a baby with similar challenges as Eden, including a rare genetic deletion and a feeding tube. Finally, after several third-hand updates (her mother told my mother who told me), I got her contact info.

She was no longer a kid with a white-blond side ponytail, two grades younger than me. She was an adept lawyer who made me laugh so hard at her one-liners about parenting that I nearly spit out my coffee. This was finally someone who knew what our life was really like. She understood all of it: the brain scans and looming surgeries, the sleepless nights and ongoing roster of therapies. We continued to meet, mostly for walks, trading resources, stories, and ideas. Our friendship was a balm that eased my utter isolation. Texts would fly afterward: clinic names, provider ideas, book titles. Our commonalities were remarkable, a shared rareness. Amazingly, we turned out to live only a few minutes away from each other, our children were in the same school district. It was another fortifying, cuburban win, even when we could only see each other every few months.

Over time, I was eventually able to build more of these types of connections. I found one friend through a beloved neighbor, and others because of my flagrant approach toward strangers who appeared to be on a similar path. I had become the kind of person who emailed random moms, like one who was active at PACER Center, a nonprofit that advocates for children with disabilities. She was featured in an article, and I took that as a personal invitation. We were already outside of the norm—or, as I had begun to say, the opposite of boring—so why not go for it? Why not try to make this life a little better? It was glaring to me now; none of us had unlimited time, including me.

My new friend was soft-spoken, as warm as a Kindergarten teacher, and seven years ahead on her path with her daughter. The first time I met her, we perched outside a bakery on wrought iron chairs. It was a put-together-enough day for me, and our conversation was first-date polite until she knew to ask a seemingly mundane question: "So how *is* your daughter doing?"

Immediate waterworks; immediate connection.

CHAPTER TWENTY-THREE

California, Nope

That December, before our annual family trip to Palm Springs, California, Eden caught another bad bout of Respiratory Syncytial Virus (RSV), some of my least favorite letters strung together. Because of her Restrictive Lung Disease (she was without full lung capacity, due to genetically influenced anatomical issues), Cedar and I hustled to do what we called *home hospital* for several weeks. It's exactly as it sounds—we ran our own little medical center, doing all the things we could to keep Eden out of the actual hospital—a pulse oximeter looming behind her crib, a nebulizer nestled into the family room couch, an oxygen compressor in her bedroom just in case, and so many medications lined up on the counter we could have been running a pharmacy franchise.

Home hospital worked, in that we managed to keep Eden out of the hospital, and that was a triumph. But the oral steroids she needed to recover gave her a withdrawal period that transformed her, for weeks, into something akin to a snarly, baby-sized puma.

"Roid rage" is real.

Although we hadn't been sure which way it was going to go, Eden recovered enough to proceed with the trip. The year before she was stuck in the hospital with pneumonia, so it had been two years since Eden had traveled anywhere outside the metro. We expected that she would love the desert rays and the well-maintained pool outside our sprawling rental home. We thought we were heading into a fun-in-the-sun vacation. The plan was to converge with the Californians—my big-hearted brother and sister-in-law, whom I didn't get to see as much as I would like, along with my boisterous Aunt Janice. My parents flew out a few days ahead of us to stock the rental house with food and supplies.

We were lucky enough to bring PCA help *and* a night nurse for parts of the trip—the night nurse's hours were still covered by our insurance. We had never brought so much support on our vacation before (Kardashians, we are not), but as a last-minute decision we had decided to splurge on it. Because Eden had been so acutely ill again for weeks, we were worn down. We thought because of this support, we would finally get some breaks.

The number of medical supplies required to travel with Eden made it look as if we were moving homes. We shipped boxes ahead of time, including exact amounts of a specialized, prescription formula unavailable in stores. We packed an IV pole for hanging her feeding tube and various other durable medical equipment.

We were quite a sight in the halls of the MSP airport, Cedar and me hauling hundreds of pounds of gear, including a mammoth duffel bag that reminded me of my first day of college. Avi and Eden led the way, weaving through the holiday crowds, with Eden in her carnation pink helmet, which she now wore at all times except when sleeping to prevent an injury from head banging, thanks to the amping up effect of the steroids.

Eight hours later, when we finally made it to our rental, Eden began saying something that perfectly illustrated her feelings about the vacation experience. She said it clearly once, and then she said it over and over again: "California, nope."

In that stunning, cloudless setting, Eden meltdowns ramped up to a level we had never seen before. One night in a fit of exhaustion, as I tried to lead her toward bed, she banged her head furiously on the wall, then sunk to the floor to kick me in the face with her hard plastic brace. As I reached down to soothe her, she clawed my lip. Blood dripped down to my mouth. I tried not to let on that she'd hurt me, which is what her behavioral therapists suggested.

I turned away so that she couldn't see my spouting tears. And I had a big scab front and center on my face for the rest of the trip. What was this? Eden's capacity for harm was startling, and she seemingly undeterred by hurting others or herself. I could not make sense of it.

The next day my mother and I tried for an outing with both kids. We decided to take them to Barnes and Noble since it was a familiar place from back home. We walked in with our heads high, hoping to spend time with a few choice selections in the comfort of the carpeted children's area. We even had the audacity to believe we would find the elusive sixth book in the Harry Potter series for Avi.

We never made it to the children's area. We'd barely stepped inside the front doors before Eden zeroed in on a stocky preschooler with a buzz cut, sprinted up to him and smacked him right in the forehead. Dazed by the sudden blow, he started to cry for his mother. When I bent down to ask if he was okay (he was), Eden started yanking books off the shelves, big, thick hardcovers, best sellers, self-help—anything she could grab, just raining them down. Then, when I reached for her, she collapsed on her back on the floor in the middle of the aisle like an insect on its back, kicking everyone in sight. The looks we got from anyone within a three-aisle radius were severe.

And the sixth HP book was out of stock.

Other than that, it was good.

My mother and I each took the hands of the children and marched them out of the mall, back into the minivan. We laugh-cried on the way back to the house while we blasted the rental's satellite radio because what else could we do? Inside, I throbbed, but to keep myself from melting down, I cracked jokes. "Do you think we should go back later this afternoon?" This was much easier to do with my mother alongside me, especially because she always had the best comeback.

"They might remember us," she smirked. "It's a legacy thing."

On day three, Cedar and I took the kids to Palm Desert Children's Museum. Concerned parents looked over nervously as Eden wailed, "No museum!" and then sprinted into a glass wall. Then she got up off the floor and banged her sweet little head against it some more until Cedar and I carried her flailing body back to the minivan, Avi trailing behind us. Now I was flooded with thoughts of despair.

I can't believe this is my girl, throwing herself at walls.

We ended up sticking close to the rental house, where Eden was slightly more at ease, for the rest of the trip. But every time one of us tried to leave to go anywhere, even for a walk, she lunged into meltdown mode. When Cedar and I tried to take a few hours to ourselves one day, within the hour we were called back by the gracious PCA who had traveled all the way out there with us. Eden had come after her, and then started slamming her own little body down on the marble floor, utterly inconsolable. She kept listing off our names. "Mommy and Daddy? Mommy and Daddy? Nana, Saba, Avi? Are they not coming back? Are they not?" We rushed back immediately.

Eden missed her routines, her normalcy, the predictability of home. She missed Julie and Marc fiercely (they were back in snowy Minnesota, although I had invited them). She needed structure and consistency. She needed the soothing cadence of familiar daily life. Vacation, with its whims and stream of family members coming and going, was terrifying for her and that anxiety spiked her aggression. We tried to establish a vacation routine; we wrote out a schedule. But it wasn't enough.

In this gorgeous, palm-tree-lined setting, we were tethered to this child in crisis. My mother even asked, during one jarring meltdown involving inconsolable screaming and head banging, whether we should take Eden to the hospital. Nobody knew the answer to that question, which was another layer of heartbreak.

Cedar and I parlayed with her doctors, set up calming routines for her, and swore up and down never to give her that steroid treatment again. There were no real or immediate solutions.

We did not bring Eden to the hospital. It didn't seem likely that a hospitalization would help her, given how much more she escalated in a medical setting. I knew that Eden's behavior was communication; she was trying to tell us about how difficult and confusing this change was for her, coupled with, perhaps, how terrible she was feeling due to the steroid withdrawal. For us, vacation was a simple stretch of days in the sun. But from Eden's perspective, she was suddenly faced with an entirely new life with no understanding of how and when we would return home, if ever.

Friends texted things like *How is California?* and *Hope you guys are having an awesome vacation!*

Wait, did this qualify as a vacation? I had no good response. How could they understand what this was like? Even among my friends who had children with disabilities, I knew no one who had a child afflicted with aggression and/or self-injurious behavior.

During the nearly two-week trip, I did not sleep much. One night, I woke at midnight and spent the rest of the night tossing and turning in our creaky bed, full of anxious energy. I tried all the recommended sleep hygiene type things and then gave up and looked at clothing rental options on my phone instead. This is not necessarily recommended for relaxation, but when down, I did like to bring some style to the moment.

Around 5:30 a.m. I got out of bed and walked into the shared kitchen, where I found my mother eating a slice of quiche. Tears streamed down my face. I asked her to come back with me into the bedroom that Cedar and I shared (he was already awake and on duty with the kids, due to the time zone change). We sat on the red pop-art bedspread, and I broke all the way down. I sobbed to her that I just didn't think I could do it anymore.

I could hear the heartache in her voice as she responded. "You can do this. And Emma, you don't really have a choice." And then, God bless her, she left for Pedal Studio for a double spin class.

Around day five, the unwelcome thoughts arrived, cresting on an exhausted wave of fear and worry: *Maybe we can't keep her with us, always. Maybe we need a new type of plan.*

I called Kate to talk through this chilling prospect, and her voice was so merciful and responsive that I began to weep. We talked about what was happening with Eden, and, after I'd pulled myself together, we also talked about her new-ish life in North Carolina, along with fashion rental, which we had come to refer to as "the important stuff." We were both trying out the same subscription clothing rental service, which Kate had discovered first. We texted each other our top picks and consulted on which *very necessary blazer* to select. It was just the kind of fluffy, light-hearted distraction I needed.

And luckily, my family jumped in to spend time with Avi. My dad, brother and sister-in-law spent hours with him splashing around in the pool, throwing a football around and floating on rafts together. My mom took Eden for stroller rides in between, and sometime during, meltdowns.

Village rallied.

As we did at home, we still found time for outings with just Avi and I walking around Palm Desert and tearing through the stack of books we brought in the evenings. I often spent time with Avi while Cedar was with Eden. Cedar's thinning hair was now clipped as short as possible, so he didn't have any hair to be yanked. Cedar was also skilled at making Eden giggle and redirecting her when she started to get ramped up.

Cedar found a sunlit park up on a hill overlooking the mountains, and we decided, for the sake of structure, to go there with the kids each morning. By day six, if we put Eden in her swing and played her favorite Lady Gaga anthems, she'd smile.

It was day ten when we finally taught Eden to say, "California, yep." She laughed, and Avi laughed, too. In their faces I saw the luster of that fierce desert sun.

She still sometimes said, "California, nope" depending on the day or hour or minute. But we had some steady moments toward the end of the trip. We waded in the pool and soaked Eden's feet in the lukewarm hot tub. She sat there dipping those toes for almost an hour, calmly.

On the plane back to Minneapolis, we crammed all our carry-on stuff into our row and sat down together on those blue pleather seats. I strapped Eden into her car seat with that satisfying click, and then she reached down so that she could hold the thick black adjustable strap, which she found soothing. We popped on the kids' tablet devices—our in-flight policy involved allowing them to embark on one long media binge (unsurprisingly, they both did well on airplanes). I breathed out a giant, lumbering sigh. We made it through vacation and, for the first winter in a long time, I could not wait to get home to our near-tundra. Minnesota, definitely.

CHAPTER TWENTY-FOUR

I've Got This

In February, I finished up my last session, wrote a quick case note, and pulled on my heaviest down coat. During my ten-minute commute home, my stomach rumbled. The day was packed with clients and despite my efforts, I hadn't brought enough to eat. And the evening—the second shift with dinner and homework and baths and stories and preparing to do it all over again the next day—hadn't even started yet.

As I was carrying in my bags (so many bags each day—the gym bag, the lunch bag, the work bag) I heard high-pitched screaming all the way from the garage.

It was Eden, of course. Bawling and slamming her little helmeted head against the back of the plastic swing because she wanted to watch Hannah Montana. I didn't know she had even heard of Hannah Montana. Cedar stood next to her, shaking his head. His hands were up in the air, a caricature of exasperation.

"This is ridiculous!" Cedar shouted as soon as I crossed the threshold. "I'm trying to make dinner; it's been like this for more than fifteen minutes."

Across the room, Avi worked furiously on a couch-cushion fort, which was one of his coping mechanisms when Eden's behavior revved up.

I dropped my bags in the hallway and got to work. I looked at Eden and wiped her cheek dry.

"I'm here to help you calm down," I whispered.

"I want to hurt her. Right now," she howled in response. As I stood there and rubbed her cheek, she told me with a red face, dripping with snot and tears, "I'm sad and mad because I want to watch Hannah Montana." It seemed like a classic case of tired/wired. I decided to try to get her to sleep. Cedar had gone back to the kitchen and was over by the sink, prepping green beans.

I brought Eden downstairs to her bedroom and lifted her thrashing body into the crib. She grabbed my hair and pulled it as hard as she could, and then smacked my glasses off my face. For over an hour I tried the things that generally worked—her favorite lullabies and calm, shushing sounds and deep pressure applied to her arms and legs. When I began to read to her, she batted at the book; it launched out of my hands and landed with a thunk. I added a dash of distraction, including a stuffed bunny dance, which went nowhere.

Eden looked me in the eye and announced, "I want to hurt you." She kicked at the air like she was powering an invisible bicycle. I leaned down to stroke her cheek and she scratched her nails into my neck. She slammed her helmeted head against various angles of the crib.

Somehow, I stayed calm, at least externally. I was in some sort of hyper-focused zone. I couldn't even feel the hunger cues that had been so present before. Eden escalated beyond her own control during these episodes, and I could hold that in my mind to stay calm, at least on the outside. She wasn't trying to hurt me; she was beyond reason.

Cedar was upstairs with Avi, who was visibly shaken by Eden's meltdown. They went for a walk in the cold sunshine, which was probably the best thing to do in this type of situation.

We did what we could to shield Avi from some of the intensity of Eden's struggles. But despite our efforts, he saw more than most. This was why we almost always had one person as primary on Eden, so that if she was struggling hard, then Avi could get some comfort, too. One of us would go with him—to his room to read with his stuffies, into the front yard to look at something, anything, that was growing. On that particular day, the window of time when Cedar had both children had been maybe a half hour.

It was clear that we couldn't do this anymore, even for a short period.

We structured our time very intentionally—all of it, including when we were able to work. Similar to most other parents of children with disabilities, the caregiving limited our earned income. We only took on as much work as we could manage well, no more and no less. The focus was on keeping the children safe, which often meant separate, in different parts of our house. That's how we crafted our schedules, and fortunately had family and PCA help to fill in the gaps.

Rabbi Zimmerman once told us that having a sibling with extraordinary needs would likely make Avi more empathetic. I hoped so. I coveted empathy the way some people coveted a trip to Vegas or the total square footage of a new house. The more, the bigger, the better.

Cedar walked in as I sat in the dark with Eden.

"I can take over," he said, standing in the doorway.

"No, I've got this," I said, shooing him away.

I've got this? I marveled at my own mind as the door closed behind my husband. *Why did I say that?* I wondered immediately. *Did I have it? What on Earth did I really have?*

Inside I thought *I can't handle this. It's too much. I don't know anyone else who has to endure this kind of thing. I cannot do this any longer.*

But I said that I *had* it. This was my automatic stress response, and it would take a lot—of my own therapy and conversations with Cedar—to even begin to shift this pattern. The technical term for it is overfunctioning. *I'm okay! I'm taking care of you and you and you and you! Everything is totally fine!* This is far from sustainable.

As I sat in the dark, leaning near the crib holding Eden's hand, who was finally calm, I thought about how this child might be out of our league. I felt a deep attachment to Eden, still, even through every heart-wrenching hit that she landed. But being the target of her outbursts and worse, watching her hurt herself without pause, even when she was causing herself pain, was eviscerating. There was no *just-leave-her-alone-for-a-few-minutes -so-that-she-can-calm-down-on-her-own* option. I knew she didn't mean to do it. I understood that her brain was wired differently, and that in certain moments she totally lacked self-control. She was missing DNA, and none of it was her fault. Regardless, it was extremely disturbing to manage, let alone witness.

I kept my outsides calm but inside I was breaking. I was accosted again by the burning thought that she would do better living somewhere else, somewhere with full-time trained behaviorists. Maybe even if she didn't do better, the rest of our little family probably would. And then I willed that thought away.

Eden was not yet five years old.

Eventually, I texted Cedar with a request to bring Eden some melatonin. He dropped off the syringe by the door, and I pushed it through her feeding tube extension in the dark, feeling that familiar plastic port opening with my fingers. This helped her, eventually, fall asleep. And then I went upstairs and warmed the Dijon chicken that Cedar made earlier that evening. I ate in silence without really tasting it.

A little bit later, I read Avi a few chapters out of a book where one of the main characters is ketchup and got him popcorn and a pretzel as if our house was some sort of carnival. We debriefed.

"I am sad when Eden acts that way," I told him. "But I want you to know that Eden's meltdowns are never your fault. We are working on helping her, Avi. We know that she needs help to learn how to calm down. How are you doing?"

It's not that I was pretending everything was okay. Most of the time, I was just trying to live like it was, to do what I could so that it would become that way. But, at times, it felt robotic, as it did in that moment. Avi took a silvery blue marble and placed it on the top of the track he had built, and then let it go. "I'm disappointed."

I wish I could have let it go like Avi did with the marble, and how he was able to do that within himself. By the time Avi brushed his teeth, it seemed as if he had forgotten the whole thing. But my overwhelmed feelings stayed with me, permeating my body with that too familiar heaviness. Eventually, it turned into an argument between Cedar and me.

"I wish you could have stayed calmer, love," I said as I walked into the kitchen briskly after Avi fell asleep. I was still in my knee-length shift dress from work, but I had put my earrings in my front pocket and thrown my hair in a ponytail. Cedar was hunched over his laptop in his pajamas, working. Probably music.

He looked at me sharply, and took a breath in, "Emma, Eden was so out of control. There was absolutely no warning. I had both kids, and I was trying to get dinner ready. She was completely flipping out, and then Avi started yelling, like he does when she gets so upset."

"I know. It's hard. It's beyond difficult. Thank you for holding it down as best you could." I could have left it there. I didn't. "But you're the adult. I mean, whenever we give up our calm, then the kids flip out. We have to stay cool," I reprimanded. My own biting tone echoed in my ears.

"Um, you should have seen it," Cedar snapped. "She was definitely the most escalated I have seen in a long time. I was calm and I tried everything. I really was managing it as well as anyone could. At a certain point, I'm just a person. You can't expect me to be more than that. It isn't realistic for me to stay cool at *every single moment*."

"I just feel like it's all on me. If you're upset, then I feel even more pressure to hold it all together. I can't always be there for everyone," I replied, almost shouting.

"No one is saying you need to be," he shot back. "Emma, you put that on yourself."

And there it went. Cedar was stressed, and then I became stressed about his stress.

"I'm so trapped in this. I felt like I couldn't leave her because then if we traded out, you might get upset, which could make it worse," I said. We were neck-deep in it now.

Cedar was one of the kindest people I had ever met, yet he also had a short-ish fuse when it came to children's meltdowns (although he was more tolerant of mine). Any negative emotional reaction could set Eden off, even so much as a tense look or an exasperated tone. And with her full-throttle intensity, it was herculean to stay completely neutral.

We kept on going like this, for at least a half an hour. This was a conversation we had hashed out already too many times before, but we were locked in the same terrible loop.

Something had to change. Something big.

CHAPTER TWENTY-FIVE

Pandemic Parenting for the Rest of Us

Well, like most of the world, I wasn't expecting a global pandemic. During those first-wave days, we mostly stayed home and sanitized the hell out of our house when the night nurse left around 7:00 a.m. When my mom got her hands on an extra can of Lysol (generally sold out before breakfast) she handed it to me proudly like a family heirloom. I cheered and went around spraying things in our home haphazardly since I had never before owned that particular type of hardcore cleaning product. Cedar waved his hands to clear the air while shooting me a look, while the fumes circulated around the kitchen. *Baby's first industrial cleaner.*

One Sunday in mid-March, after the Governor's sudden announcement to shut down schools by mid-week, our district shut down, effective immediately. Our children would not return to in-person school for six months. Gone were the peaceful days of preschool, and Avi's full days at his well-organized neighborhood elementary school. If we thought Eden's medical problems were hard on our marriage before, enter pandemic life.

We were left with two kids, two remote jobs as essential workers, and roughly zero plans for what to do with those kids while we tried to maintain our income.

My parents were not an option; we decided to stop seeing each other for the foreseeable future. They were in their seventies, and it was strongly recommended that all older adults quarantine at home for several months. Because of their age and underlying medical conditions, I was distraught about whether their deaths would come sooner than we ever anticipated. Truthfully, I had already been concerned about losing them *before* the pandemic.

In some ways, I had been living as if it was the COVID-19 era for the past five years since Eden was a baby. We'd always stuck close to home because of her medical and behavioral challenges. Over the years, we had missed countless events, outings, and activities because she couldn't participate. As a caregiver, it didn't change my social life very much.

I wasn't exactly on the club circuit.

And my hand washing routine barely shifted. I was already in the habit of vigorous hygiene, with an emphatic thirty- to sixty-second soapy hand and wrist cleanse upon entry to my home. Like a real hospital, we called it *foaming in.*

But the stakes were higher, suddenly: if Eden got the COVID-19 virus, it wasn't a given that she would make it through. It was all unknown, especially at the beginning, with her Restrictive Lung Disease. Most children seemed to do well with this disease, but Eden was not most children.

We lived under the shadow of Eden's frail health, and alongside that, the ever-present awareness that things could get worse. So much worse. As more people worldwide were hit with layoffs, economic struggle, sacrifice, and death, Cedar and I chugged along in our work, staying largely as healthy as before.

We did what we could to be grateful, although we were grateful and afraid and burned out, all at the same time. My sleeplessness skyrocketed. I had pandemic levels of insomnia. The questions were relentless in my mind: What if Cedar or I became sick? What if we both did, at the same time? What if one of us didn't come through this? How would either of us manage single parenthood?

The future is always unknown, no matter who you are. I just happened to be reminded of it every day by Eden's tubes and syringes. Yet in that collective moment of not-knowing, everyone else was holding something uncertain, too. During that initial wave of COVID, most of the world was stuck at home hoping that their loved ones didn't die—just like we'd been doing for half a decade. It was a strange and sudden connection. One that I never wanted and never expected to have. But once COVID-19 came along, I found myself in the strange position of feeling less alone than I had in years. Everyone started talking about the new normal, adjusting to a major sudden life change that had them homebound and worried. I was surrounded by people lamenting the life they had suddenly lost without warning. I was like, yes, totally, I get it.

I already knew this lost world.

At the beginning, we got by alright. On one March evening, our family came together over a shared goal: to get Eden's hair to look like Pink's, who was still one of her all-time favorite pop stars. I don't remember who started this *very important* mission-driven activity, but we all got faux-hawk focused. A little after six, after Cedar gave Eden her nightly bath, Avi, with a hot pink spray bottle in hand, assumed the role of lead stylist. Normally he wasn't so much into beauty routines, but he embraced this task with ardor. Then he hopped around spritzing water all over the carpet.

As I slid Eden's arms through her unicorn pajamas she called out, "*Walk Me Home*. Please. I want it now," pushing her lanky pointer finger toward the iPad. The video gave us a soundtrack and aesthetic inspiration. Eden interjected with her usual commentary since she had been watching this video roughly ten times a day as a general baseline. "Pink is a powerful dancer," she declared. "Can we see her live in concert?" and of course, her ever-present question, "Is it scary? Is ittt?" While I worked on soothing, Avi kept working on that hair, and after a few minutes of shaping, it was gold.

When she faced her own reflection in the mirror, Eden squealed with delight. "Like Pink," she announced, loudly and plainly. Her hands flapped as if they were producing 150 watts of mechanical power; mission accomplished.

On this particularly bright evening, I was heartened by the fact that my children understood something that I held dear: when times are tough, why not try to look good? We didn't know where things would be tomorrow or next week, especially for Eden who was more susceptible to the complications of COVID-19 or anything, really.

We had joy along with the worry, which was always my biggest hope. I knew there would be worry regardless, since Eden was always on the edge of something—bumping her head, breaking a window, a breakthrough.

The American rallying cry became *keep on keeping on, online*. Nearly everyone extolled the virtues of staying virtually connected. So, on a chilly Sunday night in late March, Mamas Group, after years of meeting monthly, more or less, in person, gathered for the first time virtually. But by the time our video call ended, I felt worse than when we started.

Normally our time was spent face-to-face on a spacious sectional, enjoying decadent, non-child-friendly food whipped up last-minute by Debra. This was generally accompanied by a crisp, budget glass of white wine. I sat with these savvy women and cried until my eyeliner gave up, and we also teared up with laughter just as much. These two-hour meetings generally made me feel lighter, stronger in my imperfections, less alone.

But this online thing, it was the pits.

I loved these women, but I left feeling *less connected* this time. Like I was failing this pandemic-parenting moment. Mostly because we talked about virtual schooling strategies and schedules. Some of the women in the group seemed born for this or their children were, or both. No one else in the group had a child who required a similar level of care as Eden. I didn't put that on anyone else, of course—I mean, I started the group. And yet, the mamas I had come to know and love who had children with significant disabilities also had barriers that stopped them from making it to a group, like steady childcare or enough energy to fully engage with others. Also, I don't think they would relate to some of the typically minded conversations at Mamas group, either. Sometimes I didn't, even though these thoughtful women were still my people.

With the children home from school, while Cedar taught high school music remotely and I ran telehealth sessions, we did the best we could do. The needs and pressures of our jobs had also greatly increased. There wasn't a lot of homeschooling going down.

Pre-pandemic, I wasn't planning on offering telehealth counseling, although I had a few colleagues who were already doing it. The ever-articulate author/psychotherapist Lori Gottlieb referred to video sessions in the *New York Times* as "Doing therapy with a condom on." Maybe there was some truth to that. But by and large, I liked it, except when there were technical difficulties.

Aside from the occasional tech-related issues, telehealth *worked*. It was huge to get to be face-to-face, via my HIPAA compliant video platform, safely with people who I had really grown to care about. And while it wasn't the same as sitting together in person, I felt a closeness with my clients that was as good as the closeness we shared when we were in the same room. We were going through something together, and I could draw from what I knew and who I was. Also, just as I had been doing for years, I continued to do my own individual therapy, but now through telehealth as well.

Sometimes I went to my office to run the telehealth sessions, but mostly I holed up in Avi's room with the door locked and the sound machine on full blast. Spaces with a door were prime real estate at our house; the only other option that had internet access was my bedroom, which felt wrong. (You know that preachy saying that declares *your bedroom should only be used for sleep and for sex*? I don't think that was meant to include deep couples and individual therapy.) So, Avi's room was my top choice, especially because of the lock on the door, and he was kind enough to let me use it without complaint, in exchange for me popping out sometimes when I had a break between clients to give him a hug or to go outside for a quick roofball challenge.

Before I started for the day, I had to rig the room to make it look a lot less like children's quarters and more like a professional telehealth outpost. I would move Avi's desk a little out from the wall, and then sit behind it, creating a blank off-white background behind me. It beat a sort-of made bed filled with twenty stuffed animals, including three different sizes of Pikachu.

I would break for as much time as possible outside with the kids, hunting around for signs of spring. Kitty would come out to check on the perennials, and we'd yell across the fence. She prepped all the garden beds for me when Eden and Avi were otherwise occupied. They weren't exactly tops with social distancing. Kitty even took over planting our window boxes with bright flowers in various shades of pink, just like I usually did each spring.

Eden was so confused about the many sudden changes in her routine that she looked at me and repeated, every few minutes, as if on a timer, "Are you not leaving?"

Her tantrums spiked like a fever (but thankfully without an *actual* fever) since we became holed up together, California style. COVID-19 in general was not something she could understand, and I didn't blame her. It was hard for adults to conceptualize this catastrophic event.

Eden's aggression continued to escalate. Her bouts would sometimes go on for thirty minutes or more, and there were times that nothing would work to calm her down. One of her most common sayings, something she repeated no matter what the person or occasion had become, "I want to hurt her/him/them." It could be directed to Cedar and me or at a character on *Sesame Street*, but that phrase was something she was repeating multiple times a day, without any clear reason or warning.

My wrists were covered in scratches, a few of which had morphed into faint scars. She kicked and threw my glasses and lunged at my face. I'd pitch my fullest effort into my poker face, since any sign of distress or injury only heightened Eden's behavior. If I let on that she caused any pain, she was emboldened.

I usually kept my composure in the moment and helped Eden calm down with a breathing video along with time in her swing. Once she finally fell asleep, I sometimes cried quietly outside her room in the hallway because that was the only place that I could be alone.

I felt so lonely after her outbursts, so frantic to escape the level of distress that Eden embodied, the one that replayed on a loop now every single day. It was nothing anyone else I knew was experiencing, or likely would ever experience. There were many moments when I thought, *I cannot do this anymore. There is absolutely no way.*

At a telehealth visit we'd be waiting on for over six months, a veteran Developmental Pediatrician declared, "You've all been under siege. Eden has a form of autism." Giving it a name helped explain her behavior, and finally, give it context. We still didn't have the official diagnosis on paper, which would require another neuropsychological exam, which came later. But we had more of an understanding of what we were looking at, day to day. Autism spectrum disorder. It was no surprise; Eden had nearly all the symptoms.

ASD presents in about as many ways as there are people who have the diagnosis, hence the spectrum. Most people who have ASD do *not* struggle with aggression, although some do. I understood why the previous doctor who had evaluated Eden didn't want to use the diagnosis; still, having it officially out there provided context for Eden's behavior.

Even with the doctor's proclamation, it was impossible to know what was sparking Eden's aggression in the first place. Was it autism or was it her rare genetic deletion, and could we even parse those out? Was it her cognitive impairment that led to her inability to communicate verbally when distressed? Eden was not fully fluent in speaking or receptive language (understanding content), although she did possess growing skills in these areas, so there was no real way to know.

I also wondered how years of medical-related trauma and chronic illness influenced Eden's volatility. Did she not have a right to be flaming hot mad about all that she had endured? To seethe with discomfort and confusion about why she had already had to go through so much, still on that damn feeding tube, while watching all the other people in her life enjoy their meals like it was nothing? And now during shelter in place, with all her routines upended, it was a huge adjustment. Her volatility was not justified—I would have done anything for her to express herself in a different way—but given all that she had faced, it was comprehendible.

And, what about the potential influence of the unique landscape of Eden's brain, which included high levels of cerebrospinal fluid and cysts? These factors had increased slightly over time but now appeared to be stable. Eden's neurosurgeon told us that the likelihood those specific structural brain differences were causing aggression was about a 10 percent chance or less—not a clear enough indication to justify surgical intervention—but there was a chance.

Whatever was the cause, through all of Eden's aggression and attempts at self-injury, I tried to remember, *this too, this too, this too,* a mantra lifted from Tara Brach, a psychologist and meditation teacher. Still, I felt as down as I had ever felt. I spent unprecedented amounts of time with my children because there was nowhere else to go, and they needed a lot of reassurance and affection. They needed a lot of everything. Cedar and I now filled all the roles that used to belong to others: teacher, friend, parent, grandparent, counselor. The net was pulled out from under us, our village suddenly so small.

When I was overwhelmed, I focused on checking off the tasks from our ever-growing to-do list. Sometimes I was hard on Cedar because he didn't match my relentless productivity. And sometimes, when Cedar was overwhelmed, he turned into a professional avoider. This was our pattern, and soon we were again in those predictable roles.

And of course, I knew that it could be much worse, which did not make it better.

CHAPTER TWENTY-SIX

If Not Now, When?

That spring, I was foraging for snacks in the kitchen between therapy sessions when Julie called. I ran into the bedroom for a semblance of privacy. "Hi Julie Bulie!," I said when I answered, using Eden's term of endearment for her. "How are you?"

"Can't complain!" she said.

"Well, you could," I said, only half-joking. "It's a pandemic." I looked out the window at the maple trees that were nearly budding. It was an early, warmer than usual spring, nature's consolation prize.

Julie laughed. "True enough. So, listen, as you know, I'm trying to go back to work," she said. "I've already interviewed, and pretty much been offered a position. But here's the thing. I'd rather work with Eden, full-time."

What? Could this be real? *Julie RN Save-the-Day Miraculous Human*? Now?

"What do you think?" she asked.

We had never had a full-time caregiver for Eden before; it had always been a piecemeal constellation of caregivers. Before the pandemic, I didn't think we needed full-time care, especially given the expense. And even if we had, we'd never found anyone willing to do it.

I practically shouted into the phone. "*Really?* You'd come back? That's amazing!"

The answer was a full-on *yes*! Julie's knee had finally healed from the injury that ended her tenure as Eden's nurse two years prior, and now suddenly was ready to take on exactly what we needed. Of course, we had been connected the whole time, along with Marc and his regular outings with Eden, which during the shelter-in-place era became innings. Marc and Julie had both been a calm and caring presence for all of us. We even loved their daughter, Rachel, who had worked with Eden as a PCA, including a recent, relieving stint.

Extended family? Villagers? Whatever we called it, I was grateful.

After some back and forth navigating the details, we determined that Julie and Marc would return as Eden's main caregivers. I could almost even call it *bashert* (meant to be), though it was a bit more complicated than that; still, this was a definitive game changer.

We decided that Eden would go over to their place to minimize the commotion at our house, which was something we'd hadn't ever done consistently before. Yet again, the only reason I was able to continue working (for pay) was because of Julie and Marc's willingness to care for Eden.

Without this aid, I probably would have become a statistic: yet another woman dropping out of the workforce because of the pressures of caregiving, given the very limited structural support provided by the United States for mothers. Our health insurance was still linked to Cedar's employment, and without that, we were toast.

We had nearly been toast, regardless.

—— ∾∾ ——

That same month, we hosted Julie and Marc for a tiny Passover Seder. The event was devoid of fuss or fanfare, scheduled for a Wednesday at 4:30 p.m. I worked a half day at my office to have time to cook beforehand; I saw three clients via telehealth in the morning, then mentally fortified by taking a phone-walk with Kate.

When I got home, I scrubbed my hands, and then got going with Ina Garden's chicken with shallots, a reliable recipe I had made many times before. I also whipped up a box of matzo ball soup mix with carrots that turned out surprisingly well. Julie made fresh matzo popovers and brought bars for dessert. We sat down well before the sun set, which is not the traditional thing, but was also the only thing for a Seder with these small children.

My parents weren't there; we were still staying away from each other to protect them. It felt so foreign to host a holiday and not include them in our plans. My mother had graciously dropped off a container of her date orange charoset (a spread that represents the mortar between the bricks that the Israelites laid as slaves) earlier that afternoon.

We gathered at our big white dining room table, with the classic Seder plate in the center. Eden kicked off the holiday conversation by yelling, on repeat, "I am pooping" because she was experiencing a painful and poorly timed bout of constipation. Avi started whine-crying because Eden was simultaneously crying and trying to hit her head on the table. After exhausting the wholesome soothing strategies, we handed her a cell phone during the Seder to watch music videos, which was probably not officially considered Kosher for Passover. But eventually, she calmed by the sacred light of the iPhone.

I had cut out little quotes and scattered them around the table, things like "If I am not for myself, who will be for me? But if I am only for myself, what am I? If not now, when?" Rabbi Hillel (Pirkei Avot 1:14). And "You are not obligated to complete the work [of repairing the world], but neither are you free to desist from it." Rabbi Tarfon (Pirkei Avot 2:21). Marc was not into it; reasonably enough, he was not into any organized activities that resembled religious school. But he indulged me with a quick discussion on freedom, which worked just fine. It wasn't about pooping, at least.

The Seder ended early and not very well. It was always going to be quick with our group. Speed Seders were the house specialty. Speed anything, really.

Somehow, afterward, we rallied for a round of "Dayenu"—a rousing Passover song of appreciation, about how it would have been enough if just one good thing had happened to us. We stood up as a group from the table, singing, following Eden, who was freestyle dancing near the couch. I admired my village's lit up faces.

Julie, Marc, Avi, Cedar, and Eden stood together clapping and stomping, totally immersed in an age-old ritual despite the force of a pandemic all around us. We each could have been alone on this holiday but instead here we were together, belting out a song I had sang every year for as long as I could remember. My battered heart swelled.

I took the kids outside to say goodbye while Cedar tackled the dishes. Marc and Julie piled into their Mini Cooper, blowing kisses and waving. Eden paced up and down the front stoop while Avi and I kicked the soccer ball between us. After our friends backed down the driveway, Eden started to cry again.

"Are they not coming back?" her dazzling baby blue eyes pleaded. "Are they not? Are they not coming back? Right now? It's hard when Marc goes," she wailed. I bent down to give her a hug.

And then she got a hold of my ponytail and yanked for dear life.

———ᴍ———

During the shelter-in-place era of COVID-19, I did not have *pandemic boredom*. I did not do 1,000-piece puzzles or take up knitting or watch copious amounts of Netflix. I did not clean my closets or accomplish amazing feats of home repair. I never once wondered, *What should I do with my spare time?*

Another day around this time, Avi looked at me, right after Eden finished banging her head against the wall of the hallway, after a long day of throwing up on the carpet, in the car, and in a cup.

He saw me sigh, took a breath and said, "Your life is hard."

I looked back at him and said, "Sometimes."

I usually added something like, "We have many good things going for us, too." And then I would name those things. But on that day, I did not.

I went on, "I know it can be hard for you, too. Let's go upstairs, sweetheart." He nodded. We walked up together to the bright, clean kitchen. It was still light out, only 5:30 p.m. Cedar stayed downstairs with Eden, completing her evening cares: washing her stoma (the wound around her feeding tube site), administering her medications, soaking her feet in warm water to soothe the ache from her braces.

After several rounds of negotiation, Avi sat at the center island and finished his broccoli, Nutella, and pretzels. Dinner of champions, especially in trying times. I leaned in close and said to him, "I want to teach you a word. It's kind of what happened today."

"Okay," Avi replied casually. I grinned to myself, knowing that I was about to upend our typical educational vocabulary lesson.

"The word is *shitshow*. It's a word adults use when everything is happening, unpleasantly, all at once. Today was a shitshow," I said, my eyes shining. I knew he would appreciate a rare opportunity for parent-sanctioned swearing.

To be clear, outside of quarantine times, I did the proper mothering things—enforcing the "pleases" and the "thank yous," the "make-your-bed -before-you-turn-on-the-TV," the well-considered natural consequences. The things that were necessary but not necessarily fun.

But what if there wasn't a future? What if that moment was it?

Avi's blue-gray eyes lit up. "Shitshow," he repeated. "It was a shitshow." He beamed, as if we had discovered something spectacular—Funfetti cupcakes at our doorstep, a double rainbow. "Shitshowshitshowshitshow," he said, nodding vigorously. I looked at his sweet round face, the giant smile plastered across it.

"Okay," I laughed, "We can use this word for like, five minutes. Tops. Then we have to go back to our not-swearing selves."

The next morning, while I washed the breakfast dishes, Eden shimmied over angrily to Avi, unprovoked, and swatted at him. I separated them quickly, but later, after I soothed him, Avi said, "I don't think I'm going to be able to do anything today now that my arm hurts. Not football, not schoolwork. Not anything. Probably for at least two weeks."

Then he told me that he had come up with a new word.

"Fuckfit," he said confidently, looking straight at me. I tried to keep my eyebrows neutral. "Eden had a fuckfit today." I looked down at the tile floor, suffocating a smile. He must have learned that prefix on the bus, back when school buses were still running. During this era, fuckfits were easy to find; I had my share of them, too.

CHAPTER TWENTY-SEVEN

The Whole House

Kate and I had no idea when we would be in the same room together again, but we were as connected as ever. We squeezed in short and long phone conversations despite our constant juggling of children and clients. We also kept up with our texting and sent each other all kinds of things via the original connector: the old school USPS.

We exchanged carefully illustrated homemade cards (Kate) and hard cider and chocolate delivery (more my thing), and activities for our children and matching bracelets for summer. We had accrued, over the years, more than a few pieces of what we called *friendship jewelry*, which was nothing more than matching modern pieces—no BFF heart-shaped adornments for us. They seemed even better knowing that we both had the same ones. I shipped her birthday bath products with dried flowers and a rose quartz rock.

I don't know when I became the kind of person who gave and received special rocks, but I was glad Kate showed up for the transformation.

We arranged countless co-walks, where we'd stroll in our respective neighborhoods at the same time, roughly thousands of miles away. Somehow, we always still had more to talk about, even at the end of one of those walks. We could go heavy (whatever was happening, online learning woes, case consultation, billing issues in our respective practices) and we could go light (summer length of pants, the home-related arts).

One Thursday afternoon, we both cried. I was wearing baggy gray sweats and a hot pink down vest, and my hair was absolutely on trend: pandemic unruly. I walked up the trail by the water to the beach and then kept going all the way to the park.

"How are you, really?" she asked with her slight East Coast lilt.

"I'm feeling the despair thing," I said, barely getting the words out. I didn't want to cry on the phone, but there it was. She knew the shorthand. When I met despair, I felt as if things would never change, that I was doomed to give up too much of myself as a caregiver. It was a sinking belief that my life was not really mine. Not because I wanted martyr status (I emphatically did not), but because of the basic equation of how many needs Eden had, and Avi, too, who approached distance learning as if he was a contestant on *The Amazing Race*, finishing up his work for the day in record time.

"Even though we are so incredibly lucky to have Julie and Marc with Eden—hyperlucky, if that was actually a word—I still can't get a break," I sighed to my long-distance friend. "Because right now, my breaks are mostly so that I can work. Which, as you know, is heavier than ever, absolutely jam packed. So much crisis, even with clients who before were so stable."

Kate listened, giving me time. She told me that she understood.

"Emma, it's a lot to carry. I get how you can feel despair about the future and also be profoundly grateful. How the responsibility of being a therapist is a lot right now. Especially given what you are holding with Eden."

"Won't it always just fall on Cedar and me, the inevitable . . . the whole struggle of her life? Her need for twenty-four/seven care?" I kept on walking, and she was walking too, in her neighborhood half a country away.

"It is so difficult," Kate acknowledged. "But I don't think it will always be exactly like this."

I liked that she said it, but I couldn't totally believe that it was true.

I looked down at the street riddled with potholes. I passed a construction site where workers hammered away on a too-big house, one that stuck out like a strip mall in a desert. Kate was probably nearing the field of lush bamboo adjacent to her home.

As I passed a patch of brittle dead grass, Kate told me she wished she had more family—actual relatives—around to help her raise her girls. Her voice caught; I could almost hear the tears. I tried to channel her empathy back to her.

"I know it's hard. Of course, you want that," I told her. "And you've already done such an amazing job of creating your own family now. You are loved by so many people." And then, "You are my sister. But better, probably."

"I wish we lived in the same place, she replied. "Especially now."

"Same, same." Would we ever?

We paused, feeling the thousands of miles between us. It was always difficult to consider anything forever. "But we have done such a good job, haven't we? Of making this work. I'm proud of us. We do great."

"Me too. We've been amazing. I love you, Emma."

"I love you, too, Kate."

We said goodbye. Kate had plans to finish her walk with a new friend, a friend who lived where she lived. I was only slightly jealous. Not jealous that she had another friend; Kate had scores of friends, many of whom I also loved. I just wanted to be there with her, sharing air together. Which during that particular historical moment meant a lot.

Later that day, I stopped by Kitty's yard. She was standing underneath a maple tree in her scuffed-up painting jeans. Two elementary schoolers, siblings from next door, sat across from one another at an old white easel. She said, "I'm leading them in art lessons from six feet away. I want to give their poor mother a break."

If we could only have more people like Kitty in this world, who were up for giving mothers a break. If we could only have systems that embodied that ethos, that could lighten the emotional and physical load for all parents.

I flashed a smile back, buoyed by the unexpectedness of this moment, "Wow, I love it—art making in the sunshine." She waved me toward a bucket at the end of the driveway, "Grab some Curly Willow to make an arrangement. They make big, rowdy bouquets." It was sitting in a white bucket with a sign which read: Please help yourself to these cuttings. And, at the bottom of the sign: *VOC Victory Over Covid.*

At that moment, one of the children tipped over in her metal patio chair and fell onto the stone path. She looked as if she might cry. I asked Kitty if I could help, but she said, "Oh no, I've got this," and turned to comfort her from afar. I walked back to my house, passing the peonies just starting to peek their red tips out of the earth.

I walked outside that evening to find Kitty's easel in my own front yard with a note attached. She had been heading out of town, it said, so she thought Avi and Eden might want to use it; she'd even disinfected it for us. *It will not need weather protection*, she'd written. *It's old and tough!*

Like her. Like I could hope to be someday.

—⁓—

I was incredibly fortunate to have my long-distance/socially distanced community and also privileged to have the support of Marc and Julie. But I felt alone and not alone at the same time; I missed the way it used to be, before the pandemic—when despair took up a room inside of me, instead of the whole house.

All through those early shelter in place months, Cedar and I fought more than I'd like to admit, about small things throughout the day, like when Cedar promised Avi he'd make chocolate croissants (from the freezer) and then totally spaced it or when I had asked Cedar for help with household tasks to get ready for Eden's birthday, and then I found him hunched over a bowl of granola reading *In Hoffa's Shadow*, a memoir about the mob. I still felt as if I was shouldering too much—and as someone with a devotion to bucking patriarchy, I seethed as I mopped the floor and cleaned the basins of the sinks each week.

I was far from the only one battling despair, of course. During that initial pandemic chaos, it seemed like everything was on fire. My stomach dropped when I saw the headlines about the brutal murder of George Floyd, at an intersection I was familiar with. This galvanized millions of people to protest with the Black Lives Matters movement, demanding an end to deep-rooted racism and police brutality.

The day the murder dominated the headlines, Avi and I sat at the dining room table together with my laptop open in front of us. Well, to be precise, I sat and Avi kind of bounced around the room. On the screen, a work-in-progress: a letter to the editor at the *Minneapolis Star Tribune*. Avi had many questions for me.

"How did he die?" he asked.

I paused, and then spoke quietly, "A police officer killed him by kneeling on him for almost ten minutes. He couldn't breathe." Avi looked down at the floor, taking it all in. I wanted to kiss the curls on top of his head, to make it easier somehow.

"Why would he do that?"

How does anyone answer a question like that? I did my best to explain white supremacy on an eight-year-old level. What a grisly world we were passing down.

In part to make myself feel better, I added, "You can help change the world."

He looked straight at me. "Oh, I know, Mom." There may have been a subtle eye roll involved. I didn't love the eye roll, but I did love that confidence. That's what I wanted for his generation, the belief that of course we can create a more just and freer place for us all.

Our world, our work to do.

"Do you think our letter will make it in the paper?" I looked over at my son's smooth skin and crooked front teeth. His eyes were bright blooms of blue. I was honest with him.

"I wouldn't count on it. But it matters that we try."

Eden and I didn't talk about ending racism or antisemitism or about anything very deep beyond the notion of love, which she instinctively understood. She couldn't parse complex concepts. And like nearly everything else with her, the future of her comprehension was uncertain. Maybe someday we would have broader conversations about social justice and civil rights, including her own as a person with disabilities. Then again, maybe we wouldn't.

CHAPTER TWENTY-EIGHT

Mother's Day Gifts

We had to keep trying to find our way through, and, eventually, for us that meant marijuana. (Not for me, though; those days had passed.) The type we landed on for Eden, for a while, had just a touch of THC, the psychoactive ingredient. It was mostly a high-quality pure form CBD. We tried CBD only at first, because of course, the gentlest version possible was ideal. I certainly didn't want my almost-five-year-old to be getting high. Although, to be fair, Eden kind of acted like she was high no matter what, in all the best and worst ways, except for the food cravings.

Yes, my pre-kindergartener was on weed.

Before Eden, if you would have told me that I would put my developing child on medical marijuana, I would not have believed you. But medical marijuana was an approved treatment for autism spectrum disorder-related aggression. We also wondered if there was pain and/or nausea sparking her aggression, which was plausible, since Eden didn't have the words to express these concerns. After a month or so it seemed to help, somewhat.

The CBD-only variety made Eden more anxious than usual. She started to repeat, "No Laura" relentlessly. "No Laura" referred to a kind and experienced swim instructor who Eden hadn't seen for months. It was Eden's code for *I don't want to go swimming*. But as "No Laura" was repeated day and night, we knew this formulation wasn't helping. So back to the dispensary Cedar went.

It had come down to cheeba or an antipsychotic; we had already tried most of the other classes of medication for Eden over the past few years. We wanted to wait on the antipsychotic for as long as we could because of the side effects, including the potentially permanent tics of tardive dyskinesia. Also because it felt hard to admit that Eden would need an antipsychotic (note the key word: *psychotic*). But it became increasingly clear that she needed it. We needed it, too.

No Hallmark card exists that could encapsulate this Mother's Day, not even close. This holiday, in my experience, has never gone quite the way Hallmark says it should—two Mother's Days previous, during a bike ride with my own mother, I got stung by a bee on my inner lower lip after roughly a block and a half. It hurt like hell, but my mother declared it better than Botox. "God, you look good," she kvelled, reflecting on my swollen mouth, as we scurried into the corner store for a handful of ice.

On this Mother's Day, by the time I got up, Cedar had already brought home a dozen bagels, and I found his rapturous note of appreciation for all my maternal efforts on the kitchen table. I surveyed the scene: Avi played video games on the iPad on the family room couch, completely zoned out. A few feet away, Cedar pushed Eden in her swing while she watched Mr. Rogers. She found it soothing to take the end of the thick rainbow strap buckling her in and hold it tightly in her hand, or put it in her mouth, or both. That morning, she happily gnawed away.

I kissed everyone good morning and sauntered into the kitchen to fix a fried egg sandwich on a sesame seed bagel. My favorite.

My bagel wasn't even toasted before Eden began to shriek.

"I want to hurt her!" This would be Lady Aberlin, King Friday's niece on Mr. Rogers. Which, of course, she couldn't (the episode was from 1985). So, she started to hit herself on the side of the head with her fist, unable to find the words to express what was going on for her, which then made her cry.

Cedar, still in his pajamas, turned toward Eden to slide her pink helmet over her head. He cooed, "It's okay, Eden," as he buckled the chin strap. In a beat, she yanked his glasses from his face and flung them toward the kitchen. They hit the floor with a clank, like a roll of dice. Eden swiped at the top of his head; a thin line of blood emerged where her nails had been. Cedar hollered, "Ow! She broke my goddamn glasses! Forget this." He stormed into our bedroom for a break, leaving me with the kids.

"Is he sad? Is he? Is he not coming back?" Eden asked, her voice suddenly pierced with pressure and longing. I tried to reassure her, but she was fully fixated. "Is he now?"

The glasses were remarkably unscathed, but I was not. I felt that familiar heaviness settling in.

I eventually got Eden soothed with a breathing routine, and when Cedar reemerged a few minutes later, we tried to rally the kids for a bike ride. Avi was having a lot of feelings.

"I won't go. I'm not going anywhere with that maniac," he shouted. I may have glared at my sweet little boy. But I understood.

In response, Eden bucked the back of her head against the hard blue plastic of the swing repeatedly. I pulled her out of the swing to try to calm her, at which point she scratched a long, sharp red line down my forearm.

I took two, maybe three breaths.

I tried. I did.

Then, when I stared down at the sight of my own blood, I lost it.

I tried not to slam the door behind me as I ran out of the house, but I failed. Hard. The cool spring air on my skin gave me some relief as I left the garage, but it was not nearly enough. My head—my heart—I was on fire. I stood stiffly, arms out to the side, facing the street. The sun streamed into my eyes. I gave in.

"IT'S TOO MUCH!!!" I yelled into the blue morning; my fists bunched by my sides. I looked down again at my forearm.

"It's just . . . too . . . MUCH," I sobbed to myself. My palms shuttered my face. The heat of tears on my cheeks felt indulgent; I was losing it in my own driveway. The release was both incredible and terrifying.

Then—

"Mom?"

Avi's thin voice behind me, threading out through the screen.

"Are you okay?"

I had thought I was out of earshot. I wiped my face as I walked back toward the house. Avi met me on the stoop, and I put my arm around his shoulder. I said—and I meant it—"Yes, baby. I'm okay."

"Mom, that was really loud," Avi chided. He was standing on the front steps in a pair of athletic shorts and his favorite white and red tank top. (I had gotten it for him one day after he saw my outfit and exclaimed sweetly, "No fair! You get to wear a tank top?!")

I looked at his face, a little bit furrowed because of the stress of the morning, the light softly reflecting off him. I had a series of thoughts then, the same series that had been plaguing me since California. *Can we keep doing this with Eden? Will this break us? If she is like this now, what will she be like when she is older, bigger, more able to hurt us? How is all this intensity affecting Avi?*

I was flooded with embarrassment. I knew the importance of keeping a peaceful home, given the intensity of Eden's challenges. I worked hard to keep our lives upbeat and seemingly smooth for Avi's sake, maybe too hard. But I also knew I was human, and therefore wouldn't always be a model citizen.

But that was my thing—the diamond-hard thing at my core—always wanting to be so fucking good.

When the pandemic started and Eden's aggression spiked, I had started to look at residential programs. Not for that exact moment, but to have as a backup plan, if and when she became capable of really hurting any of us. We didn't know how soon that future would be. Her behavior at the beginning of the pandemic, when all the usual supports had suddenly dropped away, had been almost unbearable.

Cedar and I had long since agreed that if any of us were in danger from Eden's aggression, we may have to find another place for her to live. It was gut-wrenching to think about—it felt almost like a kind of death, losing our child to a residential setting—but it also struck us as an ethical imperative, should her behavior ever get that damaging. We had Avi to think about, not just ourselves. So far, Eden had never hurt him beyond anything that a typical sibling might do. But if she became a threat to him, that was a clear line for us.

For now, on Eden's harder days we could keep them apart, using the main floor and finished basement or outside. It meant that we needed to always keep two adults on with the kids whenever Eden was home from Julie and Marc's apartment, no exceptions. This wasn't a long-term solution.

To get more information, I called our county worker to inquire about possible residential treatment options. She said, "Eden will be best in your home. There's nowhere else for a child of her age. People with developmental delays don't do well in those programs, anyway." I also asked Eden's psychologist for resources during a session around ways to manage her aggressive behavior. She suggested duct-taping gloves to her hands because of her scratching (this struck me as cruel, and I didn't try it). The psychologist shared with us that there was nothing for a child such as Eden anywhere nearby, no rehabilitation or respite, but that we could find something out of state, possibly as close as Wisconsin.

I later discovered there was nothing for her in Wisconsin, or anywhere in the surrounding states, given her complex medical and behavioral needs.

Considering all the information I received, Cedar and I decided to keep the residential treatment as a last resort. We wanted to do everything we could do to keep Eden close. To give her the best chance in her life, with consistent care and secure attachment. This meant getting her the right medication, among other interventions.

If she was going to stay in our home, we had to make this better.

We couldn't keep living like it was Mother's Day, a holiday that we recalled later, when things had eased, with a mixture of levity and anguish. It was so bad, that it was almost, but not quite, funny.

The medical marijuana seemed to make Eden tired and at certain moments, loopy, but clearly, it wasn't fully impacting her behavioral challenges. We wanted to spare her the heavier duty drugs her psychiatrist recommended, but shortly after that dire Mother's Day, when my arms were so scratched up it looked as if I had been engaging in self-harm, we started Eden on risperidone, a front-line medication for aggression related to ASD.

Gone were the days of the dispensary. If we were going to continue with the medical marijuana, we had to be able to see the results. We didn't, at least not enough.

I still put my face right next to Eden's at the end of one night to snuggle side-by-side in her twin bed. This was not always a safe place for a person's face, but she was my daughter, and I was willing to risk it.

As we lay there together, Eden gathered strands of my hair to hold them tight in her little palm. I knew the routine; when she would start with the inevitable pulling, I would get up and stand by the door in silent protest, just for a minute. I would say, "I can come back to the bed when you use gentle hands. Are you ready?" She would nod yes, and back in I would go. Sometimes, I got my hair pulled again, but it was worth it. Eventually, I would move over to the stool right beside her bed, and then she would say, "Hold my hand" and tuck her long smooth palm in mine as she fell asleep. I wanted to be there with her, to see her drift off in total peace. At her core was love. And affection and exuberance.

I still found her belly to be one of the cutest bellies I'd ever seen, her laugh a lift, no matter what. There was just a lot of other stuff going on in her brain that got in the way.

We continued to use our own DIY behavioral principles to shape her behavior for the better, since in-person therapies were out due to the pandemic. We coached Eden on expressing her feelings with words instead of with her fists, and we created clear calm-down routines. I taped lists of the routines around the house so that we could refer to them when needed.

Regrouping, by this point, was becoming a family tradition. Cedar and I started doing couples therapy online, and we each continued with our own individual therapy via telehealth, and it helped to manage the weight of it. There was a lot of therapy going down in that house, between my sessions that I was leading and then all our own work.

Bit by bit, coupled with the risperidone and the quiet, nurturing weekdays with Julie and Marc, Eden's meltdowns stopped lasting as long. It wasn't exactly what we had hoped for because the aggression continued.

It definitely wasn't what we had hoped for.

Putting Eden on an antipsychotic was an act of surrender. Since getting Eden's diagnosis, I had become a different kind of parent. A different kind of person.

Back when we first had Avi, I sobbed one summer afternoon after I knocked over a Medela bottle and a few ounces of pumped breastmilk cascaded into the cream-colored carpet. I wanted to give my baby pure, unadulterated nourishment. I felt as if he needed that gold standard of breastmilk and that it was my duty to give it to him, no matter what the cost to myself. I wanted my children to have the best of whatever I could offer them.

I still did. It's just that the specifics had become entirely more flexible.

As we measured out Eden's antipsychotic from the orange translucent bottle into a tiny syringe and pushed it through her feeding tube, I didn't feel that same jolt of guilt. I didn't feel it about the medication or anything else, really, at least not in the way that I used to.

I had come to see that it was not up to me. It never really had been. I was not in control of this, of my daughter, of her health, of circumstance. Everything was so far from perfect and strangely uncertain. And here I was, anyway, doing what I could to make a good life.

When I held that unlikely white flag, which came in the form of an orange translucent bottle, I found a surprising pocket of peace.

We are who we are. And, we are who our village helps us to become.

CHAPTER TWENTY-NINE

Short-lived and Soothing

Good morning, the email from Eden's Case Manager at the nursing company began. *I was wondering if it would be possible to have a meeting with either/both of you, myself, and the director regarding Eden's hours?*

My heart fluttered. This could not be good news.

I had been saying for years—since we got it in the first place—that night nursing was *the* component that made it possible to continue to care for Eden at home. Without sleep, I was worthless, or at least I felt like it.

I called the Case Manager right away, hoping to glean some information about what cuts we were facing. I assumed it would be a reduction in hours.

She told me that because Eden had been well since February, the nursing company planned to discontinue services in September. This, of course, made zero logical sense; we'd been following shelter-in-place guidelines since March, therefore Eden had no real opportunity to catch an illness.

Year after year, Eden had a well-documented history of pneumonia during the cold season, and pneumonia lasted weeks or more. Sometimes months.

Eden had 1,400 pages of records at Children's Hospital by the time she was two; that summer, Cedar had to go to the hospital to get copies of Eden's records. When he called to set up the transfer of paperwork, the Health Information Specialist said, "Bring a wagon. You won't be able to carry them."

After I hung up with Eden's Case Manager, I paced up and down the wooded trail near my house. I had that pit-in-the-stomach feeling, and I started to sweat. My breath heaved in and out in quick bursts. I thought about all the sleepless nights or nights with little, scattered sleep that I had done so far, and then I thought about how many more were coming.

Something inside of me was saying *I'm done.* I knew if I sacrificed that sleep and that support, I would again experience all that exhaustion sparked in me—anxiety, irritability, hopelessness, fatigue. I did not want to live that way anymore. Not coupled with Eden's vicious meltdowns, not without school in session, not without breaks on the weekends. I could not go without sleep indefinitely. And I could not spend the next several years arguing with Cedar about who gets to sleep and when.

I wanted to escape in a way that had never been more visceral, more pressing. Unexpected thoughts flashed in my mind.

Suddenly, I thought about ending my own life—jumping off a bridge, free falling away from the responsibilities that were stacked against my own well-being. *It's too much. I don't see how I can keep going, and I don't see any possible way that this can or will improve. I'm unbelievably, beyond exhausted.*

My therapist-self gently listed healthier options for me. My caregiver-self just wanted to die.

I did not have a plan to move these thoughts forward. I would never leave my family in a way that would plague them, especially my children. And I couldn't do that to my clients. But at that moment, there seemed to be no other way out of caregiving. I was done giving up too much of myself—my time, my health, my autonomy. It had been more than five years.

I called Rabbi Zimmerman right there from the woods. She answered with, "Hi Emma," in the warmest tone imaginable. She spoke delicately, "I'm at a funeral. But I can call you in an hour?"

I needed to talk with someone I trusted, someone who would know what to say and do. Cedar was tied up with the kids. I called Kate, who thankfully answered. I told her about the lost nursing hours. She knew what this meant to me without much explanation. It all poured out, "Kate, I just can't keep doing this. We will be on for Eden *every night.* I can't do it anymore. I'm . . . I'm having suicidal thoughts, Kate. And no, of course I won't do it, I promise you that . . . I know that would be so hard on everyone else. But right now, I want to."

She understood exactly. "Oh, sweetheart," my friend said. "I'm so glad you are telling me, Emma. I'm here. I understand why you feel like giving up right now. And if you feel like you can't do it anymore, really, I will come. I will find a way. I will just drive there. You have to let me know if you're at that point."

"Thank you," I sighed. "Even just knowing that you would come if I really needed you. That's really something." Of course, I knew Kate was also holding down her private practice during this tenuous time, along with homeschooling her three daughters, with no family around to help.

"I'm okay. I mean not *great,* obviously," I laughed a little, nervously. I felt that familiar mix of feelings—somewhat comforted by her reassurance, yet still desperate and terrified for what was ahead. I knew that I couldn't keep going like this, in such a precarious place. I was teetering on the edge, too close to losing myself.

After I got off the phone with Kate, I decided not to go home just yet. I continued to walk under the towering trees to talk with the Rabbi who had graciously called me back. I told her *everything.* That I didn't know if I could sacrifice so much indefinitely, for what might be the rest of my life. Eden would likely need care for as long as she lived. How could I go on, as is, when part of me wanted to die? Would I ever be free again? It seemed as if I would always be caring for this child—together with Cedar—tending to her near-constant needs around the clock.

She responded matter-of-factly, "It's okay if Eden doesn't live with you forever. Maybe it would be better because then you can be her mother instead of her nurse."

I finally went home, feeling understood. Part of me still felt like dying, but instead I put on the Punch Brothers, poured a glass of wine, and made tacos for dinner. I read stories with Eden and got into bed with her until I heard that soft, sweet snore—all the usual things. It wasn't resolved, of course. I later told my therapist about the suicidal thoughts, and Cedar, too. I knew what would save me was something essential yet difficult during a pandemic: not being alone in it.

—∿—

The next morning, I got started on appealing the nursing company's decision. During our scheduled phone meeting that Friday, the nursing director cooed in a nicey-nice Minnesota accent, "We are *so* happy that Eden has done so well, and we really want to help you come up with a new plan since she doesn't meet the criteria for nursing anymore. We are just so *thrilled* that Eden is doing so great."

What really happened while she gushed on is that I flicked off the speaker phone. I had already been in enough of those meetings to last a lifetime and heard all the felebratory (fake celebratory) language that I could take. The flick off was just for me; it wasn't a video chat.

Did it help? A little bit.

The nursing company had to justify their staffing with skilled nursing interventions and during quarantine. Eden wasn't needing many of them. Eden was tolerating a real food blend by that point, in meal-like portions (called boluses) run through the tube intermittently throughout the day, which was a step forward. She was off the continuous night feedings for the first time since the tube was placed.

Then I spoke, warmly, because by this point, I knew how to advocate like a mother. "We really appreciate everything you have done for us, and we know that at some point Eden's nursing will need to end. And yes, Eden has made progress. But this doesn't make sense to end it just as Eden will be—hopefully—if schools open, getting back into contact with peers and contracting viruses again, including, potentially COVID-19. Your plan has her nursing ending in September, the week she will be starting kindergarten. Couldn't we keep the nursing care through the fall to see how she does this year?"

Eden would attend our school district's Developmental Cognitive Disability (DCD) program in the fall. Because of her exceptional needs, she would need to attend a different school than the neighborhood school that Avi attended, but that was fine. At least she would be in school. Most likely, depending on what was happening with the virus.

The nursing director and I went back and forth, which I was used to doing. I had already appealed and advocated on school choice, countless insurance coverage issues, hospital logistics, and much more. I had written meticulous letters and emails to all kinds of places and talked until my throat was raspy. Sometimes, we got a small victory. Other times, people were just plain rude. Often, we received an overly saccharine response, which was code for *this is really not going to happen, no matter how hard you try.*

On the first appeal, the nursing company gave us one extra month of part-time coverage. This wasn't even close to solving the problem. I got the contact info of the regional manager and set up a phone meeting. A few days later, we spent a half-hour talking. I plead our case, explaining how Eden had been well because of shelter in place with no school, no therapies, no in-person doctor's appointments, no playdates, and no trips to the store.

I got the same glib response, "We understand that this is difficult for your family. This is a conversation that is hard to have. But we can't plan nursing care around what-ifs. I mean, we are so happy that Eden is doing so well. It's really exciting to celebrate this with you."

Pacing around my small office, I looked out the window at the marsh surrounded by bright green trees. "I respect and very much appreciate what you do for our community. We have loved our nurses." I glanced at the clock and mentally noted that I had to start a session in less than five minutes.

"I actually have to go in just a minute, but I need to say this before I do," my voice was even, controlled. "When you end this care, Eden will be entering back in the germ pool. And then it will all fall on us—the nights that she needs real nursing—when she gets pneumonia and my husband and I are managing her respiratory events at home. We have done that for *years.* This isn't a what-if, this is well documented in Eden's chart. Each fall the cycle begins, and then Eden is on a roller-coaster of illness until at least spring. I just need you to hear that piece," I exhaled, knowing that this was all that I could do, and then, "Thank you for taking the time to talk with me."

And then I sat down at my desk with its succulents and stack of paperwork, took a deep breath, and logged on to a telehealth session with a struggling new-ish mom. It was a difficult time to be a mother, no matter the specifics. It was a difficult time for all of us who worked so hard to maintain our well-being while caring for others.

Somehow, I was able to focus on what my client was going through, letting go of the rest temporarily. I had a lot of practice with that skill. It was almost always a reprieve, entering another world, another life, another person's challenges. Yet when the session ended, I was right back to thinking about those dreaded nights.

The next day, I got a voicemail that I listened to from home between sessions. Because of our conversation, the nursing company had decided to increase Eden's hours, for a total of one more part-time month of night nursing.

I appreciated the gesture, although it did not address our overall concerns. I also felt detached and exhausted by it. After the call, to comfort myself, I walked into the garden to cut daylilies, daisies, and cosmos, arranging them in a skinny glass vase. After checking on the other plants outside, I carried in the vase and set it down gently on the kitchen counter across from the sink. Throughout the week, I watched that vivid, sherbet-colored cluster eventually fade.

It was soothing but short-lived, just like a lot of things.

CHAPTER THIRTY

Maybe We Could Be Better Than Fine

During these gut-wrenching times, whenever I could, I turned to growing flowers in a small and manageable way. No utilitarian vegetables—not since I had children. A few herbs here and there. Mostly, I just wanted to grow bright, impractical blossoms. Feel-good flowers to cheer myself up, to gather up and plunk down in bunches inside and to give away. It was easy to leave them on a doorstep, like ding dong ditch, but prettier.

While I was immersed in my flora-therapy, Cedar and I were slowly exploring a new idea. It had come to me a few weeks before, on a pouring Thursday night over takeout with Julie. We sat in wet chairs in our backyard gazebo as sheets of rain flew down. We both looked at our arms, dotted with fading scabs and scratches from Eden, poured a glass of wine, and toasted. Our plastic glasses clinked together softly, and I said, "To getting through it." The care in Julie's eyes reflected off the glow of the globe lights strung from the ceiling, and the heavy rain heaped onto the roof above. "I'm not sure what to do now that we are losing the night nursing. Would you ever . . . have Eden at your house more often?"

I didn't exactly say what I was thinking. I wanted to feel it out first.

"Of course, we'd do anything for her, Emma," Julie said, her voice low and easy. It was one thing for me to love my own daughter unconditionally, but I was struck again by the care that streamed from these once-strangers.

We didn't finish the bottle of wine, and we didn't make a full plan either. But I felt a deep relief in my chest just knowing that our village was near and open to new possibilities. I slept better that night than I had in months.

———ɯ———

A few weeks later, on Father's Day, I sat with my aging parents on their screen porch sobbing. (I sure know how to celebrate.) We had decided to resume visits in outdoor and well-ventilated settings.

During the short drive over, Avi had been adamant about listening to KISS FM, while Eden demanded Kidz Bop radio, and it hadn't ended well. We went over a speed bump and Eden began to hit herself in the face, which culminated in her vomiting all over the car and herself.

Another holiday for the books.

I put my head in my hands; I could not rally for a more festive attitude. A willow tree outside rustled in the breeze off the bay.

But something was finally different: the idea that had been mulling around my mind since that recent conversation with Julie. I wanted to get another perspective on it—Cedar had already responded with an emphatic *definitely.*

"It will be okay," my dad offered, rocking back and forth vigorously in his favorite wicker chair.

I stared down at the fabric of my dress and spoke wearily, "I'd like to make it more okay. It's breaking me." I looked out at that old willow tree and thought about how my brother had once tried to swing from it, with his own brand of sound effects. "What would you think . . . if I asked Marc and Julie whether Eden could spend a few nights there a week? Every week." I spoke tentatively.

My mother quickly jumped in, "That's a yes. I like your thinking on this, Emma. Would they do it?"

"I don't know if they would . . . I sort of alluded to it with Julie. I'd like to ask them."

My father spoke, his face solemn and still. "I know it's . . . not what you expected. But I get it. Definitely, talk to them. What have you got to lose?" He looked at me and nodded a few times, in his very specific understanding way. My mother's eyes reflected her commitment to me, decades of nurturance.

They got it—got me—in the way that I had always longed for, for as long as I remembered. I didn't have to explain much. I didn't have to justify who I was or what I needed. They had seen it all firsthand.

Somehow, despite the car ride over, Father's Day became the opposite of Mother's Day. It was suddenly filled with possibility.

As Cedar and I talked through all kinds of possibilities in a series of short and long conversations, I twirled my hair, a habit from high school that revved up when I got nervous. A lot of hair twirling was going down.

By the next Saturday, we had a well-researched proposal for Julie and Marc, which we began to refer to as our respite plan.

Julie, Marc, Cedar, and I met in our backyard to discuss the details. It was humid, and in my nervousness, I chugged a can of fizzy water and started on a second. I was uneasy, mostly because of how badly I wanted the respite. Not just the respite, but respite with these genuine, devoted, loving people. There was no other option even close to this, nothing else really to even consider with Eden still so young.

They listened. We listened. They talked. We talked. We put it all out there. Finally, Marc, in his signature baseball hat, leaned back in his chair and said, "I want what is best for my best friend. That's all I care about."

Avi, who was in the house with Eden and an ace PCA, sensed that we were in a serious meeting, so was doing his best to maximize it. He kept yelling things to us out the kitchen window like, "Can I have dessert?" and "Is it okay if I play *Minecraft*?"

Here's what we came up with: Eden would live with Marc and Julie part-time, three nights a week. She would get her own bedroom in their house, a rainbow picture hanging on her wall, a soft bed with a sherpa blanket, all of it just like her bed at home. Eden would get the assistance she needed during the night, lots of hugs and wagon rides and trips to the park during the day, along with the necessary tube feedings, medications, and therapies.

It was unconventional, for sure. It was a big step toward letting our village take care of us, especially during a time when villages felt as scarce as sanitizer.

The idea was to lessen the intensity on Cedar and me, along with Avi, yet provide Eden with sensitive, attuned care. For three nights a week we could sleep, soundly (or at least as soundly as we could muster) off-call for the first time in years. The aim was to give us some semblance of freedom, of rest, of normalcy—or at least our own version of it—to connect and decompress without the weight of relentless caregiving.

The hope was to feel more hope for the future.

Over an hour, we talked through most everything, including the financial arrangement, and the logistics of Julie and Marc moving to a different apartment within their building so that Eden could have her own room. They had already planned to move anyway, but Marc and Julie felt that the unit they had planned on taking was too cramped and wouldn't be conducive for any one of them, including Eden, to thrive. We also mused about the future, about how if this went well, that Julie and Marc might move closer to us, closer than the current eleven-mile trip, once their lease was up the following summer.

I knew I didn't even have to ask Eden because her boundless love and nearly life-long attachment to Julie and Marc was obvious, but to be fair, I did. Later, I looked over at her wispy blond curls and beatific face and asked, "What do you think about spending more time at Marc and Julie's house, like sleeping over there a few nights each week? Would you like to have your own room there?"

She replied, simply and emphatically, "Yes." And then she said, "Is Marc coming? I want to see him *today*."

After some consideration of the specifics, we each decided: we were in. Yet the plan was contingent on Julie and Marc landing the new apartment. We waited several long days for the management to get back to us with the news about the switch. I think someone was on vacation, or at least it seemed like it.

And then Marc texted, *They just approved our new apartment that has the room for Eden.*

I texted back, *Fabulous!* along with a full row of party hat emojis, which for some reason felt right, probably because I was a child of the eighties.

We agreed to start the respite in August, the very next month.

I thought all about Eden's new room as we made these plans, a room where our daughter would spend three out of seven nights each week away from us. It was a strange thing to consider; Eden's bedroom in Julie and Marc's home, with its gray walls and smooth wood floors near the shores of one of Minneapolis' bustling city lakes. We would decorate it with pictures of us, her original village, and the same little floral pillow she had at our house. I felt pangs of sadness as I gathered up the reassuring things to put in her new room, and while selecting photos to frame and send with her. It wasn't something I ever would have or could have anticipated, especially back when I became Eden's mother, and I held her tiny body against my chest for the first time. As I packed up her colorful t-shirts, size 5T (including a rainbow-striped one that for unknown reasons she called *her Kidz Bop shirt*) and soft, worn cotton pajamas, there was a heaviness. That heaviness, in various permutations, had been with me since we got the first phone call about her sizable genetic deletion.

Paradoxically, I also felt released from the all-encompassing sense of duty that I had been lugging around for years. I would no longer be a full-time caregiver, at least for a spell. I knew this decision would be hard to explain to some people who had no idea what it was like to raise a child like Eden. It was counter to the customary approach to family. This creative approach to kinship was, in some ways, informed by the chosen family ethos of the LGBTQ+ community; ours was also an alternative family structure built by necessity. Ours was not born from difficult rejection or judgment by our family of origin (like so many of my fellow LGBTQ + friends have faced), but we, too, needed solid support from people who were not blood relatives. Extended family.

It was outside the norm, but so were we. And really, isn't everyone?

I had learned my whole life that good mothers *must* sacrifice themselves for their children. And I had sacrificed myself enough, and then almost completely, and I never wanted to be there again. Respite was a way for me to reclaim my own life, to have something left. If I wasn't a perfect mother, or in the eyes of some, even a very good one, at least I was alive.

It would be a reprieve from so many elements of caregiving: washing syringes, doling out medication, changing diapers, cleaning up vomit, obscene amounts of laundry, scanning constantly for any possible harm that Eden might inflict on herself or others. It would be a reprieve from giving too much; the thing I never wanted in the first place. As I envisioned this shift, I felt a slight slowing of my breathing. My stomach began to settle. I almost felt relaxed.

I certainly never expected that our child would live part-time away from us with extended family and a view of the city (a lovely one, with her window facing the sunrise and sailboats dotting the lake). But after living in another zone for so long, the zone well beyond traditional family life, with frequent meltdowns and the persistent beep of a feeding tube, with endless appointments and the constant vigilance required to keep Eden safe, Cedar and I had a humbling understanding that we could not do this alone.

Eden would be fine, I knew, much better than fine—she would be loved unconditionally, at all hours, by her beloved people. People who she had been close with for more than 4/5 of her life, since before she was even a year old. She would go to sleep holding hands with Julie, who'd be by her side, stroking her hair, softly singing, as if Eden was her own. In the night, anytime she needed care, Julie would be there. Eden would wake up in the morning with Marc grinning, and then she could start the day saying, "Markie Barkie, watch this!" and show off her newest dance move. Her best friend would smile and chuckle, and the day would begin.

And maybe we would be fine, too.

Because of this respite, maybe we *all* would be better than fine.

CHAPTER THIRTY-ONE

No More Crying at the Sink

The weeks pre-respite flew by, summer in full throttle. With such monumental relief on the horizon, Cedar and I were not fighting as much.

Yet it wasn't solely the respite plan that softened things between us; we had changed. After years of arguing, and a whole lot of therapy, Cedar started to mop the floor, throw in a load of laundry, and let me sleep past seven (which was the new ten). He initiated trail walks with Avi and ushered the kids to the beach while I worked or spent unscheduled hours alone. And most of all, Cedar took on managing Eden's appointments, medications, and tube-feeding regimen. He was steadfast in executing the copious medical details. Some days, I may have even appeared to be the supporting-role partner, the one who got up later and did less of the health-related coordination.

All of that was big, yet the biggest shift was this: Cedar fully took over the nights. Whenever needed, he kept the baby monitor that we still used to ensure Eden's safety and slept by Eden's side if she was sick. He got up with her for the day at four or five when she wouldn't go back to sleep. After I hit the wall of despair, he did this for me, for us. And he kept it up.

Most of the time, I felt that we were partners. We were working together to keep patriarchy out of our house, among various other tasks.

Was I becoming something akin to World's Best Dad? Or maybe just a good enough mother, something I'd always extolled in *theory* yet grappled with in real life.

Cedar was awarded a week-long artist residency through the Everwood Farmstead Foundation (a quiet farm retreat in which to freely create), and I became a little bit envious again, but this time I also had my own passions to lean on—writing and working contentedly in my private practice. Something big had shifted: I no longer wanted to be him. This time, unlike during the touring days, I could be more supportive. It wasn't easy with him away. But there was no crying at the sink anymore, there was no roiling pneumonia, or rushing to the ER.

By that point, Eden hadn't been in the hospital for almost two years.

When Eden's care plan fell apart on day one of Cedar's trip (I had over-optimistically planned to work my usual hours with clients), I called Julie, and she answered on the first ring.

"Hi sweetness, what's up?" She was at an outdoor dinner party, but told me she could come over at eight, right afterward, and she did.

Kitty often puttered in our yard, rescuing this hydrangea or that one. She had mentioned to me, as we gathered in her driveway the week before, surrounded (but not too close) by a bunch of neighbors, that she planned to be around all week. "Let me know if you need me, in a pinch, I can waltz around outside with Eden."

I didn't feel alone because I wasn't. I even had time to arrange a bouquet for Cedar to honor his return, filled with coneflower, bee balm, and lilac-colored balloon flowers. I set it on his nightstand with a little note, and I meant it: *Welcome home, love.*

Almost every night, once the children were asleep, or nearly, we came together to hold hands on the crumb-strewn couch. One evening in late July, around eight, I made a beeline over to it from Avi's room. My hair was in a messy bun, and I was already wearing pajamas, my face wiped clean and shiny with lotion. Cedar stood at the kitchen sink in shorts while he rinsed syringes. He dried his hands on a striped hand towel and walked over to me.

"I'm passing out," I announced as I slumped on the faded couch. "I'm done for."

"Long day, huh?"

"The longest."

"Well, it is near the solstice," Cedar said as he reached over to me and started to rub my shoulders. "How was work today?"

I sighed. "This is such a hard time for people, especially in Minneapolis."

"That makes sense."

"But here's a first: I actually forgot that I had a nine o'clock today, and one of my clients called me while I was running on the trail. I was like oh yeah . . . be there in five, and then I ran home and got the professional shirt on and did the comfy pants on the bottom thing. My first time. I was a little bit sweaty, but not bad. It was pretty funny, actually. Apparently, I'm a very sporty therapist now." I leaned back into Cedar and felt my body relax a little.

"Keeping it spontaneous. I like it," Cedar quipped. "I think everyone gets to have a day like that, where you lose track of time. I mean, what is time anyway?"

"I didn't have it on my radar at all. I didn't even know that it was scheduled for today. I thought I was starting at ten. It's so weird working from home."

"Happens to the best of them," he replied.

"I didn't even beat myself up about it, which I knew would impress you."

"Nice work," He looked at me, his eyes crinkling a little with amusement. Then he continued. "So, today I saw Spike again, one of the little puppies from next door. With his sweet little face." He held up his hands like he was squeezing a dog's snout inside his grip. "I know it might be a while, but I'm so glad we are on the list. The ones at the farm were ridiculously cute."

"Oh, I'm into it. It will probably take forever, though. We aren't the only ones with that idea right now. But yeah, I think our next baby is going to be canine. I guess the other ship has sailed." I looked away.

"Are you okay with that? I mean, I know you really wanted one more."

"It is okay. Not like, awesome. I thought it might be something I would always regret if we didn't. But now I feel that having another child and then having it break us apart would be worse. I know . . . it's not what you want."

"I just think, as things are, it would be too much. I'd like to be able to enjoy what we have more."

"I get that, I do. You have a very reasonable take. I am sort of settled with it. But I don't think it's going to be something that feels 100 percent resolved for me. It's beyond logic. It's strange, with everything we have been through, that part of me still really wants like five kids running around here. Is that deranged?" I put my feet into Cedar's lap.

"Is that the part of you that's blocked out what it's really like to have a newborn? Is that because of the nitrous they gave you?"

"Absolutely." I looked up at him. "Maybe it's wired into me. I don't know. I do like the idea of getting a puppy. I can train it as a therapy dog."

"It seems . . . manageable. I mean, not easy. But we can do it. I'm warming up."

"I have wanted a dog since I was, I think, nine and my dad pretended he was allergic. You know, I had those Dog Fancy posters up above my bed. Other kids had Whitney Houston or Madonna, and I had centerfolds of Chow Chows. Later he told me it was a *psychological* allergy." I paused, shaking my head. "My parents think it's a terrible idea," we looked at each other. "And there's some truth in that. I mean, any living being will require a lot of work. But I want to do it. It's probably good not to please your parents too much."

"Babe, I agree. Let's fuck shit up and get a dog in the suburbs."

I turned to Cedar and said, "Um, that's the funniest thing I've ever heard."

He looked at me, shaking his head. "Emma, you can't say that every other day. I think it cancels itself out."

And then we laughed, in the same way that we'd been laughing together for years.

CHAPTER THIRTY-TWO

Humble, Extraordinary Devotion

On a humid Friday afternoon on the last day of July, we crammed several big boxes into our Prius station wagon and drove over as a family to Marc and Julie's. Masks on, we rode the elevator up to the new apartment. Eden ran down the gray hallway shrieking ahead of Avi, who trailed behind with us. Eden already knew the way.

The two-bedroom was decorated with scores of family photos, ornate Jewish books and art, and various keepsakes. It was the opposite of my austere dorm walls back in Santa Cruz, in the most loving way. The many framed photos featured their (now adult) children and their cousins, sisters, brothers, mothers, and fathers, and Eden. Pictures of her with Marc and Julie, snapshots taken at her birthdays, all mixed in with the rest of the family. A depiction of the beachside moment when Eden took her first steps with Marc, etched into a stained-glass piece, hung on the wall outside of Eden's door; their artsy friend had created the memento for them after they proudly showed him the video. The focal point was Eden and Marc holding hands. And at eye level, a framed photo of Eden and Rachel, Julie and Marc's daughter, sat on a glass shelf. Their faces were pressed together, beaming.

How did this happen again? How did we get to know such gracious, holy people? I was shocked by the enormity of it all. By the amount of pure chance involved every step of the way, and by the humble, extraordinary devotion of Julie and Marc. It could have gone any other way but this, but there we were, in the home of people who were once strangers, but were now family-ish, surrounded by framed pictures of our child.

We came to get Eden's room set up, and we got right to work. Cedar began by assembling Eden's twin bed, the exact same one that she had at home, right down to the mattress. As we started to hang the photos that we had brought, Julie asked if we wanted to kick off happy hour while we worked.

She grinned and offered, "You guys, it's five o'clock somewhere!"

I always admired her wisdom. We each cracked open a lime hard seltzer as we continued to make the room shine.

Marc, Eden, and Avi watched *Ugly Dolls* in the den while we ran Eden's tube bolus. Avi just wanted to snuggle with CJ, their aging rescue Chug (Chihuahua and Pug mix). When Avi approached the pup, he growled and burrowed in Marc's lap. Marc motioned to Avi to give a little space, explaining, "CJ gets a little nervous. He just gets scared around new people."

I looked at Marc, who was gently cradling a whimpering CJ, and tilted my head a little. I said, "I can't believe you. You're such a great whisperer for sweet and spicy beings." He shook his head, waving me away. Smiling.

A little later in the afternoon, I scanned the apartment; Avi was nowhere to be found.

"Has anyone seen Avi?" I asked.

"He's in their room." Cedar grinned as he motioned in the direction of Marc and Julie's bedroom. "He's been in there for a while, painting a rock."

As I walked into Marc and Julie's bedroom to find Avi, I was struck by their lush view of Lake of the Isles. I was so glad Eden would have this. Avi said, "Look! You can see for infinite miles." He was right. And as always, startlingly poetic.

He was seated at Julie's antique desk facing the window, which was covered in the art pens and markers that she used for her mandala art. Julie meticulously painted rocks with bright, intricate patterns, and then gifted them to her loved ones and others deserving appreciation, like Eden's teachers.

Avi focused keenly on his rainbow-colored rock. He spent a long time letting the red, yellow, and blue layers dry. When it was finally ready, Julie asked, "Do you want to write a word on the back?" I was certain he wouldn't since as a lefty, handwriting didn't come easy for him. Avi nodded yes decisively. He took a white pen, and confidently spelled out the four-letter word. I was relieved that it wasn't a swear. It read, "Nope."

"Like California," he said, laughing. I kissed him on the back of his head.

"I love it," I exclaimed. "I think you really summed it up, Avi."

He knew how desperately hard it could be to raise a complex child such as Eden, and he also knew how she united us. He knew about medical challenges, about meltdowns, about sticking together. He knew about helping others and being helped.

He probably knew entirely too much for his age.

For dinner, Julie made a tuna pasta salad, garlic bread, and roasted veggies. She even baked chicken tenders for Avi. After we said the Shabbat blessings and lit the candles, we spread around the living room to eat. Julie and I sat at the table with Eden, who was steady in her Bumbo seat between us. Our family often reviews our highs and lows of the week at Shabbat dinner, so I asked Julie what hers were for the week. "Well, I think getting the room ready was my high," she shared quickly.

"Me too," I later told her, and I meant it. I thought that getting Eden's bedroom ready might be sorrowful, but it wasn't. With all the love and joy in that home, I couldn't help but feel it, too.

I personally would live there. Happily.

Eden didn't stay at Marc and Julie's that night—we were just there to set up the space together—although that would happen soon enough. I hoped what I felt in this moment would endure once we started the respite. I knew there would likely be a stiff cocktail of feelings (per the usual).

Julie packed up what seemed like six pounds of leftovers and most of a chocolate cake for us, along with a rock decorating kit for Avi that she gleaned from her supplies. As we left, I thanked her and Marc profusely, but there was no way to thank them enough. There were no words of gratitude that could come close to matching the love and support they were giving us. The generosity of time and space and spirit.

Sometimes in the face of such unconditional love, all you can do is let it in.

—⁓—

That summer, Cedar and I managed to carve out two consecutive nights alone together to celebrate our ten-year wedding anniversary. We escaped to a cabin in the pines Up North, at a resort my mother and I had visited three years earlier. Avi stayed at my parents' house; Julie and Marc had Eden. This was before the respite plan had officially started. We thought of it as "pregaming".

Cedar and I decided to make it a creative retreat, which was something we both always wanted. Cedar packed up his midi controller and various electronic equipment for the trip so he could arrange the music he composed during his lingering days at Everwood Farmstead a few weeks before. I put my trusty laptop in the trunk, all charged up and ready for writing, along with a cooler filled with enough groceries for an entire week, which Cedar had organized. I had not under packed on clothes, or anything, this time around.

Khruangbin's *Con Todo El Mundo*, one of our favorite albums, sailed through the car speakers as we made our way North in Cedar's station wagon. I put my feet up on the passenger side dashboard and opened the windows; we already smelled like sunscreen. "Let's stop at the next Culver's," I said. "I'm hungry, and this fruit we packed as a snack only gets me so far."

"I think I'm going to wait until we get there," Cedar told me as we pulled off the main road, "I've got these turkey veggie wraps I want to make for lunch."

"You've gone soft," I replied. "When we met, you were all desserts, all the time."

"Those were the days," he said.

When we arrived at the cabin, after I sanitized the hell out of it, we stepped into the dusty screen porch and sunk into the chairs overlooking the still lake.

"I'm happy to be here, Cedar," I said. The breeze circled us. Ducks honked nearby. "I'm just . . . glad we made it this far."

"I agree, Emma. It's good." His beard was graying ever so slightly, and he looked at me with big, brave, weathered eyes.

It was good, and I loved him.

I loved us again.

CHAPTER THIRTY-THREE

If Not for Eden

For a major milestone birthday, some people might splurge on a cruise to Alaska, if they can swing it, or have dinner at a fine restaurant in town. But for her seventieth birthday, Kitty went full force on a tradition she had long been building toward: she bought a whole wheelbarrow full of bulbs—hyacinth, lilies, allium, tulips, and daffodils—and decided to plant these perennials for her neighbors and friends.

Muddy hands on her hips, out in our front yard, she told me, "I'm lucky that I've made it this far. I know so many people who haven't." Then, without any fanfare, she got to planting. Kitty organized a curved border along our front yard with handfuls of bulbs. She kept on planting well beyond that birthday, through every single year.

Those blooms blew kisses of color beneath the trees like we were living in a fairy forest. One day, on a whim, Kitty stocked her pond with koi that she bought for Avi. Each day he would go check on them, feed them, and observe how much they had grown. "My fish are really looking good!" he'd exclaim.

Whenever I passed Kitty's garden, I thought about the many giving, gracious souls who had held me through our family's—through Eden's—struggles. People who cared for the sick, people who cared for the earth. People who lived like "Yes, this is what it's all about." Not me or you or mine or yours.

We, us.

It doesn't mean I never again felt lonely. Sometimes, I still did. This isn't a happily ever after story; it's just a story of a regular, sort of not regular life.

If not for the insufferable nights of caregiving, we never would have moved out to the woods or met these radiant humans. Without Eden, I would not know Julie or Marc or Kitty, and maybe not even Kate, or at least not in the same way. There would be scores of people I never would have gotten to meet. And without my daughter, I would not know my mother, never would have known how steadily she walked beside me, step by step (while somehow looking fabulous the entire time.)

If not for Eden, I would not know Cedar, or at least the Cedar who became more himself because of this tumultuous time. I may not have even been able to fully appreciate Avi, with his originality and sense of awe. I would not know the depths of high-mindedness within both of my parents.

And I would not know myself in the way that I am now.

Without Eden, we wouldn't be here. We wouldn't be anywhere near it.

We wouldn't be living in this woodsy rambler that gets surprisingly good sunlight in the afternoons. Maybe instead I would be running around Lake Harriet in the city or maybe I would get really into cleaning my car—it could use it, but generally I have other things to do. Better ones.

Eden was my one and only girl, in my one and only existence. The more I sat with that, with what was actually happening, instead of imagining the measureless iterations of what could have been, should have been, what I thought was going to happen or *might have been if I would have only*, the better I felt.

Oh Eden, so tender and sweet, and tough and scrappy and daring. I had never wanted to raise a pushover, and that was *definitely* not a problem. My one-of-a-kind daughter sometimes knocks me off my feet, literally—on purpose. And then suddenly, Eden does something, gives me a tender look or makes a friend at school—a very real friend who sings "Ring Around the Rosy" with her while holding hands after class, and it strikes me: it is going to be okay.

It is going to be better than okay, this wild, magical adventure.

We have a house in the woods, we have each other. We live under trees with leaves that miraculously shoot out in the springtime, complete and new, regardless of what is happening in the world. We sometimes sit around the fire pit in the backyard together (although never for very long) singing like we are at summer camp. This family—this village—sings the way we did most everything in our lives: a little off-key.

Yet when we are together, we are almost, sort of, free.

—— ∽ ——

On the May morning that we celebrated Eden's sixth birthday, it was 70 degrees and sunny, which never happens in Minnesota, especially when any kind of enjoyable event is planned. We'd been talking up the party with Eden for weeks, reviewing the guest list and reminding her that, yes, at this llama farm, there would be real live llamas.

"We can sing and then we go home? Llamas are not scary? Are they?" Eden asked repeatedly during the week leading up to the party. Our puppy Benny, who was already almost six months old, paced around looking for scraps under the table, and then jumped up to snag Eden's silky pink ribbon, which she held for comfort. His smooth chestnut fur was especially shiny; Cedar had just given him a bath the day before.

When we first got Benny, one of Eden's nurses said that having a puppy was like having another child, and she wasn't the only one who made that comment.

"Have you met my children?" I'd asked. It certainly wasn't the same as a child for us. Benny required work, sure, but he didn't even need to use the nebulizer. He also sat whenever I wanted him to, which never got old.

Eden was still repeating her llama-related questions when I left to go pick up the cupcakes (and eight bags of garden mulch on the way). Cedar stood in the kitchen fielding her questions, which was Edenese for "I'm really anxious right now." He had become so patient with her and joined in wholeheartedly on whatever song or game or conversation she wanted to explore (usually, pop music trivia).

Unfortunately, Eden was more fearful than ever of trying something new. This acute anxiety caused her to vomit, which affected nearly everything outside of her regular routines, including her ability to attend school.

School had been a battle all year, requiring countless hours of our fiercest advocacy. Because of her anxiety-related vomiting and too many behavioral incidents to count, the district wanted to move Eden to a more restrictive environment than our local public school system offered—a level four placement. We fielded incessant calls and emails from the school, and there were many days where Eden was sent home early (like the morning that I was called to pick her up at 8:15 a.m., after an 8:00 a.m. drop off), even though Eden had already had her school hours reduced by the district to only a few hours per day. We were looking for a new school.

My mother had planned this llama farm party, which we knew would be a stretch for Eden. But my mom was so pumped up about the pastoral venue—and Cedar and I were so relieved not to have to coordinate a celebration ourselves—that we breezed along with it. We all understood full well that it might be a complete bust, with the birthday girl possibly unable to attend her own party, but why not try? Her track record with birthdays had been, to my continued amazement, stellar.

Marc and Julie's forest green Mini was ahead of my chalky Prius as we wound around the dirt roads leading up to the farm. As we pulled up to the weathered red barn, I ended my Bluetooth phone call with Kate, who lamented with a lilt in her voice, "Of all the days, I really do miss Eden's birthdays, like extra."

"Me too. I mean, I miss you especially," I replied. I had already snapped a picture that morning of the pink and bronze bracelets adorning my wrist that day, ones that Kate had sent over the past three years that she had been in Durham. I texted it to her, *Today we are celebrating Eden's birthday. You're here.*

Cedar helped Eden out of her new booster seat. She emerged from the car in a flouncy floral dress and pink knee pads which cushioned her frequent floor dives. Eden took one look at the small, familiar crowd and without so much as a hello, directed, "Sing *Happy Birthday.*"

Of course, we sang, including Eden, who was jubilantly celebrating herself. When the song ended, Eden shouted across the lush, rolling hills of the farm, "Everybody is so happy! Everybody is here for my birthday!"

Cedar and I exchanged relieved looks. My mother, decked out in puffed sleeves and perfect sunglasses, didn't say *I told you so*, but she easily could have.

After we toured the grounds, fed the llamas and donkey, and then ogled the Icelandic sheep, Eden took some bites of blueberry yogurt. There was finally something in this world that she sort-of liked to eat.

We sang *Happy Birthday* to Eden again over the cupcakes. When we got to "Happy birthday dear Eeeeedennnn," Eden's face was a shiny circle of glee, those long hands flapping eagerly, her high white-blond ponytail bouncing and a royal blue bandana tied around her neck. Her smile was expansive. Julie and Marc beamed alongside her, soaking in her exuberance. Eden had been doing respite care with them for almost a year at this point, and they were about to move to a new apartment much closer to our house. The only notable issue was that inevitably, in nearly every transition between homes, we forgot a medication or some essential medical supply, which necessitated a lot of driving back and forth. But we had all agreed to keep the arrangement going for at least another year, and as far as Cedar and I were concerned, for as long as humanly possible.

I still feel occasional pangs of guilt. As beautiful as this life can be, some facts still remain: my daughter is still dependent on a feeding tube for nearly all of her calories, she wakes up in another home three mornings a week, and no matter which home she wakes up in, she still struggles with bouts of aggression and self-injury, although less than she used to.

It isn't what my vision was for her, my hope for my role as a mother, for the *excellence* I sometimes still chase, even against my better judgment. Maybe I was prone to those pangs regardless of what my parenting was or wasn't. Maybe what I thought was guilt was really that other persistent village member—grief.

I imagine this grief and I will be roommates for the rest of my life.

The future was a tender, slippery thing. But I was no longer so afraid of it.

Eden was content at both places, comfortable, cared for exceedingly well. She was full of giddiness and grins—at home in two homes. She was not racked with longing, with expectations of how things should or could be, with wanting to be so very good.

Eden did not care much about being good.

She adored us all, her unlikely village, and, in return, she was faithfully, wildly adored. Even with her complexities, her bursts of combativeness, with everything that she embodied. She was our girl.

After the singing ended, Eden relaxed in her wagon with a feeding tube bolus that Cedar had started. I helped her pull her birthday presents out of glossy, brightly colored gift bags. Eden barely glanced at any of it; she had little interest in things. For her, it was always about the people. Avi read a few of the birthday cards aloud to her, and then just as quickly, without being asked, he grabbed up the gift bags and loaded them into the trunk of my car.

"I'm helping," he told me.

"I can see that, sweetheart." When he smiled, his eyes crinkled at the sides.

Blue skies above us, green fields below. The air smelled like dry grass mixed with dirt, with the slightest breeze. Eden, in that lush little voice of hers, made another announcement.

"This is the best day ever. Raise your hand if you love this birthday." Every single person within earshot raised their hands. My mother cheered as if it were a baseball game. I caught my father's gaze, despite his dark wraparound sunglasses; I could tell that he was feeling it, too. Even the gracious owner of the llama farm had overheard Eden, and even from over by the tractor, I could tell she was moved. Tears pooled in her eyes.

I looked at Cedar. He raised both hands. Then, so did I.

I wanted her, and only her, my daughter. I wanted this life, *ours*, even with its undertow of heartbreak. I loved Eden, bonkers-ly, the kind of love that transcended tomorrow, that transcended what she might do for me when I was old, that transcended the plans I had before I first whispered her name, and transcended everything that came after that. I wanted Avi too, always. And I wanted Cedar. Along with the rest of our unlikely village.

This was family. We had nothing else to offer each other but this moment. It was equal parts what I'd always imagined and could never, ever have imagined.

I stretched both my arms into the ultramarine sky as far as they could go. I was loving this unlikely birthday, surrounded by these unlikely people.

My hands were up, and I was not alone.

Epilogue

The fall after Eden turned six, she started a full-time ABA day program at Fraser, a wonderful nonprofit organization. Through hours of warm, consistent, repetitive behavioral modification, Eden slowly traded head banging and hitting for hugs and high-fives. Several of the staff members came to our home to train us, task by task, in administering these principles at home. When Eden, instead of grabbing my hair or bopping me in the face, gently rested her long fingers on my arm in order to get my attention, I thought, *people could live like this.*

This was workable.

This was hope.

After a year, Eden was set to graduate. Well, technically she aged out of the Fraser program, and Cedar and I spent countless hours researching and applying for the next one. It was like the college admissions process, without the prestige. The waitlists were often epic. Summer was nearly over when we found out the news that Eden got into another excellent therapy program, this time in a school setting.

On her last day at Fraser, the entire group of ABA therapists stood outside the building, as Eden, the last child out of the clinic that day, ran down the sidewalk toward Julie and Marc. Almost thirty staff members—people of various ages, races, and histories, stood together in an arc around her. Some danced, as a nod to what they had shared throughout the year. Eden looked around at the cheering faces, flapped her hands enthusiastically, and squealed, "I did the whole thing! Everyone is clapping for me!" There was hardly a dry eye as Eden sauntered toward the car. Except for Eden, whose smile lit up the parking lot. This child, and those who surrounded her, could make even a suburban storefront lot shine.

Love doesn't generally go like we think it will. In fact, it usually doesn't. Love often unfolds, just like a day, a season, a year, a childhood, a coming of age, a growing older.

Love, like life, always changes, so we change with it.

ACKNOWLEDGMENTS

I hope that this book (and ideally, best-case scenario, my life) is already an acknowledgment to the people who have shown me love and bolstered my family.

Thank you to all the hardworking clergy and staff of Temple Israel, especially Rabbi Marcia Zimmerman, Rabbi Jen Hartman, Cantor Emeritus Barry Abelson, and Rabbi Jason Klein. To the skilled, patient PCAs and nurses who delivered crucial care to Eden, a few standouts: Brittany, Gretchen, Megan, and ChunCha. Thanks to Eden's first teacher, Kate Whiting, who gave her a top-notch introduction to school, and to all the skilled educators and therapists since. To the healthcare professionals who tirelessly treat complex needs with the whole child in mind, we are fortunate to have met many.

A huge thank you to my agent, Lara Love Hardin of True Literary, who quickly understood the bigger picture of this story and helped clarify the vision of the project. I will be ever grateful that you decided to champion this story. Thanks to Ty Love who joyfully helped bring this manuscript into fruition along with the entire team at Idea Architects: Sarah Rainone, Bella Roberts, Doug Abrams, and Rachel Neumann. Thanks to Jenny Davis for the steadfast developmental editing along with Kate Hopper for your guidance through an early draft of this manuscript. Thank you so much to everyone at Central Recovery Press, including Valerie Killeen, Nancy Schenck, Jennifer Mutz, and John Davis, who graciously helped to bring this book to readers.

To Jill, who had the courage to connect me with Julie in the first place and for the bountiful weekly dinners; I'll never forget it. To Rachel Kessler, thank you for the care and the welcoming spirit. Gratitude to Muffy and Larry Rudnick, who accompanied us during breathing-related scares and other adventures in the early days. Thank you to Renee and Dr. Mike Popkin and Marge and Irv Weiser, among others, for sustaining us with meals during tough stretches. To Joanna Woolman, Mike and Jack, one-of-a-kind friends to Avi. And to my local villagers Karen Stombaugh, the Sigels, the Fligges, and the Conlins—through the pandemic and beyond, thank you. Thanks to Justin Vernon and Middle West for your generous support. Billy Rosenberg and Betsy and James Schwartz, thank you for your kindness (and James specifically, for your photography over the years). Thank you to Jay Eidsness and Maja Gamble for showing up warmly on days that would have been harder without you, and the entire Eidsness family.

I am so grateful for Dr. Kirsten Lind Seal who provided a nuanced ethical lens to therapy, writing and the intersection of both. To Nick Wallace, along with Carole Cera, an early mentor. And to my clients who bring new perspectives, wholehearted work, and insight on what it means to be human.

A monumental thank you to Kate Cosgriff who waded through various versions of this manuscript, and life, alongside me. An abundance of gratitude for my friends who have been integral to this story: Melissa, Sara, Debra, Laurie, Sarah, Beth, Jeannie, Vanessa, Meggan, Jamie and Randy, Angela and Ben, Mel and Amanda, Kara, Carly, both Danas, Anna, Tamar, June and Ron.

To my unstoppable parents, Candice and Charles Nadler, who model grit, generosity, and meaning making. Thank you for all that you have contributed as grandparents, parents, and for your unwavering affection. To Julie and Marc, who share their home and hopeful outlook. You brought joy into our lives from the very first *kickasserole*, but I had no idea how much you would impact us for the better. Thank you for trusting me with our story. To my brother and sister-in-law Geoffrey Nadler and Cat Manalo, I love you. Janice Nadler, thank you for your compassion and unconditional warmth.

To Avi, who surprises and delights me daily, I love you forever. To Christopher Thomson, who will always be Cedar to me, my favorite person to talk with (and kiss) in the world, whose superpower is making me laugh even when I am crying. Thank you for loving me steadily during this series of adventures we never planned on having. To Eden Ayelet, for the most all-in smile, passion, and robust dance moves I have ever seen. You gave us a rare, lovestruck adventure. Without you, I think I may have gotten lost.